BALLET MUSIC—AN INTRODUCTION

BALLET MUSIC

AN INTRODUCTION

By

HUMPHREY SEARLE

**SECOND REVISED
EDITION**

DOVER PUBLICATIONS, INC.
NEW YORK

Published in Canada by General Publishing Company, Ltd., 30 Lesmill Road, Don Mills, Toronto, Ontario.
Published in the United Kingdom by Constable and Company, Ltd., 10 Orange Street, London WC 2.

This Dover edition, first published in 1973, is a revised and enlarged edition of the work originally published by Cassell, London, in 1958.

International Standard Book Number: 0-486-22917-3
Library of Congress Catalog Card Number: 73-75233

Manufactured in the United States of America
Dover Publications, Inc.
180 Varick Street
New York, N. Y. 10014

PREFACE TO THE DOVER EDITION

The second edition contains a new chapter describing developments from 1957–72, as well as revisions of the previous chapters. There are also an additional bibliography, an updated discography, and a further list of first performances. I should like to record my indebtedness to two books on modern ballet which I have found invaluable, Peter Brinson and Clement Crisp's *Ballet for All* and John Percival's *Modern Ballet.*

London   H.S.
February 1972

PREFACE TO THE FIRST EDITION

THERE have been many books about ballet-dancing; this book is an attempt to give some account of the musical side of ballet. Music is, of course, only one element in a ballet, and it is perhaps wrong to isolate it from the choreography and décor; on the other hand, the music can make or mar a ballet almost more than any one of its other components, and there are very few ballets surviving in the modern repertoire where the music is recognized as being very poor. This was not always so, of course; in fact it was not until this century that the real importance of music in ballet was appreciated, and even now many ballets show a discrepancy between the choreographer's ideas and the musical score.

This book can only claim to give a general introduction to an enormous subject; it attempts to give an assessment of the most important scores written for ballet, but it naturally cannot include full details of all ballet scores. Technical details regarding the music of a number of ballets and its relationship to the stage action will be found in *The Decca Book of Ballet* (London, first published in 1958), and the libretti of many important ballets are described in detail in Cyril W. Beaumont's invaluable book; *The Complete Book of Ballets* (London, 1951) and its supplement, as well as his *Ballets of Today* (London, 1954) and *Ballets Past and Present* (London, 1955).

Finally, I would like to thank Mr. Robert Irving for being kind enough to read this book in proof and for his many helpful comments; and Dr. Walter Beckett for his valuable assistance.

H. S.

[vii]

CONTENTS

[ix]

LIST OF ILLUSTRATIONS

I

The Earlier History of Ballet Music

IT is an obvious fact that the dance is as old as man: but the
ballet in the form we know it to-day is a very much more
recent creation. However it is perhaps worth briefly recalling
the stages by which dance has developed into ballet, and the
various vicissitudes which have occurred in this process, especially in so far as they affect present-day ballet. In primitive
societies dancing was mainly confined to the two purposes of
popular enjoyment at festivals and celebrations, and of form-
ing part of a religious ritual: later came a third function, that
of dramatic entertainment, either sacred or secular, in which
the dance often took an important part. The music was of
course purely ancillary, being provided in the first place by
some kind of percussion instrument simply to mark the
rhythm, by the human voice, or by some kind of pipe instrument—a primitive flute or oboe. This kind of pattern held good
throughout many centuries of history, and indeed till well on
into the Middle Ages, when the invention of polyphony on
the one hand and the greater instrumental resources available on the other, made a more elaborate musical accompaniment possible. But the original pattern remains to this day in
many primitive communities, though in some cases with
certain modifications—some African negroes, for instance,
have greatly elaborated the rhythmical complexity of the
music with which they accompany their dances, chiefly by
subdivision of the main beat, but the fundamental rhythmical
units remain constant, and so does the unison singing which
often goes on simultaneously with the dancing.

[1]

Both ritual and popular dancing took place in ancient Egypt: in ancient Greece there were popular dances like the Cordax and the Sikinnis, reputed to be of a somewhat obscene nature, which were part of the old Attic comedy, and later, dancing took a considerable part in the performances of the classical Greek tragedies. In Rome dancing was an essential part of the old *feriae* and also of the popular *Ludi Romani*: the former were originally religious ceremonies, but gradually developed into public feasts and holidays, while the latter were actual entertainments organized by the State. The *Ludi* contained both religious and popular elements, beginning with a procession in honour of Jupiter in which dancers and flute-players took part: then came chariot-racing and other festivities. In later years these degenerated into gladiatorial shows: but music and dancing still continued as part of the dramas, or *ludi scaenici*. The Latin comedy had originated in the rude fun of country festivals and harvest amusements, but reached a high literary standard by the second century B.C. About 50 B.C. the era of the mimes began. Singing and dancing continued to be part of these entertainments, and also of the later pantomimes, in which the actor mimed without speaking: in some cases the lines were recited by another actor while music supported the miming. Here we have something like a primitive form of ballet: and indeed the principal *pantomimi* became extremely popular and famous, such as Pylades and Bathyllus, the favourite of Maecenas in the Augustan age. But the Roman theatre lacked a real virility like that of the Greeks, and the pantomimes became increasingly associated with gladiatorial shows and entertainments of a somewhat crude nature in the later years of the Roman Empire.

When the Christian Church became dominant in the Roman world all entertainments, and particularly the theatre, were regarded as exceedingly immoral, and as a result the dance theatre as such disappeared for nearly a thousand years. At one stage the reformers tried to divest church music of any secular tendencies by banning the use of two of the Greek modes, the Ionian and Aeolian—our present major and minor scales—as being too worldly and too easy to dance to. They used the remaining, less popular modes in Gregorian chant, which with its rhythmical flexibility and lack of regular beats provided a more austere and unworldly atmosphere. Nevertheless dancing continued, both within the church and outside it. Thus there are such things as the mediæval Dance of Death, and the ritual dances of the Flagellants: some Spanish churches even permitted dances with tambourine accompaniment, and there are similar religious dances recorded in the Languedoc in the sixteenth century. Also, of course, there continued to be dancing at peasant festivals and gatherings of all kinds. Towards the end of the mediæval period popular song and dance again began to approximate to an art form, with such manifestations as the Minnesinger in Germany, the Morris dances in England, and the Troubadours in Italy and Spain. The Church was compelled to take some notice of this popular activity, and borrowed the melodies of a number of popular dance songs for use as hymn tunes. But it was above all the rise of the secular power which led to the reinstatement of song and dance as an artistic entertainment. Birthdays, marriages, and other events important to noble houses were celebrated with ceremonies which became more and more elaborate as the period went on. There were still no theatres, but courtyards did just as well, and in these private court ceremonies was the genesis of the modern ballet theatre. Indeed from this period there dates the story of the *ballets des ardents,* the court masque of King Charles VI of France in the early fifteenth century, in which the shaggy costumes of some of the dancers who represented savages caught fire from a torch; two noblemen were burnt to death, and the shock is supposed to have unhinged the King's mind.

But it was in the Renaissance period that ballet, as such, really began to develop. Its basis was still the court entertainment,

the masques held in noble houses, with ballets as interludes
in operas and plays, and sometimes even taking the form
of independent pantomimes, especially in Italy. In 1489, for
instance, there was a celebrated masque on the occasion of
the marriage of the Duke of Milan to Isabella of Aragon. This
was composed by a Lombard, Begonzo di Botta, and it represented a number of classical myths—Jason and the Argonauts,
Mercury, Diana, Orpheus, and others. This was talked of all
over Europe, and is perhaps the earliest example of what we
mean by ballet. In Italy, and indeed throughout Europe, music
was turning away from the austerity of the Gregorian chant
and was developing a more sustained melodic line with stronger
rhythmical accents. Examples of this may be found in the
'Carnival Songs' of Heinrich Isaak (*circa* 1500) and in the
sung and danced 'Ballo' form: the diminutive version of
this, the 'Balletto' or 'Ballett' is well known to us from
Elizabethan music. These balletts were short, light compositions—Thomas Morley called them 'Fa Las' because of their
conventional refrains. In 1591 Gastoldi published a collection
of balletti, described as 'to be sung, played, and danced', and
Morley and Weelkes followed with similar collections within
a few years.

In fact the whole history of this period is that of the gradual
infiltration of dance rhythms into serious music, which had
so long been under the influence of the a-rhythmic Gregorian
chant. The old-fashioned *Chanson mondaine* was given a new
lease of life by the introduction of rhythms derived from
popular song and dance, and the influence of this may be
observed both in many of the madrigals of the later sixteenth
century and also in the lighter Frottole and Villanellas. Normally, however, the more serious madrigals remained un-
affected by regular rhythmical beats, while the lighter ones
approximated more to dance forms. And of course the rise
of opera and oratorio during this period did much to hasten
the process.

[4]

At first the more strongly rhythmical movements in opera were confined to choruses and ritornelli, or interludes, while the dramatic action took place in free recitative without regular rhythmical accents. Thus the final chorus of Peri's *Euridice* (1600) is marked 'Ballo a 3', and Monteverdi's *Orfeo* ends with a Moresca which is itself preceded by a highly rhythmical chorus. There is also a ballo in Monteverdi's *Ulisse*, but only the words are preserved. Similarly the influence of popular dance songs may be seen in the oratorios of this time, particularly in the choruses: Cavalieri's *La Rappresentazione di Anima e di Corpo* (1600) provides good examples of the Italian approach, while in Germany the use of chorales, encouraged by Luther, brought a strongly rhythmical element back into religious music. Similarly the early French Protestants based many of their hymns on popular tunes: and the old tradition of the mediæval mystery play, which had always included singing and dancing, was thus revived through the entry of popular music into the oratorio.

This was also the period in which the dance forms which we know to-day, and which in fact are still the basis of many movements in modern ballets, finally crystallized, as it were, into their recognizable forms. They came from two sources: the *haute danse* of the peasants, who leapt nimbly and gaily in the air, and the *basse danse* of the courts, in which the aristocrats eschewed violent leg movements for sake of greater complexity and sophistication in the movements of their other limbs. For theatrical purposes both methods were fused and used as and when needed: and in addition the composers of Italy, France, and the Netherlands drew together in their common use of dance rhythms, whether in the Italian opera or in the choral compositions of Paris and Fontainebleau. The dance suite as an entity arose: these might be called 'ordres', as Couperin did later on, or 'Partitas', as they were known in Germany, but their essentials remained the same. The basic dances were the pavane (later replaced by the allemande), the

[5]

courante, the sarabande and the gigue: but other dances, such as the minuet, gavotte, rigaudon or passepied, and bourrée were also later inserted in the suites. In their later instrumental form these suites became the basis of the classical sonata and symphony: but in the theatre the dances remained more or less separate entities, in spite of the conventional order in which they were often arranged.

The pavane, in $\frac{4}{4}$ time, was slow and stately, and suitable for the processional entry of the courtiers: the allemande which replaced it in the instrumental dance suites, was normally written in equal semiquavers in $\frac{4}{4}$ time, and was more vigorous in character. The galliard, which often followed the pavane in the early suites, was a gay dance in $\frac{3}{4}$ time: the courante, which was popular in three different forms between 1550 and 1750, was of Franco-Italian origin, also vigorous, and mainly based on running quaver passages. The sarabande, a slow dance in $\frac{3}{4}$ time, is reputed to be of Mozarabic origin dating back to the twelfth century, and castanets or bells were sometimes used in it: it was associated with the languorous movements of the courtesans. The gigue, called 'hot and hasty' by Shakespeare, was in $\frac{6}{8}$, $\frac{9}{8}$, or $\frac{12}{8}$ time: it probably originated in Britain, but France and Italy also developed forms of it. The minuet started as a fairly vigorous and fast dance, the bransle, from Poitou: but after its introduction to the French Court about 1650 it was considerably moderated in both tempo and style. The chaconne existed in two forms: the better known type was based on an ostinato, or regularly repeated, theme, usually of four or eight bars' length, while the other type is really the ancestor of the rondo form; it was often used as the final dance in a ball, consisting of eight bars danced by the whole company, then a passage for two or three dancers only, then another eight bars for the whole company, then another solo passage for different dancers, and so on, the music for the solo dancers varying while that for the company remained the same. At one time it became the convention in France to

[6]

end operas with a chaconne of this type, until Rameau ended this practice. Other dance forms current at this time were the cheerful bourrée, and the gavotte with its central musette: the latter was written over a drone bass which is reminiscent of bagpipe music. The list of the major dance forms is completed by the passacaglia, a dance similar to the chaconne in its use of a regularly repeated ostinato theme but in $\frac{4}{4}$ instead of $\frac{3}{4}$ time: originally it was lighter in style than the chaconne, but in the hands of later composers such as Bach and Handel it became extended into towering proportions.

It is interesting to reflect how much our musical forms even to-day owe to the dance forms of the early seventeenth century. The A–B–A form, as seen in the minuet and trio or gavotte and musette, is still used by practically every composer of to-day when writing a scherzo movement, and the rondo form is still used in symphonic finales: the passacaglia is still a favourite with many composers, and even the first movement sonata form was developed out of the ternary form of the minuet.

The period from 1550 onwards saw the real birth of ballet as an artistic entity—though as yet it was not an independent one. The French Court had long loved entertainments of all kinds, and in the early sixteenth century the prevalent form was the mascarade. This consisted of a miscellaneous sequence of events, including dancing, recitations of poetry, processions and tournaments, all to sing the praises of the reigning monarch. But in the second half of the century a group of poets and musicians banded themselves together in an attempt to raise the general artistic standards of the time, and in 1570 the Académie de Musique et de Poésie was officially instituted by Charles IX. Académies of this type had already existed in Italy: they were not, of course, conservatoires, but, following the Greek model, were societies in which artists collaborated in technical research in order to promote the better production of their works. The moving spirits in the new French Académie

[7]

were the poet Jean Antoine de Baïf and the musician Joachim
Thibault de Courville. Baïf was trying to create a new kind
of union of poetry and music, in which the musical rhythm
was to correspond with the metre of the verse, and in addition he wanted to create a single dramatic entertainment
which would combine poetry, music, dance, and scenery
into an organic whole. The first result of this was the *Ballet
Comique de la Reine Louise,* on the subject of Circe, first
produced before the court in 1581, in honour of the marriage
of the Duc de Joyeux. The music was by Baltasar de Beau-
joyeulx (an Italian violinist whose real name was Belgiojoso):
it replaced the loosely knit scenes of the earlier mascarades
by a unified treatment of the subject, and while it was full of
the influence of Italian opera, oratorio, and dance music, it
was sung in French and marked the foundation of the French
school of opera-ballet.

This new entertainment was not an unqualified success,
mainly because of its expense, and the old mascarades continued
to be performed, though in a slightly altered form, with more
dancing included. These ballets-mascarades were in great
favour in the reign of Henri IV (1589–1610), and over eighty
of them are reported to have been given during this period.
Meanwhile operatic music had been developing in Italy,
particularly the *dramma per musica* with its sung recitatives,
and the latter were introduced into French music from about
1610 onwards: the dramatic tension of the entertainments
was considerably increased thereby. This melodramatic form
of ballet, which almost amounted to a miniature opera, only
flourished for about ten years, and was then replaced by the
ballet de cour.

This type of ballet, which was raised to its greatest heights
later in the century by Lully, began somewhat in the manner
of the mascarades, as a mixture of song, recitative, spoken
dialogue, choruses, and dances. In these the dances were normally written by second-rate composers or by the ballet-

masters themselves, while the vocal numbers were written by the composers responsible for the Musique de la Chambre du Roy: among these were Pierre Guédron and his successor Antoine Boesset. It is noteworthy that until Lully's time Baïf's principle of the musical rhythm corresponding exactly with the metre of the verses was still observed in the choruses. To mark still further the difference between the dances and the rest of the entertainment, the former were played by the Vingt-Quatre Violons du Roy, a string band famous for its precise rhythm, and the vocal music was accompanied by a mixed band of members of the Chambre du Roy playing on theorbos, lutes, guitars, flutes, hautboys, cornets, cors de chasse, and so on.

This extremely hybrid art-form was revolutionized by Lully, who joined the royal band as a player and dancer at the age of twenty in 1652. He soon began to collaborate in the composition of the music for the dances. His talent was then observed by Cardinal Mazarin, for the wedding of whose niece he wrote a divertissement in the Italian manner: Lully himself had been born in Florence and came to France when he was fourteen. Mazarin was one of the chief supporters of Italian music in France: Rossi's *Orfeo,* staged in Paris in 1643, had been France's first introduction to Italian opera, and Mazarin had imported a company of Italian singers to popularize the new form of entertainment. But the court ballets remained firmly in the lines of French tradition, and curiously enough, it was the Italian-born Lully who realized that the Italian line of development could not succeed in Paris, though he was astute enough to write music in the Italian style when it was needed for specific purposes. Thus when Cavalli's operas *Xerse* and *Ercole Amante* were performed in Paris in 1660 and 1662 it was Lully who wrote the ballet music which French taste demanded should be inserted into them. And it was through another ballet which included arias in Italian, the *Ballet de la Galanterie du Temps,* written at Mazarin's request and performed before the whole court, with the King taking the leading part himself, that Lully's genius as a composer was finally recognized, and he was officially appointed court composer instead of merely appearing as dancer and violinist: he even persuaded the King to create a new orchestra specially for him, called the Petits Violons, as opposed to the Vingt-Quatre Violons with whom Lully had quarrelled. So within four years of his first appearance at court Lully had succeeded in being entrusted with the composition of all the purely instrumental music in the royal ballets, and it was not long before he took control of the vocal composition as well.

These royal ballets were a real State institution. Every Carnival season the King danced in his own ballet, surrounded by princes of the blood and the chief aristocrats, before an audience of three thousand people or more. These ballets were eagerly awaited events, and their brilliance showed up the poverty of the public theatres of the time. The King and his courtiers, masked and richly caparisoned, took part in certain numbers of the ballet, while other numbers were danced and sung by professionals. Each ballet had a theme of a somewhat vague character; for instance, the *Ballet de la Nuit* (1653), the first ballet in which Lully appeared as a dancer—if not as a composer too—portrayed various events, chiefly based on classical myths, occurring between sunset and sunrise. The general theme of the ballet and the production, such as it was, was in the charge of a minor court official and a poet was employed to write the sung verses, and up to Lully's time the music, as we have seen, was composed by various hands. Lully changed all this. For the *Ballet de la Galanterie du Temps* he was responsible for the subject, the music, and the dance movements as well, realizing that the ballet could never be made into an artistic form unless the prevailing hodge-podge system was replaced by some kind of unified control.

After the success of his *L'Amour Malade* (1657) and *Ballet d'Alcidiane* (1658) Lully was able to develop his ideas during the next six years, and to arrive at the unification of the singing and dancing elements within the ballet. The *ballet de cour* really became a unified musical-dramatic form. But he was still obliged to rely on mediocre poets for his texts until in 1664 he began his collaboration with Molière. This combination of a great dramatic poet and a great musician produced the new form of the comédie-ballet, which began with *Le Mariage Forcé* in 1664 and reached its climax with *Le Bourgeois Gentilhomme* in 1670. Molière and Lully were able to write for an audience whose tastes they knew exactly and who wished to see on the stage a mixture of drama and music which corresponded with those tastes. The court festivities of Louis XIV provided opportunities for cultivating this new medium before an intelligent and highly sophisticated audience. It was not enough simply to repeat the same formula year after year, but each new work had to have a new form and contain new elements which would arouse interest and provoke discussion. The seven years from 1664 to the breach between Molière and Lully in 1671 saw the French court theatre rise to a hitherto unsurpassed standard, and the experience which Lully had acquired in writing music for the *comédies-ballets* was of immeasurable help to him when he embarked on the composition of operas in the years between 1672 and his death in 1687.

Lully's period at the French court showed the gradual transformation of the ballet from an amateur into a professional entertainment; although it was originally designed for the courtiers to disport and amuse themselves in the dance, they now tended to appear in fewer and fewer of the numbers or *entrées,* and the rôle of the professional dancers increased correspondingly. Eventually only the opening and closing *entrées* of the King and courtiers remained in the *ballet de cour,* and even these disappeared in the *comédies-ballets.* Thus the ballroom dancing of the courtiers was replaced by the mime and dance of the professionals: popular dances were banished from the *ballet de cour*, only appearing when justified by the scenario, for instance in a ball scene or country festival. And if a gavotte, courante, or bourrée, for instance, appeared as part of the music, the dancers would not use the ballroom dance steps for them, but would adapt to the rhythm of these dances the steps and gestures which fitted the rôles they were portraying. One can see from the surviving drawings of dancers of this period the importance given to miming in these dances: the gestures portrayed are often violent and even bizarre, and are far removed from the stately choreography which is usually provided for 'period' dances in modern ballets. French theatrical dancing of this time was extremely bold and realistic, and the courtiers, when they did take part in the ballets, were limited to the easier dances and were usually surrounded by professionals who could see that they did not make too many mistakes.

But the ballet as we know it to-day had still not developed into an independent entity: the music consisted of a very large number of short numbers—overtures, ritournelles, airs (often purely instrumental), sarabandes, gavottes, bourrées, galliards, etc.,—interspersed with spoken dialogue or singing. The comédies-ballets were plays with music in which the dancing was more or less incidental: and the next step forward was the creation of the *opéra-ballet,* in which spoken dialogue disappeared, and which was a complete musical and dramatic entertainment given in a public theatre.

In 1669 Louis XIV granted letters patent to the Abbé Perrin, Robert Cambert, and the Marquis de Sourdéac for the establishment of an 'Académie Royale de Musique' which should present in public 'operas and dramas in music, and in French verse' on the model of the Italian opera houses. This marked the foundation of what is now the Paris Opéra, and it opened in 1671 with Cambert's opera *Pomone.* However Lully, who had recently broken with Molière, by a series of intrigues managed to obtain control of the new opera house, and he remained its director till his death in 1687. During this period he not only produced a large number of operas of his own, but he also laid down the lines on which the Opéra was to continue for many years—in fact until the advent of Rameau some forty years later. After his death his work was carried on by his pupils strictly according to his principles; in fact even in his lifetime those who disagreed with his methods were compelled to break away, and they founded what is now the Opéra-Comique. Nevertheless Lully did lay the foundations of French opera: and ballet was an integral part of it from the start. Hence, no doubt, the French insistence, which was only relaxed not so very many years ago, that every opera must contain a ballet: to them an opera without a ballet was quite unthinkable. Lully considerably developed the musical side of opera and also increased the resources of the orchestra: he also followed Cambert in obtaining sanction for the appearance of women on the stage. Noble ladies did dance occasionally in court ballets, but usually female parts were taken either by boys or by men wearing masks, and this was certainly a step forward: in addition the lords and ladies of the court were now given royal permission to appear on the stage at the Académie as performers if they so wished. The mixture of vocal music and dancing in Lully's operas still did not give ballet a really independent status: but the founding of the Académie did mean that opera and ballet had now been put on a permanent basis in a proper theatre with a professional company. Some years later the entertainments organized by the Duchesse du Maine at Sceaux showed the beginning of the *ballet d'action*: for these consisted of classical legends mimed to music, and performed by well-known dancers who had never attempted pantomime before. The first of these, *Les Horaces,* was so successful that the Duchess's musical director, Mouret, was emboldened to compose several ballets for the Académie on similar lines. In

Lully's operas the ballets were introduced at suitable moments in the dramatic action and formed an integral part of the plot: the remainder of the music consisted mainly of an arioso type of recitative, with occasional arias interspersed. This was also the type of opera which was later developed by Rameau.

Meanwhile in England dramatic music had been following a course mainly parallel to that in France, if at a rather slower pace. The innate conservatism of the English character made them wary of assimilating foreign styles and habits until they had been carefully weighed and tested. The birth of opera in Italy at the end of the sixteenth century had not affected the normal English custom of using music merely as an incidental addition to the structure of a play, although the solo song and the lute-song were, of course, recognized and accepted and the new sung recitative had been introduced into the court masques. In England, as in France, dramatic entertainment on a large scale could only be found at the royal court. These masques, like the French mascarades, included dialogue, singing and dancing: they were a hybrid form of entertainment which provided greater opportunities to the scenic artist and the musician. They flourished under James I and Charles I. No expense was spared in their production, and the stage settings and machinery were elaborate. The most famous masque of this period was Milton's *Comus,* with music by Henry Lawes, produced at Ludlow Castle in 1634.

The Civil War ended the elaborate royal divertissements but did not kill the masque, which was carried on by less exalted performers. Cromwell's régime banned stage plays but did not object to musical entertainments as such. Thus in 1653 Shirley's *Cupid and Death,* with music by Matthew Locke and Christopher Gibbons, was performed privately in honour of the Portuguese Ambassador. Meanwhile, as we have seen, Italian opera had been brought to Paris by Cardinal Mazarin, and the young Prince Charles, later to become Charles II, attended several performances while living in exile there.

This was to affect musical developments in England after the Restoration. At the same time the Italian type of opera was introduced into England, but in a somewhat hole-and-corner manner. In 1656 D'Avenant's opera *The Siege of Rhodes,* with music by Henry Lawes, Matthew Locke, and three other composers, was performed before a small audience at Rutland House, Aldersgate, in the City of London. But in general this kind of opera, with no spoken dialogue, did not meet with success in England, though after the Restoration Cambert came to London, when Lully had wrested control of the Paris Académie, bringing with him Perrin's opera *Ariane, ou le Mariage de Bacchus.* This was set to music by Grabu, the Master of the King's Musick, and was performed at the Theatre Royal in 1674 by the 'Royal Academy of Music', an institution obviously modelled on the French Académie. Grabu later collaborated with Dryden in an English opera on the French model, *Albion and Albanius,* but this was a failure, and the only other performance of a complete opera in England at this time seems to have been one of Lully's *Cadmus et Hermione* in 1686, given by a French company. Purcell was probably present at this performance: at any rate he appropriated one of the airs and used it in his music for *The Tempest,* and it is clear from his Welcome Songs that he was familiar with Lully's instrumental style.

But English taste on the whole was against opera on the French or Italian models and turned to a hybrid form of entertainment—the dramatic spectacle in which music played a large and important part. Some of these were adaptations of existing plays, including Shakespeare's, while others were specially written for operatic performance. These began as imitations of the Molière-Lully *comédies-ballets,* the first of them being Shadwell's *Psyche,* first performed in 1675, and a French *comédie-ballet, Rare en Tout,* was performed at court in 1677. This vogue for the semi-opera did not last much longer than the end of the seventeenth century, but the majority of Purcell's dramatic works are cast in this form. And with the Restoration the masque again became a court entertainment, often being produced on a lavish scale.

Cupid and Death, for which the music had been written by Locke and Gibbons, contains a large number of dances and short instrumental pieces as well as songs, both florid and lyrical, declamatory recitative-like movements, and choruses. the last usually being combined with parts for the solo singers. The Restoration masques followed much the same pattern: and though *Psyche,* for which Locke and Draghi wrote the music, is described as an opera, it is in all essentials a masque, designed for public rather than private performances. The theatres had now been reopened, and dramatic performances no longer had to be restricted to private gatherings. The first masque of real musical importance was *Venus and Adonis,* by John Blow, produced some time between 1680 and 1687. The music shows an acquaintance both with Lully's instrumental style and with the operatic declamation of the Italians. There is no spoken dialogue, and the work is a small-scale opera rather than a true masque, but it contains a number of instrumental movements for dancing. It is interesting as a forerunner of Purcell's *Dido and Aeneas;* the music has a great deal of charm, and the work has been revived many times on the modern stage with success.

Dido and Aeneas, Purcell's best-known dramatic work, is also his only opera: but it is not an opera on a grand scale, having been written for private performance at a ladies' boarding-school in Chelsea, and in this it follows the tradition of the pre-Restoration masques. Like *Venus and Adonis,* it contains no spoken dialogue; but dancing is prominent, both alone and together with choral singing. Though it is divided into three acts, it only lasts about an hour in performance. Standing between the English masque and the Italian cantata, it was a prelude to a development that never took place— the founding of an English operatic form. When Italian opera finally came to London in the eighteenth century, it mainly consisted of a number of arias linked by recitatives, and the more concise dramatic form seen in *Dido*, and consisting of choruses and dancing as well as recitatives and arias, never bore fruit. Indeed Purcell's other dramatic works are operas only in name. They are really combinations of heroic drama and music, the music not being purely incidental but making a considerable contribution of its own; but the principal actors do not sing—this was apparently due to the lack of experienced opera singers in London at the time. Dancing however becomes of great importance in these works, especially in the numerous divertissements which intersperse the action. In *Dioclesian*, for instance, which was produced in the year after *Dido and Aeneas*, there is a sumptuous masque, consisting of both dancing and singing, which occupies the greater part of Act V, as well as two ceremonial occasions earlier in the work which are similarly celebrated with song and dance, and various incidental dances and songs are interspersed from time to time. The masque in *Dioclesian* has become one of Purcell's best-known works and is frequently performed in concerts. In the original production the stage was divided into four levels, representing the palaces of Flora, Pomona, Bacchus, and the Sun respectively, and the singers and dancers took the parts of the three gods as well as Silvanus and the gods of the rivers: there were also fauns, nymphs, heroes, heroines, shepherds, shepherdesses, and the Graces and Pleasures with their followers. The music contains two breezy bacchanals and a charming duet for the shepherd and shepherdess, as well as an impressive final chaconne. In fact it was successful enough to attract the attention of Dryden, who was in search of a composer who he felt could match his verse in music, and the result of this was the collaboration of Dryden and Purcell in *King Arthur*.

King Arthur, a strange mixture of fantasy and historical legend, was deliberately designed by Dryden as a semi-opera, and he made ample provision for songs, choruses and dances in it. In fact the music is more important here than in *Dioclesian*. But a concert performance of the music alone is not satisfactory; it is intimately linked to the stage action, and for this reason *King Arthur,* in spite of its somewhat absurd plot, does make a successful fusion of drama and music which can hold the stage even to-day. The *Fairy Queen,* on the other hand, which was produced in 1692, is simply a succession of masques which have little to do with the subject of the play: this was adapted from *A Midsummer Night's Dream,* but one would be hard put to it to guess the fact. All sorts of characters are introduced who do not figure in the original— gods and goddesses, spirits, nymphs, shepherds, monkeys, Chinese dancers, and the four seasons. Oberon and Titania, and Bottom and his crew appear as speaking characters, and the action is constantly being interrupted for singing and dancing. Nevertheless if staged as a lavish spectacle, as was done at Covent Garden soon after the war, *The Fairy Queen* can provide a very effective entertainment, and it contains a good deal of Purcell's best music.

Purcell's last two semi-operas, *The Indian Queen* and *The Tempest*—the latter being an adaptation of Shakespeare by Shadwell—show him at the height of his musical powers. The music is smaller in quantity than in *King Arthur* and *The Fairy Queen,* but its quality is at least equal to that of the earlier works, and it certainly deserves to be more frequently performed. In *The Tempest,* as we have seen, Purcell borrowed the melody of the dance which immediately follows the well-known air 'Arise, ye subterranean winds' from Lully's *Cadmus et Hermione,* but he was evidently not content to accept Lully's harmony—or that of his assistants—without question, and he radically altered the bass. Purcell's early death brought to an end the hopes of creating an English operatic style of the kind that Lully had achieved in France. In his last two stage works Purcell had thoroughly absorbed the Italian style, and with more time he might have been able to forge a national form of opera which would have been strong enough to stand up to the Italian invasion later in the eighteenth century. But it is useless to regret what might have happened, and we can merely be glad that Purcell left us as much fine dramatic music as he did; apart from the semi-operas he wrote incidental music for over forty plays.

In France little changed between the death of Lully and the arrival of Rameau on the French operatic scene. In Lully's later years the *ballet de cour* was tending to lose its own distinctive character and to become merged with the opera-ballet, and several of Lully's later operatic productions emphasize the dancing at the expense of the singing and dramatic action. The most famous of these, *Le Triomphe de l'Amour* (1685) provides the best fusion of opera and ballet of its time. Most of the other ballets, so-called, differed from the operas only in being based on lyrical and pastoral rather than heroic subjects. However the operas and ballets of Quinault and Lully did offer a unified form of entertainment in which a single theme was developed throughout five acts. The eighteenth-century ballet provided a new form in which each act treated a different subject. This was the invention of the poet Antoine Houdar de la Motte, who, in collaboration with the composer Campra, produced in 1697 the ballet *L'Europe Galante*. This set a new vogue and was followed by other ballets of the same type. In fact it now became possible to differentiate between the opera and the opera-ballet for the first time: in general an opera was based on a tragic or heroic subject, which it developed throughout its five acts, and the dancing in it merely served the purpose of adding variety to the action, whilst a ballet was based on a lyrical, fantastic or gay subject, had no fixed number of acts—varying between one and four, but three was the most common number—and each of these dealt with a different theme and had its own title. Finally, though the ballet still contained solo and choral singing, these were inserted merely to explain the course of the action, and the dance was paramount.

Rameau's most famous ballet, *Les Indes Galantes,* was first produced at the Opéra in 1735. The tradition of *L'Europe Galante* had by then been established for nearly forty years, and though writers like Jean-Jacques Rousseau might object to the loose sequence of themes in the ballets of this type, they had become firmly fixed in the popular favour, and Rameau had to conform to it. The libretto of *Les Indes Galantes,* by Louis Fuselier, a well-known stage writer of the time, originally consisted of a prologue and three entrées or acts, all depicting vaguely oriental or Indian themes—'Le Turc Généreux', 'Les Incas du Pérou', and 'Les Fleurs, Fête Persane'. For the second production in the following year Rameau and his collaborator added a fourth act, 'Les Sauvages', set in savage America. This was done in order that Rameau could introduce into it his *Air des Sauvages,* written ten years earlier for the Comédie Italienne, which had become very popular. The principal male rôle in the early productions was taken by the well-known dancer Dupré, and the part of the Rose in the Flower Scene was danced by Mlle. Sallé in the first production, and in later productions by Mlle. Camargo. At the time of the first performance Mlle. Sallé had just returned from London, where she had danced in the fables of *Pygmalion* and of *Bacchus and Ariadne.* In the former she created history by discarding the formal and elaborate costumes which all ballet dancers still wore and appearing in a simple Greek dress. But the tradition of the court ballets of Louis XIV still persisted at the Opéra, so far as costumes were concerned, and Rameau was one of those principally responsible for liberating the dancers from their cumbrous conventional garments and giving them freedom of movement. He is even reputed to have taught Dupré how to dance the chaconne in 'Les Sauvages', when the famous dancer found difficulty in executing the steps himself. Rameau was certainly in constant difficulties with dancers who had their own fixed ideas of what to do on the stage, and demanded that he should write dances which would show off their own particular capabilities without any regard for the effect of the ballet as a whole—Mlle. Prévost demanded passepieds, Mlle. Sallé musettes, Mlle. Camargo tambourins, while Dupré insisted on chaconnes and passacaglias, which suited his style of dancing best. At this time the ballet company had considerably increased beyond the four men, later joined by four women, with which Lully had begun at the Opéra, and the company now consisted of fourteen solo dancers and twenty-six who formed the corps de ballet. And Rameau, by the sheer dramatic power of his music as much as by anything else, was able to widen the scope of the dancers' capabilities and lay the foundation of the modern pantomime ballet.

Nevertheless, if one looks at the score of Les Indes Galantes, one is bound to notice how few numbers in it, as compared with the vocal numbers, are for dancing alone. Individual dance numbers are certainly interspersed between the songs and choruses throughout the work, but the only considerable ballet section, as such, comes in the third entrée, 'Les Fleurs', which ends with an elaborate ballet consisting of two airs danced, not sung, by the Flowers, a gavotte en rondeau, a storm scene, an air for Boreas and two for Zephyrus, another air for the Flowers and a final gavotte. This section of the work is the only one that is in the present-day ballet repertoire, having been revived in a lavish production by the Paris Opera Ballet, with choreography by Harald Lander. It certainly makes an attractive spectacle, but one cannot honestly say that it is more than a period piece. Rameau's music, incidentally, does not attempt orientalism anywhere in Les Indes Galantes; even the conventional 'Turkish music' of bass drum, cymbals and triangle which occurs in Mozart's Il Seraglio and many later eighteenth-century works finds no place here, and Incas and Persians alike dance to courtly French measures. But *Les Indes Galantes* was undoubtedly a success in its time, and did a great deal to increase Rameau's reputation. It remained in the repertoire of the Opéra, as a whole or in separate acts, till 1773.

Rameau's operas contain almost as much dance music as *Les Indes Galantes* does: in *Castor and Pollux* (1737), which many regard as his masterpiece, each act contains a separate section for dancing only, and the number of minor characters who are portrayed by dancers is immense—they include, in the Prologue, the Graces, Arts and Pleasures, and in the main action athletes, warriors and Spartiates, followers of Hebe, demons, spectres and monsters, blessed spirits, stars, constellations, planets, satellites, and many others. This was typical of the French opera, which insisted on lavish spectacle, but the dances in themselves were not complicated, and chiefly acted as interludes in the dramatic action, the chaconne— which was the inevitable ending of the old *ballets de cour*— here appearing immediately before the final chorus in the last act. A good deal of the ballet music of *Castor and Pollux* has become well known, particularly the menuet chanté 'Naissez, dons de Flore' from the Prologue; and there is also a good deal of admirable ballet music in *Hippolyte et Aricie* and many of Rameau's other operas. But with Rameau, as with Lully, each dance is a short, self-contained unit—apart from certain exceptions for dramatic purposes and also the final chaconnes, which are usually more elaborate and extended. For modern ballet they would really only be suitable for a divertissement type of ballet of a rather formal kind. In spite of their many beauties and felicities they still breathe the air of the conventionally regulated court dance.

Thus Rameau's achievement was not a revolutionary one. It consisted more in breathing new life into traditional forms. Certain of the dances which were popular in Louis XIV's time had now fallen out of favour under his successor: allemandes and courantes are rarely found in Rameau's operas, and the sarabandes are only of the 'tendre' type, such as that for Hebe in *Castor and Pollux*. The gavotte and minuet occur more frequently, here often invested with a nostalgic undercurrent which was lacking in Lully's music, and the loure in Rameau's later ballet *Les Fêtes d'Hébé* (1739) almost acquires a character of religious solemnity: similarly Rameau's gigues tend to be civilized and subtle rather than extrovertly gay. But Rameau also used the dance forms of the common people —rigaudons, bourrées, tambourins, musettes, and contredanses, and he saw to it these were practical for dancing to, unlike the more stylized contrapuntal dances of Couperin and Bach.

Side by side with the more formal type of ballet, the new form of pantomime ballet was steadily developing in the middle of the eighteenth century, Noverre in Paris being one of its leading exponents. Noverre's ideas spread to other countries, and in 1761 Gluck's ballet *Don Juan* was produced in Vienna. This marked a turning-point both in the history of ballet and in Gluck's own career. It was the first pantomime ballet with music by a really important composer, and it also marks the dividing line between Gluck's early and mature works. The scenario is based on Molière's *Le Festin de Pierre*, and the ballet consists entirely of dances, without singing or speaking of any kind. The preface to the score states, perhaps with some exaggeration, that *Don Juan* is the first ballet to return to the pantomime of the ancients; at any rate it certainly marked a considerable step forward in the development of ballet as we know it to-day, and it was successfully revived in 1936 with choreography by Fokine. The music consists of some thirty short numbers; some, like the gavotte and fandango, use traditional dance forms, but most are short symphonic pieces, and some are extremely dramatic. Gluck was forty-seven when he composed this ballet. Although he had written one ballet, *Alessandro*, about six years previously, he had chiefly been occupied with the conventional form of

Italian opera then in vogue, which consisted mostly of giving the singers opportunities to display their technique, to the detriment of the dramatic action, just as the ballets of the time contained little but posturing and acrobatics. *Don Juan* thus marked a revolution both in the choreography, which attempted to give a serious representation of a drama by means of pantomimic dancing, and in the music, which is written with a simplicity and directness new for Gluck, and which anticipates the style of his *Orfeo,* produced in the following year, and his other mature operas. The irrelevancies and trappings of his earlier Italian operas have now disappeared, and we are presented with a series of self-contained movements, some admittedly rather conventional, but many which are full of dramatic expressiveness. The final Larghetto and Allegro in particular admirably express the climax of the drama, the Statue's revenge on Don Juan, and they must have been in Mozart's mind when he himself came to write *Don Giovanni.* The chromatic harmony and the use of the trombones are strikingly similar.

Don Juan was originally divided into three acts. In the first Don Juan serenades Elvira: the Commendatore intervenes and is killed by Juan. The second act represents a feast at Don Juan's house. The statue of the Commendatore appears, and invites Don Juan to return his visit. The third act takes place in the cemetery: when Don Juan appears, the Statue leaves its pedestal, demands that Don Juan recant his wickedness, and consigns him to hell. This scenario had been adapted from Molière by the Italian dancing master Angiolini, who had been living in Vienna for some years. Angiolini was responsible for the choreography of all Gluck's ballets apart from those in his Paris operas, where Gluck collaborated with Noverre. Angiolini and Noverre were of the same generation, and shared the same ideas on the importance of creating a really dramatic pantomime ballet; but there were several points on which they disagreed. It was Noverre's habit to distribute to the audience a programme giving the plot of the ballet to be performed: Angiolini considered a ballet to have failed if the audience could not grasp the meaning of the mimed action without being primed in this way. In addition, Angiolini was attempting to develop a system of choreographic notation, which Noverre regarded as impracticable. There seems to have been some considerable jealousy between the two choreographers, but Angiolini was not too proud to learn from his rival. It can hardly be a coincidence that Don Juan was produced within a year of the publication of Noverre's famous *Lettres sur la Danse et les Ballets,* in which he set forth his principles of mimed dancing: Noverre had been working on these ideas for some years, and seems to have been impressed by, among other things, the miming of Garrick, whom he saw in London in 1755, and with whom he had a good many discussions on artistic problems.

Gluck's other ballets, all produced in Vienna, did not achieve the importance of *Don Juan.* Apart from *Alessandro,* the date of which is uncertain, and which does not seem ever to have been properly finished, they consist of *Semiramide,* produced in 1765, and *L'Orfano della China,* which appears to date from the following year or thereabouts. *Semiramide* was adapted from Voltaire's drama by Calzabigi, the librettist of Gluck's *Orfeo.* Although, like *Don Juan,* it is in three acts, it is comparatively short, only containing about thirty minutes of music. A good deal of this music was later used by Gluck for *Armide* and the two *Iphigénies. L'Orfano della China,* also adapted from Voltaire, is based on the story of a contest between the civilized Chinese and the barbarous Tartars, and though Gluck does not make any attempt at orientalism in his music, he does contrast the two races stylistically in the individual dances.

In addition to his actual ballets, Gluck of course wrote a considerable amount of ballet music in his operas. *Orfeo,* for instance, has an expressive ballo with mimed action early in

the first act, where Orpheus sends the chorus away, wishing
to be alone with his grief. The first scene of the second act,
set in Hades, contains the famous chorus and ballet of Furies,
full of tremolandi and bustling scales. For the Paris production
of the opera Gluck added to this scene the dramatic Dance of
the Furies from *Don Juan*. In the next scene, set in the Elysian
Fields, the beautiful and well-known Ballet of the Blessed
Spirits comes as a superb contrast, and even the last act ends
with a festive ballet of celebration—the first performance of
Orfeo in Vienna took place on the Emperor's name day,
and it was therefore found necessary to change the tragic
ending of the classical myth by means of a *deus ex machina*.
Similarly *Iphigénie en Aulide*, Gluck's first opera written for
Paris, ends with a grand ballet—with a solo for soprano
sandwiched in the middle of it—and solo singers and a chorus
also taking part. In spite of the tragic and dramatic nature of
the story it would have been impossible for Gluck to defy the
tradition of the Paris opera ballet. *Armide,* a setting of the
same libretto by Quinault which Lully had used some ninety
years earlier, contains several ballets, some danced by Armida's
companions, some by nymphs and naiads, an important
ballet of evil spirits and an impressive chaconne in the final
act. In *Iphigénie en Tauride* the most remarkable dance numbers are those for the Scythians in the first act and the Eumen-
ides in the second—apart, of course, for the inevitable festive
ballet at the end, again brought about by divine intervention.
The Scythian chorus which precedes the dances in the first
act contains parts for side drum and cymbals, at that time a
fairly rare effect in dramatic music, and it was a later conductor's attempt to improve on Gluck by adding cymbals
to the first dance as well that so enraged Berlioz when he
saw the opera as a student in 1824. 'As to the cymbals,' he
writes in his *Memoirs,* 'which Gluck has introduced so happily
in the first Scythian chorus, I do not know who had taken
upon himself to import them into the dance, thus falsifying

the colour and marring the sinister silence of that weird ballet. . . . Boiling with anger, I nevertheless contained myself until the piece was finished, and then, seizing the occasion of the momentary lull which preceded the next piece, I shouted out with all my might, "There are no cymbals there: who has dared to correct Gluck?" The hubbub may be imagined. The public, who are not very sharp-sighted in matters connected with art, and to whom changes in an author's work are matters of complete indifference, could not understand what made the young lunatic in the pit so angry. But in all subsequent performances order was restored: the cymbals were silent, and I listened content, muttering through my teeth, "All right".'

Gluck's ballet music hardly rouses such passions nowadays, but as a master of dramatic effect Gluck did see that his ballets were an integral part of the action and did not unnecessarily hold up the course of the drama—apart, perhaps, from the final celebrations in several of his operas, which he was forced to include for extraneous reasons. And though Gluck's strength lay in vocal melody and in orchestral effect, much of his ballet music is more than competent, and, as in *Orfeo* and *Iphigénie en Tauride,* often inspired. Gluck certainly gave the ballet a new dignity and impressiveness which was to have far-reaching consequences in later years.

A curious sideline to the ballet music of the period may be found in the *Ballet Espagnol* of the Italian composer Luigi Boccherini, who, in spite of having written 155 quintets, ninety-one quartets, forty-two trios, twenty symphonies, and sixteen sextets, is now known to us almost exclusively by one minuet. Boccherini was a more or less exact contemporary of Haydn, whom he somewhat resembled in style, though he was romantic and colourful rather than strictly classical in feeling. It is this feeling for colour which makes his *Spanish Ballet* specially interesting. He held an appointment in Spain for sixteen years, and later returned to end his

days in Madrid. He obviously had a considerable acquaintance with Spanish popular music, and was one of the earliest
Italian composers, apart from Domenico Scarlatti, to introduce Spanish elements into his works. He even wrote three
quintets for guitar and strings, one of which has a finale in
fandango rhythm, while another is called *The Retreat from
Madrid* and has a Turkish March for the finale. In one of his
string quintets the second cello is played pizzicato throughout
and is directed to be held on the knees like a guitar.

The *Ballet Espagnol* was written in 1774, five years after
Boccherini's arrival in Spain, and was given in Vienna and
Moscow in the following year. The choreography may have
been by Boccherini's brother-in-law Onorato Vigano, the
father of Salvatore Vigano, the choreographer of Beethoven's
Prometheus, and it is even possible that young Salvatore
danced in it before the Spanish court. The music uses a number of Spanish effects, including syncopations, roulades, and
guitar-like pizzicato accompaniments. The third movement,
unusually, introduces two dulcimers into the score. These
instruments, like the cimbalom, consisted of wires struck by
hammers held in the hands, and their use in this particular
context again suggests the imitation of a guitar effect. Other
effects include the use of violas playing sul ponticello, long
drone basses and much use of divided strings. It would certainly be interesting to hear this ballet under modern conditions. Boccherini's music was used in recent times in *Scuola
di Ballo,* and there is plenty to interest choreographers among
his enormous output. A start in the rehabilitation of Boccherini has in fact been made by various Italian chamber
music ensembles who regularly play his works, and there is
no reason why this process should not go further.

Though Haydn wrote a good deal of both stage and dance
music, he did not concern himself with ballet as such, and we
may now pass on to the story of Mozart's brief flirtation with
the ballet—a flirtation which might have become more of a

regular affair if Mozart had had the necessary opportunities, for he was clearly attracted to the art. His only surviving ballet is *Les Petits Riens,* written in 1778 when he was on a visit to Paris. The twenty-two-year-old composer had met Noverre, and had hoped to be commissioned to write an opera for Paris. But Noverre asked for a ballet instead, and Mozart appears to have suggested the libretto of *Les Petits Riens,* which had already been performed in Vienna in 1768 with music by Asplmayr. Mozart wrote to his father on 9 July 1778: 'Because of Noverre's ballet I have written nothing else. . . . He used just half a ballet, and I wrote the music for it—that is, there will be six pieces by others in it, which however only consist of wretched old French airs. This ballet has already been given four times with great applause. But I absolutely won't do anything if I don't know in advance what I'm getting for it: I only did this out of friendship for Noverre.'

The ballet was given six performances, together with Piccinni's *Fausses Jumelles;* then the music was forgotten, and was only rediscovered in 1872. In consists of an Overture and twenty dances, of which seven are probably not by Mozart. A theme from the Overture was later used in *Figaro.* It also appears from sketches for a ballet intermezzo with indications for the action, which is preserved in the Paris Bibliothèque Nationale, and from another page of sketches in the German State Library in Berlin, that Mozart was planning to write another ballet for Noverre, but evidently this came to nothing. Another Mozart ballet, *L'Épreuve d'Amour,* was discovered in manuscript at Graz in the 1930's and was first performed at Monte Carlo on 4 April 1936, with choreography and book by Fokine and décor and costumes by Derain: but the authenticity of the music is doubtful—some numbers are clearly based on some of Mozart's Kontretänze, while others appear to be by different hands. It remains also to mention Mozart's incomplete *Music to a Pantomime* which dates from 1783.

Though Mozart wrote no more actual ballets, a good deal of dance music naturally comes in his operas, the most famous numbers perhaps being the fandango which forms part of the wedding festivities in *Figaro,* and the celebrated ball scene in *Don Giovanni.* The latter calls for three orchestras on the stage: the first, composed of oboes, horns and strings, leads off with a minuet. Then the second orchestra, of strings only, is heard tuning up—the actual notes for this are indicated in the score—and then begins a gavotte which is heard simultaneously with the minuet, each bar of the gavotte occupying the same time as two beats of the minuet. Then the third orchestra, also of strings, tunes up and begins a German waltz, each bar of which occupies one beat of the minuet. The simultaneous combination of these three dances is one of Mozart's most characteristic and ingenious effects.

Beethoven's principal contribution to ballet, apart from the early *Ritterballett,* was *The Creations of Prometheus,* written in the latter part of 1800, when the composer was thirty, and produced at the Burgtheater, Vienna, on 28 March 1801. It was a great success, receiving sixteen performances in 1801 and another thirteen in the following year. The piano score was published immediately, and Beethoven was given time to breathe and probably some cash to spare before embarking on other enterprises. The choreography was by the Italian dancer Salvatore Vigano, who had come to Vienna in 1793 and had recently returned there after a tour of Germany. The subject is said to have been suggested by Haydn's *The Creation,* and the piece is called a 'heroic allegorical ballet', in two acts. The score consists of an overture, which is frequently played as a concert item, a short and stormy 'Introduction' and sixteen numbers. The actual libretto has been lost, but a synopsis of it survives from a theatre bill. Prometheus is 'a lofty spirit who found the men of his day in a state of ignorance and civilized them by giving them the arts and sciences. Starting from this idea, the ballet shows us two statues brought to life and made susceptible to all the passions of human life by the power of harmony. Act II is placed in Parnassus and shows the apotheosis of Prometheus, who brings the men created by him to be instructed by Apollo and the Muses, thus endowing them with the blessings of culture.' It seems more than likely that some, at any rate, of the ideas in this libretto stem not from Vigano but from Beethoven, who regarded Prometheus, as 'the liberator of mankind from sorrow', to be in some ways symbolic of himself. And in fact *Prometheus* does mark the turning point in Beethoven's development and the boundary between his first and second periods. Beethoven himself attached considerable importance to the work, and the principal theme of the finale, which in the ballet accompanies the apotheosis of Prometheus in his rôle of the liberator of mankind, was subsequently used by him as the basis of the Variations in E flat for piano, Op. 35 and also of the finale of the 'Eroica' Symphony, written two years after *Prometheus*—it is clear that this theme, which, incidentally, also appears in a small contredanse written by Beethoven about the same time, had a considerable symbolic significance for him. He evidently regarded it as representing 'creative power and divine completion', as one writer has put it.

The overture to *Prometheus* bears a marked resemblance to the first movement of Beethoven's first symphony, which had been written a few months earlier: the 'Introduction' which precedes the ballet itself has much in common with the 'Representation of Chaos' in Haydn's *Creation* and fulfils a similar purpose. The dances which follow are real ballet music in that they are not symphonically constructed but mostly fall into short sections in contrasting moods and tempi which follow the stage action. Beethoven must clearly have worked very closely with Vigano and carried out his wishes in detail. There are many contrasts of colour and a considerable use of solo instruments; the fifth number introduces a harp, an unusual instrument in the orchestras of the time, and also contains a cadenza for solo 'cello, while the fourteenth number has an elaborate part for the basset horn. In the finale the 'Eroica' theme appears, not as a basis for a set of variations, but in a rondo-like manner, alternating with other themes. *Prometheus* was certainly an important step forward, not only for Beethoven himself, but in the whole history of ballet music, and it has been successfully revived in modern times.

Beethoven's only other excursion into ballet, the *Ritterballett,* was produced for the Bonn nobility in 1791, when Beethoven was only twenty-one: in fact he was asked to act as the 'ghost' of Count Waldstein, but the true authorship of the music soon became known. The ballet, which is Beethoven's earliest orchestral work of undoubted authenticity, is a straightforward score in eight numbers. The second of these, a 'Deutscher Gesang', bears a curious resemblance to the vivace of Beethoven's piano sonata in G, Op. 79—that movement too is marked 'presto alla tedesca'.

The story of Schubert's unfortunate experiences in the theatre is too well known to need repetition here, nor did Schubert ever write a ballet as such. However he did write two pieces of ballet music which have become world-famous, particularly the second one. These come in the eleven pieces of incidental music which he composed in 1823 for the play *Rosamunde, Princess of Cyprus.* The text was by the well-known bluestocking Helmine von Chezy, who also was responsible for the somewhat absurd libretto of Weber's *Euryanthe.* The play of *Rosamunde* has been lost, but a contemporary synopsis of the plot shows it to have been even more absurd, if possible, than *Euryanthe. Rosamunde* was produced at the Theater an der Wien on 20 December 1823, Schubert having completed the music in five days. Although only one orchestral rehearsal of two hours was possible, the music was so well received that the overture was encored and Schubert himself was accorded an ovation at the end of the performance. But the play had only one further performance, and the music remained forgotten till 1867, when it was discovered in Vienna by Sir George Grove and Sir Arthur Sullivan in the course of their quest for Schubert MSS. The first of the two ballets in *Rosamunde* is the third piece in the set of incidental music. It is in B minor, and somewhat dramatic in character, with a strongly marked rhythm. It begins with a repetition of the first nine bars of the first entr'acte, no doubt for dramatic reasons, and then continues with a fairly brilliant section in B major which includes a restatement of the opening bars. It ends with a short lyrical section in G major, in a somewhat slower tempo. The second ballet, in G major, is the last piece in the score. It has become one of Schubert's best-known works, as indeed it deserves to be, and it is absurd to think that it was lost until forty years after its composer's death!

II

Ballet Music in Opera during the Nineteenth Century

AFTER the death of Gluck ballet continued to be an integral part of French opera, as indeed it remained up to the end of the nineteenth century. But there was a somewhat closer integration, in that a good many of the dance numbers contained solo or choral singing—as happens in the ball scene in *Don Giovanni*—and the ballet was not invariably left on its own as a separate item or interlude. It would be tedious and indeed impossible to give complete details of all the ballet music written for late eighteenth- and early nineteenth-century operas by such composers as Méhul, Gossec, Grétry, Auber, Boieldieu and others. Most of it is now forgotten, though some operas of this period have been raided by modern choreographers to provide music for their ballets—a procedure which will be discussed in a later chapter —and in other cases conductors and arrangers have made suites out of the music which have become popular concert items. Among the best known of these are the suites arranged from Grétry's *Céphale et Procris, Zémire et Azore,* and *La Rosière Républicaine.* The last of these is interesting for several reasons: it was produced in 1794, when revolutionary feeling was at its height, and its original title was *La Fête de la Raison.* It is a short opera in one act only, and it is really a kind of divertissement which leads up to the elaborate ballet with which it closes. The theme is anti-clerical in that priests and nuns are shown as yielding, somewhat unwillingly, to the popular rejoicing which accompanies the crowning of the May Queen at a village Spring Festival and even taking part in the dancing of the carmagnole. There is a vigorous and inelegant 'Danse Générale' with a definitely earthy flavour: then follows a pas de trois in which a dancer—the part was taken by Vestris at the first performance—stops two nuns on their way to Mass and persuades them to take off their veils and dance a 'gavotte retenue', followed by the carmagnole in which all join and which ends the opera. This certainly shows Grétry in a different vein from the elegant and classical music which he wrote for the rest of his fifty operas, mostly on safe historical subjects: but he was not a composer of great personality even at the best of times.

Much the same may be said of Méhul, Gossec, and Boieldieu, whose music remains unperformed to-day, apart from a few overtures. Auber, who came later, had a less frigidly classical approach and was also possessed of the gift of writing catchy tunes. His *Masaniello,* the scene of which is laid in Naples under the Spanish occupation, contains a guaracca and a bolero as well as the famous tarantella which Liszt made into a virtuoso piano piece. *Les Diamants de la Couronne* contains a sarabande for a ball scene at the Portuguese court, as well as a sung bolero, and Auber's music has been successfully used in modern times for the ballet *Les Rendezvous.*

Weber's operas do not contain any ballets as such, but there are of course a number of dance movements introduced as aids to the dramatic action. In his early opera *Sylvana* there is a pantomime scene in which the dumb heroine dances in front of a mirror to a graceful piece of music. Later there is a duet in which her voice is represented by a 'cello solo, and at the end there comes a torch dance. *Preciosa,* the scene of which is laid in Spain, contains some Spanish and gipsy dances. There is a short and lively ballet movement in Act I, and in Act III comes a set of three Spanish national dances, Allegro , Andante, with the flavour of a bolero, and Molto vivace.

Der Freischütz has a rustic waltz for the villagers early in the first act, and in *Euryanthe* there is a Maestoso dance somewhat in the style of a polonaise after the opening chorus: during this the ladies crown their knights. Weber also composed an additional ballet movement, a pas de cinq, for the performance of the opera in Berlin. This is a fair-sized group of dances consisting of a short introduction, an Andante quasi allegretto , a Vivace and a Presto . Finally *Oberon* contains some fairy dances and the well-known chorus-barcarolle.

One of the most curious ballets of the earlier romantic period comes in the third act of Flotow's *Martha* (1847). The scene is laid in England, and the ballet celebrates the picking of the hops. In the first number the maids dance holding a mug in one hand and a beer-jug in the other. Then after a pas de trois (a waltz) and two 'echo-dances' comes a final waltz in which the girls each carry a hop branch which they give to the young men, each claiming that her branch will make the best beer. The style is that of a rustic dance.

Although a large number of modern ballets have been based on music by Rossini—*La Boutique Fantasque* being of course the most famous example—ballet music in fact played a fairly unimportant part in his numerous operas. This was because the Italian opera, as in the previous century, did not normally include a ballet, and most of Rossini's ballet music comes from those of his operas which were produced in Paris in his later years. For these he usually strung together a few numbers from one of his previous operas or other works, to make up the obligatory divertissement: thus in *Il Viaggio a Reims,* an opera which he wrote specially for the Théâtre Italien in 1825, he introduced in the ballet an air with variations for two clarinets from a cantata which he had composed six years earlier in honour of the restoration to health of the King of Naples. Similarly in *Moïse,* a French version of his earlier serious opera-oratorio *Mosè,* which was produced at the Opéra in 1827, he made up a ballet of three numbers taken from his *Armida* and *Ciro in Babilonia*. The third of these is an effective hunting piece which begins with trills for the horns —an unusual piece of orchestration for the time. After *William Tell*, when Rossini had given up operatic composing for good, several of his operas were produced in French versions in Paris: *Otello*, for instance, was given in 1844 with a ballet arranged from airs in *Mathilde de Sabran* and *Armida*. Two years later came *Robert Bruce*, a pasticcio adapted by Niedermeyer to parts of the *Donna del Lago*, *Zelmira* and *Armida*. Rossini certainly gave permission for this to be done, but it is not clear whether he took any active part in its preparation. *Robert Bruce* contains two dances in the first act, a pas de cinq and an Écossaise, the latter in the conventional dotted rhythm which is characteristic of the Écossaises of Beethoven and Chopin. In the third act come a pas de trois and a pas de deux, the former being identical with the first dance in the ballet music of *Moïse*, while the latter is in the form of a Polonaise. The failure of *Robert Bruce* set Rossini against having any more of his operas produced on the French stage for some time, but in 1857 he authorized the production of *Bruschino* at the Bouffes Parisiens, and in 1860 *Sémiramis* was produced at the Opéra. For the production of the latter opera Rossini could not even be bothered to rescue some ballet music from his earlier operas, and the recitatives and dances were written by Carafa.

However in his operatic masterpiece *William Tell* Rossini did treat the dance in a rather less cavalier manner, and this ballet music has become world-famous. It consists of the well-known F major pas de six in the first act, and the long scene in the third act in which both dancers and chorus take part. This consists of a pas de trois in G major, leading to a Tyrolean chorus and dance, followed by the 'Soldiers' Dance', with which the Tyrolean dance alternates. Many later choreographers have seized on this music for their ballets—for instance Walter Gore in his *Plaisances*, produced for the

[37]

Rambert Company—and the 'Soldiers' Dance' has also become famous in Britten's arrangement as the first of his set of *Soirées Musicales*. Both these and his *Matinées Musicales* have been used for dancing.

Rossini's original *Soirées Musicales,* or *Serate Musicali*, were a set of twelve songs with piano published in 1834—that is, five years after Rossini had given up operatic composition. Their title arises from the fact that Rossini wrote them for evening parties in which he and his friends used to make music. They soon became popular. Liszt wrote two elaborate fantasies for piano on them, and also transcribed the whole set for piano in a rather simpler style. Respighi drew on some of these for *La Boutique Fantasque,* but his main source for that ballet was the collection of small piano pieces which Rossini wrote during the remaining thirty-five years of his life. Most of these came into the possession of the Italian publisher Ricordi after Rossini's death, and many of them are in manuscript even to-day. Some of them have absurd titles, such as 'Valse anti-dansante', 'Fausse couche de polka-mazurka', 'Ouf! les petits pois' etc. The Italian critic Luigi Rognoni is preparing an edition of many of these unpublished pieces, and it will certainly be interesting to see more of Rossini's 'last sins of my old age', as he described them him-self. (In recent years some volumes of them have been published by the Rossini Foundation of Pesaro and are available via Universal Edition.)

Donizetti, like Rossini, wrote little actual ballet music, and what he did write comes mainly in those of his operas which were produced in Paris. In 1840 his *Les Martyres* was staged at the Opéra: this was an adaptation of his *Poliuto,* an opera on the subject of the early Christian martyrs in the days of the Roman Empire, which had been banned by the Neapolitan censorship. It contains a short ballet of three dances, the first of which represents a gladiatorial combat and is suitably dramatic in style, while the others are divided into a number of sections in varying moods and tempi. In this and his other ballet music Donizetti showed that he understood the nature of dance music a good deal better than most of the other operatic composers of his time, who were usually content to provide their choreographers with longish symphonic movements which contained little or no variation of any kind. By including as much variety as possible in his dances Donizetti was able to facilitate the tasks of choreographers and dancers and to give his ballets an added interest.

This may also be seen in the ballet music in *La Favorita*, which was also produced at the Opéra in 1840. Here the ballet is intended as a celebration of the return of the hero from a successful military campaign, and the first number consists of an introduction in which the King makes a sign for all to be seated and enjoy the spectacle. Then follows a pas de trois, again in various short sections of different speeds and rhythms. Next comes a pas de six, which begins slowly and gradually gets quicker and quicker, and then a finale which again shows considerable variation of tempo. In *Dom Sébastian*, produced at the Opéra in 1843, the setting of the ballet is laid in Africa, and after the pas de trois and pas de deux comes a dance of Moroccan slaves which does include some orientalisms of a rather simple kind, such as the use of the augmented second, but these only occur in the opening section of the dance, and the remainder of the music is in the normal operatic style of the day. While Donizetti's best music is certainly not to be found in his ballets, he at least made an attempt to write music which would be properly balletic, and some of it has been used for modern ballets. The most notable of these was *Veneziana*, produced at Covent Garden in 1953 with choreography by Andrée Howard and the music arranged by Denis Aplvor. Some rearrangement was necessary in this case as not all the music was taken from Donizetti's actual ballet music, and several numbers were based on arias or choruses in which the vocal parts had to be fitted into a purely orchestral score.

With Verdi, as with Rossini and most other Italian operatic composers, dancing was a mere adjunct to the plot and chiefly appeared in festal or ballroom scenes. Separate ballets are rare. There are of course exceptions, such as *Jerusalem,* the reworking of *I Lombardi,* which was produced in Paris in 1847. Here there is a ballet of four dances, set in the harem gardens, which comes in the third act. Each of the dances except the last contains sections in different tempi. There is also a ballet in *Les Vêpres Siciliennes,* written specially for Paris in 1855. It is an elaborate ballet of the Four Seasons, beginning in this case with Winter and ending with Autumn. As well as a number of short dances, there are several recitative-like mimed sections and the whole ballet ends in a dramatic climax. For the Paris production of *Il Trovatore* in 1857 Verdi wrote a four-number ballet which is danced by the gipsies in Act III after the soldiers' chorus; it consists of an Entrée and Gitanilla, Sevillana, Bohémienne, and Galop. *Macbeth,* too, contains a short ballet in the third act. Here the dancers are the witches whom Macbeth is coming to consult. First comes a dance for the witches; in the second dance Hecate appears and in mime gives the witches instruction as to what they are to tell Macbeth. The ballet ends with a curious waltz, in which appoggiaturas are prominent. *Macbeth* was originally produced in Florence in 1847. The ballet was added for the French production of 1865. For the first production of *Don Carlos* in Paris two years later Verdi wrote an allegorical ballet for the third act. Three dancers represent pearls and a fourth the Queen of the Waters, who comes to punish the fisherman who has dared to dance with her pearls; then from a golden shell there emerges the most radiant jewel of the Spanish crown, La Peregrina, who is in fact the Princess Eboli dressed in the Queen's robes—so the ballet is integrated into the action of the opera.

It is unnecessary to go into the details of all the stage and ballroom music which appears in Verdi's other operas—for instance *Rigoletto,* with its stage band in the first scene playing a minuet curiously like that in *Don Giovanni*, and *Un Ballo in Maschera* with its ball scene which forms the climax of the story. And there are many examples of choral dances, such as the fête scenes in *La Traviata* and *La Forza del Destino*. The opera in which ballet music is most closely integrated into the action is *Aïda*: in the final scene of the first act (the scene of Radames' consecration), the sacred chorus and dance of the priestesses admirably catch the oriental atmosphere in a highly original way. In the first scene of the second act the dance of the Moorish slaves acts as an excellent foil to the song of Amneris and her women which surrounds it, and in the second scene of the same act the ballet heightens the climax of Radames' triumphal procession—being surrounded by the march, as it were, one feels that it is an integral part of the celebrations and not just something tacked on for effect. In Verdi's last two operas, *Otello* and *Falstaff,* there are normally no ballets as such, though he did write a ballabile for the third act of *Otello* which is occasionally performed in some productions. (This begins after the arrival of the Venetian ambassadors; first there is a dance of Turkish slave girls, then one of Greek girls and afterwards a group of Venetians dancing a Muranese; after a pas de deux there is a warriors' dance for men only and then a final dance for the whole company. The whole ballet lasts only six minutes: it was Verdi's final music for the stage, and was written for the Paris production of *Otello* in 1894.) But the choruses of women and sailors in the second act of *Otello* act as a kind of ceremonial interlude in the course of the drama, and in the last act of *Falstaff* the song and dance of the supposed fairies and sprites round Herne the Hunter's oak again makes a fusion of music, drama and ballet.

Verdi's music has been used in a number of modern ballets. One of the most successful of these is *The Lady and the Fool*, originally produced at Sadler's Wells in 1954 and later transferred to Covent Garden. The choreography is by John Cranko, and the music has been adapted by Charles Mackerras from a number of Verdi's earlier operas. Adaptation of operatic arias and choruses to the needs of a purely orchestral ballet score often entails considerable filling-up and rescoring, especially in the case of arias which were lightly accompanied in the original score in order to give greater prominence to the voice; and while one can say that Mackerras has done his work extremely effectively, it must be admitted that the scoring is sometimes over-elaborate, thick, and heavy. However the ballet does give one the opportunity of hearing a good deal of music by Verdi which would otherwise never reach the stage nowadays. Admittedly some of Verdi's earlier music tends towards brassy vulgarity, but it is always alive and healthy.

Berlioz was hardly a ballet composer in the proper sense, but dance movements of one kind or another come in all his works and often play an extremely important part in them. His first opera, *Benvenuto Cellini,* was produced at the Paris Opera in 1838, after a good deal of intrigue on Berlioz's part. The second scene of the second act portrays a carnival on the Piazza Colonna in Rome. The composer was not allowed to conduct the work himself—that being the custom of the time in French theatres—and he was furious at the slow tempo adopted by the conductor, Habeneck, for the saltarello which is danced and sung in this scene. Berlioz's own description of the rehearsal is worth quoting: 'The dancers, not being able to adapt themselves to Habeneck's dragging time, complained to me, and I kept on repeating: "Faster, faster! Put more life into it!" Habeneck struck the desk in irritation, and broke one violin bow after another. Having witnessed four or five of such outbursts, I ended at last by saying, with a coolness that exasperated him: "Good heavens! if you were to break fifty bows, that would not prevent your time from being too slow by half. It is a saltarello that you are conducting!" At which Habeneck, in pique, stopped the rehearsal altogether.'

However Berlioz had his revenge some years later. After

the failure of *Benvenuto Cellini*—it only ran for four performances at the Opéra—he determined to salvage at any rate some of the music, and transformed most of that of the carnival scene into the overture *Carnaval Romain,* which has now become one of his best-known works. On the night of the first performance of this overture Habeneck happened to be in the green-room of the concert hall. To continue in Berlioz's words: 'He had heard that we had rehearsed it in the morning without the wind instruments, part of the band having been called off for the National Guard. "Good!" he said to himself. "There will certainly be a catastrophe at the concert this evening. I must be there." On my arrival, indeed, I was surrounded by the wind players, who were in terror at the idea of having to play an overture of which they did not know a note. "Don't be afraid," I said. "The parts are correct: you all know your jobs: watch my beat as often as you can, count your bars correctly and it will be all right." Not a single mistake occurred. I launched the "allegro" in the whirlwind time of the Transteverine dancers. The public cried "Bis!" We played the overture again: it was even better done the second time. And as I passed back through the green-room, where Habeneck stood looking a little disappointed, I just flung these few words at him: "That is how it *ought* to go!" to which he took care to make no reply.' And Berlioz goes on to point the moral: 'Unhappy composers! learn how to conduct, and how to conduct yourselves well, (pun or no pun) for do not forget that the most dangerous of your interpreters is the conductor himself.'

After the failure of *Benvenuto Cellini* Berlioz avoided the operatic stage for more than twenty years, but meanwhile he wrote the dramatic cantata *The Damnation of Faust* which has often been successfully presented on the stage. Like many of Berlioz's works, it falls between two stools: while parts of it seem too dramatic for the concert hall, other sections are too static to be staged without a great deal of ingenuity. The famous 'Hungarian March', for instance, which is a most

exciting concert piece, needs considerable invention on the
choreographer's or producer's part if visual movement is to
be added to it, and some recent producers of the work have
avoided this responsibility by using the cyclorama or a film.
However the score contains two genuine pieces of ballet
music, the 'Dance of the Sylphs' and the 'Minuet of the
Will-o'-the-Wisps'. The first of these comes in a scene by
the banks of the Elbe: Faust, lulled to sleep by a chorus of
sylphs and gnomes, is shown by Mephistopheles a vision of
Marguerite, and the scene ends with the dance of the sylphs
themselves. The music is of magical lightness, and the whole
scene lends itself admirably to balletic treatment. The 'Dance
of the Will-o'-the-Wisps' occurs later: Faust has found his
way to Marguerite's house, and, hidden behind the curtains,
watches and listens as she sings the pathetic ballad of the
King of Thule. Mephistopheles, outside, summons up the
spirits of inconstancy and caprice to make Marguerite yield
to Faust; their dance, beginning as a minuet, is sardonic,
mocking, brilliant, and capricious. *The Damnation of Faust*
has always been one of Berlioz's most successful works, and
the march and the two dances are familiar concert items.

Berlioz's next opera, *Les Troyens,* was completed in 1858.
It was originally planned as a single opera in five acts, lasting
about five hours, but Berlioz failed to find an opening for it
at the Paris Opéra, and was eventually persuaded by the
director of the Théâtre Lyrique to allow him to put on the
second part of the work, 'Les Troyens à Carthage', by itself.
The first part, 'La Prise de Troie', was never performed in
Berlioz's lifetime, and even to-day performances of the whole
work are rare. Though both parts of the opera contain a
number of ceremonial and crowd scenes, the amount of
actual ballet music in it is small. In the second act of 'La Prise
de Troie' the Trojans are celebrating the apparent departure
of the Greeks with a chorus, which is followed by a short
'Wrestlers' Dance'. This acts as a foil to the pantomime scene
in which Hector's widow, Andromache, brings her infant

[44]

son to receive the blessing of King Priam and his queen—
one of the most moving passages in the whole opera. 'Les
Troyens à Carthage' begins with an elaborate ceremonial
scene with processions of builders, sailors, and workers. In the
second act there is a ballet to celebrate the victory of Aeneas
over the Numidian king, Iarbas. The dances, which are sometimes heard as concert items, do not perhaps show Berlioz at
his most characteristic, though they are full of interesting
ideas. The final dance, that of the Nubian slaves, introduces
some oriental colour, both by the use of an E minor scale
with a flattened second, and also in the instrumentation, which
contains parts for Tarbuka (a kind of drum) and miniature
cymbals, the melody being mainly entrusted to piccolo, oboe,
and cor anglais, in octaves. Women's voices also join in from
time to time, singing what are presumably meant to be Arabic
words. 'Les Troyens à Carthage' also contains the famous
pantomime scene, the Royal Hunt and Storm, in which Dido
and Aeneas, while taking part in a hunt, are compelled to seek
refuge from a storm in a cave, where their mutual love is
consummated. Here Berlioz called for a number of dancers
to set the scene for the entry of the lovers, including naiads,
huntsmen, nymphs, fauns, and satyrs. Needless to say, poor
Berlioz met with enormous difficulties at the first performance
of this scene. 'The mise en scène of the hunting interlude was
wretched,' he says. 'Instead of real waterfalls there was a
painted one: the dancing satyrs were represented by little
girls of twelve, and the blazing branches which they ought to
have waved were forbidden for fear of fire. There were no
dishevelled nymphs flying through the forest crying "Italy!"
The chorus singers who represented them were placed in the
wings and could not be heard in the theatre. The stage thunder
was scarcely audible, notwithstanding the weakness of the
orchestra. And always after this contemptible parody the
scene-shifter took at least forty minutes to change the scene.
I myself therefore requested that the interlude might be sup-
pressed.' And in fact this scene, which has now become one

[45]

of the most popular works in the orchestral repertoire, was not even printed in the first edition of the vocal score of 'Les Troyens à Carthage', and first appeared in an appendix to the second edition.

Berlioz's last opera, *Beatrice and Benedict,* based on Shakespeare's *Much Ado about Nothing,* contains no ballet music apart from a short Sicilienne in the first act, but Berlioz has achieved fame as a ballet composer through Massine's production in 1936 of his *Symphonie Fantastique* as a ballet. The question of the value of symphonic ballets as a whole will be discussed later. One would have thought in the abstract that the *Symphonie Fantastique,* with its detailed story and its series of dramatic orchestral effects, would have made a much better ballet than either Tchaikovsky's fifth symphony or Brahms' fourth, which Massine had previously made into *Les Présages* and *Choreartium* respectively. But curiously enough this was not so in practice. In spite of its dramatic details, the symphonic construction of the work moves at a slower pace than is really suitable for choreography—for one thing, Berlioz's themes tend to long lines which are difficult to parallel with dance movements, and there are also some repetitions of complete sections which are not easy for the choreographer to get over. So that in fact *Symphonie Fantastique* was much less successful than another ballet on the same story, *Apparitions,* which was produced in the same year at Sadler's Wells with choreography by Frederick Ashton and music chosen from a number of Liszt's later pieces by Constant Lambert. Here the comparative shortness of the pieces simplified Ashton's task.

The operas of Meyerbeer were lavish spectacles in which ballet played an extremely important part—a practice to which the present Paris Opéra seems to be returning in some of their productions. In *Robert le Diable,* as well as a pas de cinq in six movements in Act II, there occurs in Act III the extraordinary ballet of the ghosts of nuns who have been unfaithful to their vows, and who are raised from their graves by the Devil in order to tempt Robert to seize a mystic cypress branch from the grave of St. Rosalie. The 'Bacchanale', in four movements shows Robert being tempted with drink, sports, and love: finally he succumbs and seizes the branch. This scene was one of the most celebrated in all nineteenth-century opera, though it would appear somewhat grotesque to us to-day. The 'Valse Infernale', from the same opera was effectively arranged for the piano by Liszt. *Les Huguenots*, in addition to its gripping dramatic scenes, contains two ballets, one in the third act, beginning with a 'Danse Bohémienne' and an allemande, and including two other movements before the 'Danse Bohémienne' is repeated, and another shorter one in the fifth act. In *Le Prophète* comes the famous skating ballet which Constant Lambert used as the basis of the music for the Sadler's Wells production *Les Patineurs*— though he added a good deal of other music by Meyerbeer to it. In its original form it consisted of four numbers, a valse, a 'Pas de Rédowa', a 'Quadrille des Patineurs', and a galop. In some productions the dancers were on roller-skates, and sometimes two of the dancers would disappear down a trap and return carrying a large fish. Liszt also made a brilliant piano transcription of the waltz from this ballet. In the finale of Act V of *Le Prophète* there is a 'Bacchanale' and some 'couplets Bacchiques' as the Prophet and his henchmen feast before the final catastrophe of the story. *L'Africaine* contains an exotic Indian march and ballet in Act IV, and the most famous number of *Dinorah* is the 'Shadow Song', in which the heroine dances to her own shadow.

The tradition of elaborate ballets in French opera continued throughout the nineteenth century and well on into the twentieth. Thus even in a perfectly serious opera like Ambroise Thomas's *Hamlet* we find a ballet of eight numbers danced by country folk. The music is bucolic, cheerful, even including a cornet solo, but effective of its kind. Delibes, as an experienced ballet composer, naturally included a divertissement in *Lakmé*. The scene being laid in India, this has a somewhat oriental flavour, and the dances are a terana, a slow $\frac{6}{8}$ movement, a rektah, allegretto vivo, lighter in style, a 'Persian Dance' which includes a wordless chorus against wailing chromatic scales on the oboe, and an extended coda which also includes a part for chorus. Gounod's *Faust* contains the celebrated ballet music which he wrote for the production at the Paris Opéra. This comes at the beginning of the fifth act, and is supposed to represent Faust being shown the celebrated courtesans of history by Mephistopheles—Thaïs, Cleopatra, Helen of Troy, Phryne, and others. There are seven dances altogether, effective as dance music pure and simple, but hardly giving any idea of the atmosphere of the scenes they are supposed to accompany. In Gounod's *Romeo and Juliet* the occasion for the ballet are the nuptials between Juliet and the Count of Paris in the fourth act. This consists of six numbers, 'Entry of the Jewellers', 'The Bride and the Flowers', 'Valse of the Flowers', Dance of the Bride', the 'Girl with the Veil', and 'Gipsy Dance'. Gounod's *Queen of Sheba* also contains a four-movement divertissement in Act IV. The scene is Solomon's palace, and the arrival of the Queen is awaited. *Philémon et Baucis* contains an 'Entrée et Danse des Bacchantes' in Act II. This is not a ballet of great importance.

It would be tedious to continue the catalogue of ballets in French nineteenth-century operas, and we may conclude this survey with a brief glance at some of the ballet music of Bizet, Massenet, and Saint-Saëns. Bizet's operas were mainly opéras-comiques, in which ballet music was not obligatory. *Les Pêcheurs de Perles* includes a choral dance at the beginning of Act I and another in the second scene of Act III, and *Djamileh* contains an important solo dance for the heroine. Better known is the 'Danse Bohémienne' from the *Fair Maid of Perth*. This is often played as a concert piece, and is sometimes inserted into *Carmen* to form part of the ballet in the fourth act—this ballet is generally made up out of various dances by Bizet from other sources: that is, where it is not omitted altogether. Many of the other numbers in *Carmen* are, of course, in the form of dances, notably the well-known habanera, seguidilla, and the gipsy dance in Act II: but these were designed as sung dances, and the dancing is incidental. Massenet's operas were mainly designed for the Opéra, and so contain elaborate ballets, some of the music of which has become known from concert performances. These include *Le Cid, Le Roi de Lahore,* and *Hérodiade.* The last has dances for Egyptiennes, Babyloniennes, Gauloises and Phéniciennes, and one of the dances in *Le Roi de Lahore* is based on a Hindu theme. Saint-Saëns' best-known piece of ballet music is the Bacchanale from *Samson and Delilah,* which is often played as a concert piece. This again has a vaguely oriental flavour. The opera also contains a dance for the Priestesses of Dagon.*

Wagner's longest and most elaborate ballet comes in the second act of *Rienzi,* written between 1837 and 1839, during his sojourn in Riga. Wagner had Paris in mind for the production of *Rienzi,* but, in spite of some assistance from Meyerbeer, whom Wagner had got to know on his first arrival in France in 1839, the doors of the Opéra remained obstinately closed to him, and *Rienzi* was first produced at Dresden in 1842. Wagner wrote in later years: 'Grand opera, with all its scenic and musical splendour, its wealth of effect, its volume of musical passion, was present in my mind: and it was my artistic ambition not only to imitate this, but to surpass all previous creations of the kind in reckless prodigality. Yet,' he adds 'the subject of *Rienzi* really inspired me, and I added nothing to my scheme that did not stand in direct relation to the source of my inspiration. . . . For instance, I did not seek a pretext for a ballet in my subject, but with the eye of an operatic composer I automatically perceived a festival, which Rienzi was bound to give to the people, and

---

* César Franck's somewhat Wagnerian opera *Hulda* contains an allegorical ballet at the beginning of Act IV for the entrance of the royal court.

in which he would have to present a telling scene from ancient Roman history in the form of a pageant. This was the story of Lucretia, and in connection with it that of the expulsion of the Tarquins from Rome. That this pantomime had to be cut in such theatres as produced *Rienzi* was a distinct drawback to me: for the ballet which took its place misled criticism with regard to my more worthy intentions and caused this scene to appear in the light of an ordinary operatic device.'

The ballet is given by Rienzi as an entertainment for the people of Rome after his victory over the nobles: and the story of the expulsion of the Tarquins was obviously chosen as a parallel to Rienzi's own actions against the aristocracy of his time. The ballet music, which occupies fifty-five pages of piano score and lasts nearly half an hour in performance, consists as much of pantomime as of actual dancing: it begins with a short pantomime scene in which Collatinus, Brutus, and their friends express their regret at having to leave Lucretia alone with her maidens while they wait on Tarquin. When the men have gone Virginia and the maidens entertain Lucretia with a dance in polonaise rhythm. This is interrupted by the entrance of Tarquin and his soldiers, who carry off the girls and leave Tarquin alone with Lucretia. Now follows a long dramatic pantomime in which he attempts to seduce her, but, rather than give way to him, she stabs herself. Tarquin flees on hearing of Collatinus' imminent return. The latter appears with Virginia and his friends—they grieve over Lucretia's death and swear vengeance on Tarquin. Next Tarquin and his retainers are seen in flight, and finally Brutus and Collatinus re-enter victorious. They dance a sword dance; then the allegorical object of the ballet is made even clearer by the entry of a cortège of knights in mediæval costume, who challenge the ancient Romans to a battle. Finally the Goddess of Peace appears and unites the two factions in a 'Festal Dance' 'depicting the union between the old and the new Rome'. This somewhat pretentious scenario gave Wagner the opportunity of writing some effective music in the Meyerbeerian manner. Little of his own personality emerges, but it is at any rate interesting to see how even in this comparatively early opera Wagner was already thinking in terms of dramatic unity in opera, and wished to make even ballet fit into his dramatic scheme rather than remain a mere excrescence for the purpose of pure entertainment.

Wagner's next venture into ballet music was of a very different kind. None of his next few operas contained ballet music of any sort, but when, in 1860, Mme. de Metternich managed to persuade the Emperor Napoleon III to order the mounting of *Tannhäuser* at the Opéra, Wagner was faced with the necessity of adding a ballet to it at some point—a full-scale ballet was still considered an essential feature of any production in this august establishment. The only place where Wagner felt he could suitably insert a ballet was in the Venusberg scene at the very beginning of the opera, and this naturally infuriated those powerful and numerous members of the audience who were accustomed to arriving late for the performances and who came with the express purpose of seeing the ballet, which was of course normally placed later in the evening. The result was the celebrated riot which drove the opera off the stage after only three performances. Wagner's music probably also contributed to this failure. *Tannhäuser* itself had been written sixteen years earlier when Wagner's chromatic style was comparatively undeveloped, and the music, though considered slightly 'modern' in some quarters, held no undue alarm for the average operatic audience. But since then Wagner's style had changed radically: he had completed *Tristan* in 1859, and his new ballet music did not hark back to the past. Indeed it palpitates with violent passion, and even to-day it remains one of the most extravagant outpourings in all stage music. No wonder then that the audience, subjected to this violent assault on their ears immediately after the rise of the curtain, refused to listen to the quieter and more lyrical sections which follow. The music of the ballet, though by no

means ballet music of a normal type, starts straight out of the
Venusberg music at the climax of the overture, and keeps up
a pitch of orgiastic excitement for a considerable time. It is
only when our emotions have been thoroughly exhausted
that it sinks back into a more lyrical mood with the voices
of unseen Sirens heard faintly offstage. Wagner never again
attempted to insert a ballet into his operas, but there are two
dance scenes in his later operas which are worth mentioning
—the 'Dance of the Apprentices' in *Die Meistersinger* and the
'Flower Maidens' Scene' in *Parsifal*. The former comes in the
last scene of the opera, a public gathering on the banks of
the river Pegnitz where the people of Nuremberg have assembled to hear the song contest between Beckmesser and Walter.
Before the Mastersingers arrive in solemn procession, a boat
appears full of girls in peasant costumes, and in the ensuing
waltz-like dance the apprentices and journeymen rival each
other in their attempts to seize the girls. David joins in the
game too. The music shows Wagner at his most charming
and least heavy-handed, and is unusual in being written mainly
in phrases of seven bars' length.

The 'Flower Maidens' Scene' is very different in intention.
This comes in the middle of the second act of *Parsifal,* where
the magician Klingsor creates a magic garden to enrapture
Parsifal's senses. The maidens, divided into four groups, sing
and dance to a delicate waltz-like theme of the utmost sen-
suousness, as they entrance Parsifal with colours and scents.
Both these dance scenes, different as they are, show Wagner's
wonderful capacity for creating atmosphere when he wished
to—one could wish that he had written more scenes of this
kind and fewer monologues for Wotan.

Ballets were not common in German operas unless these
were produced in opera houses like that of Vienna, which
had a resident ballet: as was Goldmark's *Queen of Sheba,* given
in Vienna in 1875. Apart from a chorus and dance of the women
in the first act, this contains an elaborate ballet in the third.
The scene is a banquet at which the women of the harem

dance, and the ballet includes a solo dance with veil and a bee and also a Bacchanale —but the music is in the normal German romantic style with little use of orientalisms. We should not leave the subject of German opera without mentioning the dances in the most famous of all operettas— Johann Strauss' *Die Fledermaus*. These come in the ballroom scene in Act II, and consist of a Spanish Dance, a Schottische with dotted rhythm and bagpipe effects, a Russian Dance , a polka, in which the chorus joins, and the well-known csárdás with its traditional slow opening section and furious finale. These are interesting examples of what Strauss could do in the styles of other nations when he turned away from his famous waltzes.

The dances in Slavonic operas are mainly based on national themes, such as those in Smetana's *The Bartered Bride*. These consist of a polka, a furiant, and the 'Dance of the Comedians' —the last is an extremely effective piece which works up to a powerful climax. In Russia we find orientalism creeping into many of the dances: apart from *Le Coq d'Or,* which has been successfully given in ballet form, as we shall see later, Rimsky-Korsakov's main contribution to operatic dancing is the opera-ballet *Mlada,* which contains a great number of dances throughout. These include a rédowa (or mazurka) in the first act, a 'Ronde Fantastique' for sixty to eighty dancers in the third. a set of dances for squires, courtiers and warriors later in the same act, and Lithuanian and Indian dances in the fifth— the latter embellished with vocal parts and handclaps. In addition the parts of the shade of Mlada and the shade of Cléopâtre are taken by dancers, who play an important part in the action throughout. Many dances, of course, occur in Rimsky-Korsakov's other operas, perhaps the best-known being the 'Dance of the Tumblers' from the *Snow-Maiden,* and his music has been frequently drawn on by modern choreographers for new ballets, as we shall see later.

Of the other Russian composers, the most striking and vivid dance music comes from Mussorgsky: in *The Fair at Sorochinsk* we find the well-known gopak at the end of the opera, and also the fantastic 'Night on the Bare Mountain' scene, which calls for considerable choreographic invention if this vision of evil spirits and witches is to be properly interpreted in visual terms. In *Boris Godunov* the only important dance music comes in the Polish act, with its fine Polonaise: and in *Khovan-shchina* come the magnificent set of Persian dances in the fourth act, which have been staged as a separate ballet by the Diaghilev and de Basil companies.

Tchaikovsky's *Eugene Onegin* contains the well-known Waltz and Polonaise, frequently heard in the concert hall, as well as a less-known Mazurka. In the *Queen of Spades* the episode of the masked ball in Act II allows Tchaikovsky an opportunity of period pastiche in the form of a 'Sarabande of Shepherds and Shepherdesses'. His otherwise unremarkable opera *Mazeppa* contains a 'Cossack Dance' which is also frequently played as a concert piece. Mention should also be made of the numerous and effective dances in Glinka's operas *Russlan and Ludmila* and *A Life for the Tsar*.

We shall return to the Polovtsian Dances from Borodin's opera *Prince Igor* in Chapter 4, and may conclude this brief and necessarily incomplete survey of ballet music in nine-teenth-century opera with an account of a piece of Italian ballet music which, though world-famous, is rarely seen on the stage outside Italy—the 'Dance of the Hours' from Pon-chielli's opera *La Gioconda*. The scene is a sumptuous hall in a great house on the Grand Canal, Venice. The dances are intro-duced by a recitative and are punctuated at intervals by the chorus. There are four main entries: the 'Dance of the Dawn Hours', of the 'Day Hours', of the 'Evening Hours' and of the 'Night', and all join together in the finale. The whole makes an impressive spectacle when properly presented. The salon versions we so often hear of this piece are a mere tra-vesty.

III

The Grand Romantic Ballets

DURING the eighteenth century ballet had begun to spread outside its original homes in France and Italy, and by 1800 it was firmly established in several other countries, notably in Russia, where Empress Anne founded a State School of Dancing in 1735. The Royal Danish Ballet also dates from this period, and it is in fact one of the oldest companies with an uninterrupted history. This company was fortunate in having the gifted choreographer Bournonville at its disposal in the early part of the nineteenth century, and he created for it a number of ballets which are still performed by the company to-day. (The Royal Danish Ballet even have a ballet in their repertoire with eighteenth-century choreography, *The Whims of Cupid and the Dancing Master*, but this is little more than a curiosity). The ballets of Bournonville mark the beginning of the romantic ballet of the type we know in *Giselle*, for instance; that is to say, the dancing is not purely classical, but includes a good deal of mime, and the subject is usually based on some poetical idea, as for instance in Bournonville's version of *La Sylphide*—not to be confused with *Les Sylphides* of many years later. Other ballets in the Royal Danish Ballet's repertoire include *Napoli* and *A Folk Tale*: these are all full-length ballets lasting the whole evening, as indeed was the usual practice in nineteenth-century ballet, and they include a good deal of mime and are extremely realistically staged. Unfortunately the musical side of these ballets does not match the choreography or staging: the music is mostly a hotchpotch of tunes by various Danish composers, of whom Niels Gade, a contemporary and follower of Mendelssohn, and Lumbye, a composer of popular dance tunes, are the only ones to be known outside Denmark. Of course this kind of musical hotch-potch was quite common in the days of the purely classical ballet, when the dancing had complete primacy and the music was considered of little or no importance, provided it gave a reasonable background to the dancer's movements. But in the Romantic period mime was becoming more and more important, and it was essential that the music should be properly fitted to the stage action, and, what is more, should be a unified conception. It is true that this ideal was not satis-factorily attained until the days of Delibes and Tchaikovsky, but at any rate the nineteenth century saw a gradual tendency towards a more serious conception of the ballet as a whole.

During this period France remained, as before, the chief home of the ballet, and a very large number of ballets were produced in Paris which have since passed into oblivion. These were mostly full-length ballets in three or four acts, lasting a whole evening. Usually there was some kind of fairly simple story which was mimed, interspersed with a good deal of dancing—general dances for the corps de ballet, variations for solo dancers, pas de deux, pas de trois, pas de quatre etc. The dénouement of the story normally came at the beginning of the last act, and the remainder of the ballet usually consisted of a divertissement containing a number of dances which had nothing to do with the story, but sometimes had a separate theme of their own. This pattern has, indeed, survived into the full-length ballets of to-day. We need waste no time in discussing those French ballets which have dropped out of the modern repertoire: but there are three, or perhaps three and a half, which should be discussed in some detail.

The earliest full-length ballet to remain in the present-day repertoire is *Giselle,* originally produced at the Académie Royale de Musique in Paris on 28 June 1841, with Grisi as Giselle and L. Petipa as Albrecht. The scenario was evolved by Théophile Gautier and Vernoy de St. Georges. Gautier got his original idea for it when reviewing Heine's book *De l'Allemagne*, and he wrote to Heine saying how charmed he was with 'all those delicious apparitions you have encountered in the Harz Mountains and on the banks of the Ilse, in a mist softened by German moonlight.' This quotation gives a very fair idea of the atmosphere of the ballet, even if the 'German moonlight' is seen here through French eyes. The choreography was by Coralli and Perrot, and the music by Adolphe Adam, a composer who lived from 1803 to 1856 and devoted his life to the theatre; but of all his numerous grand and comic operas and ballets only *Giselle* and some extracts from his comic opera *Le Postillon de Longjumeau* have survived into the present-day repertoire. He probably learnt his theatrical sense from Boieldieu, with whom he studied at the Paris Conservatoire, but he was not a composer of a very strong personality; in fact he is severely attacked in the first edition of Grove's Dictionary of Music, published in 1890, where it is stated that: 'His melodies are frequently trivial to absolute vulgarity: the structure of his concerted pieces is of the flimsiest kind: all this, no less than the choice of *hasardé* subjects, seems to indicate the gradual decline from the serene heights of Boieldieu's humour to the miry slough which has swamped that sweetest growth of French national art, the comic opera, and the murky surface of which reflects the features of Beethoven's countryman, Jacques Offenbach. It is a fact of ominous significance that Adam regarded with interest, and gave his journalistic aid to the theatrical creation of that enterprising composer—the *Bouffes Parisiens*.' We do not feel so harshly about poor Adam these days, but there is no doubt that the continued success of *Giselle* depends far more on its dancing than on its music.

Nevertheless Adam's score for *Giselle* is, at least, extremely competent, and often very apt for the dramatic action. Indeed the music is very closely related to the dance, and there is no elaborate symphonic development; it is more in the style of the older dance suites. Though the melodies often seem commonplace and even perfunctory at times, nevertheless they do fulfil their function in providing danceable numbers. The score is written in a series of short, almost fragmentary sections, and the composer's skill is shown in the way in which he alters and varies the speed and character of each successive dance, so that the score does add up to a dramatic whole. One can say, in fact, that the whole is greater than the parts, and many a greater composer, or one who could have written more distinguished individual dances, may well envy Adam's dramatic skill in building up a large structure out of somewhat unpromising material. In a sense this is what ballet music should aim at, at any rate in a dramatic ballet: if one is too taken by individual numbers one tends to think of a ballet as consisting of a chain of separate dances rather than a dramatic whole. Such music is of course ineffective in the concert hall— but that is not its place. It is intended to be listened to as an adjunct to the dance, and it supports the dancing by adding its rhythmical, emotional, atmospheric, or dramatic qualities. I am not saying that all ballet music should be like *Giselle*— Heaven forbid—but I do feel that the simplicity of the music here does disguise a greater dramatic power than many people realize.

The first act of the ballet is concerned with the love of Count Albrecht, who is disguised as a peasant, for the peasant girl Giselle, her discovery of his deception and her death. The simplicity of Giselle's character is well expressed in the music, but the dramatic scenes tend to be somewhat naïve musically. However the unison passage associated with Hilarion is very effective despite its extreme simplicity. But, as we saw above, Adam never attempts to develop a musical theme, though as the act proceeds he does use some of the material that has already been heard, and his handling of these reminiscences of

earlier themes is often very apt; for instance, the restatement of the pastorale theme from the first part of the act
in the later mad scene. There is a certain similarity
to Donizetti in the cast of melody and in the alternation between lyricism and drama. The chief aim of
the music is to express the story clearly and make a
direct appeal to the audience, and in this it succeeds very
well.

The second act is concerned with the Wilis, brides who
have died before their wedding day. Giselle rises from her
grave and joins them. Then Albrecht returns, not realizing
what has happened: the Wilis make him their victim, and the
act ends with his prostration over Giselle's grave. Although
this act, in contrast to the first, is chiefly concerned with supernatural beings, Adam makes no attempt to express this in the
music, which continues much as in the first act; and many of
the dramatic passages are underplayed. However, the lyrical
passages are expressive and effective, and the music at least
provides an adequate support for the dancing. A number of
interpolations have crept into the score, the chief of which is
the 'Peasant' pas de deux by Burgmüller in Act I, which was
already included in the first performance. However, some
companies, such as the Scottish Theatre Ballet, have gone back
to Adam's complete original score. In the versions used by some
companies considerable rescoring has taken place, but at any
rate Giselle does remain in the repertoire of practically every
important ballet company of to-day, and it has always remained
a favourite with the public. It may be added that Adam also
composed ballet scores for Faust for a London production in
1832, and for La Jolie Fille de Gand in 1839. Neither of these
has remained in the repertoire; nor has his score for Le Corsaire.

The French nineteenth-century ballet composer who is best
known to us to-day is Léo Delibes, who lived from 1836 to
1891. He was a pupil of Adolphe Adam at the Conservatoire

and thus had an early apprenticeship in the French theatrical tradition. His first works were comic operas and operettas which achieved some success. In 1863 he became an accompanist at the Opéra itself, and three years later he was commissioned to write the music for the ballet *La Source,* in collaboration with the Russian ballet composer Minkus. Minkus was well known as a composer of ballet music of an extremely conventional type, and this direct comparison of the two composers gave Delibes the chance of really making his reputation. Of the four scenes of the ballet Minkus wrote the first and fourth and Delibes the second and third, and after the first performance on 12 November 1866 the following notice appeared in *La France Musicale*: 'The style of the two composers is essentially different and easily recognizable at a first hearing. Minkus's music has a vague, indolent and melancholic character, full of grace and languor. That of Delibes, fresher and more rhythmic, is much more complicated in orchestration, and sometimes a little more ordinary. I should add that this difference in style is perfectly justified by the contrasting character of the two parts of the ballet.' The critic of *Le Ménestrel* went even further and wrote: 'The first act, despite several pretty details, seemed a little thin, but the music of the last scene contains some charming and often very expressive melodies. The second act is brilliant and does great credit to Delibes: it is certainly the most successful and noteworthy portion. The whole of the score could have been entrusted to the young composer, and this will doubtless be done on another occasion.'

The story of *La Source* is concerned with Naïla, the Spirit of Spring, who influences an intrigue at the court of the Khan of Ghendjib. The somewhat conventionally oriental plot contains magic flowers, evil mists, and other trappings of this kind. The concert suite from Delibes' music has become well known, and a favourite item from the ballet is the 'Naïla Waltz', which has been effectively transcribed for piano as a concert piece by Dohnányi. At any rate, *La Source* made Delibes' reputation: he was immediately asked to write a divertissement, 'Le Pas de Fleurs', for insertion in *Le Corsaire,* a ballet by his old master, Adolphe Adam, and shortly afterwards he was commissioned to write *Coppélia.*

Delibes' first full-length ballet, *Coppélia, ou La Fille aux Yeux d'Émail,* to give it its full title, was first produced at the Paris Opéra on 25 May 1870, with choreography by St. Léon. The book, by Nuitter and St. Léon, was suggested by E. T. A. Hoffmann's character of Dr. Coppelius, the inventor and controller of mechanical puppets who also appears in Offenbach's opera *The Tales of Hoffmann.* Delibes' music made an immediate impression. Writing three days after the première, the critic of *Le Figaro* said: 'M. Léo Delibes has composed for the three scenes of *Coppélia* a distinguished, piquant, and colourful score, excellently orchestrated. . . . It is very difficult to write for dancing with a little artistry, taste, and style. . . . M. Delibes has succeeded in avoiding the commonplace.' Accustomed as they were to an extremely mediocre standard of ballet music in French theatres—Adam's *Giselle,* though hardly a very original work, was a masterpiece compared with the average ballet score of the mid-nineteenth century—it is no wonder that the critics acclaimed Delibes' work, for it combines successfully the art of pure ballet music—music which is solely concerned with the dance and is incapable of standing alone without it—with that of attractive dramatic music of the lighter kind. Delibes' score contains both these kinds of music, and its tunefulness and effectiveness has kept it alive to this day.

The two main elements in the plot are Dr. Coppelius, the doll-maker, trying to impart life to his creations, and the simple love story of Swanilda and Franz. Apart from the set dances, Delibes' score simply but effectively portrays the course of the story. There is little music of symphonic stature but the ballet nevertheless makes a definite dramatic entity.

The ballet is in three acts (or tableaux, as they are called). Before the first act comes a Prelude, beginning slowly with a suave passage for four horns followed by a flowing string melody. A short 'working-up' passage leads to the brilliant Mazurka, which we are to hear again in the first act. Then follow short cadenza-like passages for woodwind which lead to the first act itself. This begins with a waltz, which, though attractive and tuneful in its own right, also serves as a suitable accompaniment to Swanilda's dance and her gestures of friendship to the doll seated in the window—it is this combination of tunefulness and choreographic suitability which has ensured the success of Delibes' ballet music. Next comes a scene in which Franz makes his bow to the doll: to his delight she responds, and her jerky movements are admirably expressed by the double-dotted woodwind rhythm. Next follows the Mazurka, already heard in the overture; this has become familiar as a concert number. There follows the scene of the Burgomaster's entry and the general interest expressed in the happenings in Coppelius's house, and then a Ballade, a simple violin solo containing the 'Hungarian cadence', during which Swanilda tests Franz's fidelity with an ear of wheat. The next dance is a 'Slavonic theme' with four variations and a coda in quicker tempo. Then follows the well-known csárdás, beginning with a broad and well-marked melody in D which leads to a more lively Allegretto and finally an Allegro and Presto—but though the form of the traditional Hungarian csárdás is observed here, the music hardly has the authentic Hungarian flavour. Then there is a sortie for the dancers, and the finale of the act, a movement in C minor which is linked rhythmically with the doll music heard earlier, hints at the mystery of Dr. Coppelius' house, which we are to explore in the following act.

The entr'acte before this act begins in the same way as the finale of the previous act, as if to remind us that it is Dr. Coppelius who will shortly be our concern. Then it leads into a repeat of the waltz from the first act. The curtain rises on the entry of the girls into the room where the Doctor keeps his mechanical puppets. Their hesitation is delightfully expressed by a featherweight melody for muted violins staccato. Then comes another descriptive scene, while Swanilda explores the room: suddenly the dolls are awakened and set in motion, and we have the noisy 'Musique des Automates'. Next follow descriptive scenes for the successive entries of Coppelius and Franz. In a rather heavy, Germanic type of dance Coppelius invites Franz to drink with him. Swanilda, who has now taken the place of the doll Coppélia, is produced, and we have the 'Danse de la Poupée', followed by her bolero, to which she does a Spanish dance, and her gigue, a Scottish dance. The act ends with a dramatic scene in which the plot is discovered and the girls are chased out of the house. Throughout this act, the most dramatic in the ballet, Delibes alternates sections of dramatic music with set dances, and the combination of the two is extremely effective.

The third act consists almost entirely of a divertissement, beginning with the 'Marche de la Cloche', the scene of the Presentation of the Bell, which serves as a simple but well-proportioned overture. Then follows the 'Fête de La Cloche', a series of dances of various characters. The first is the 'Valse des Heures' (Heures Matinales), the well-known waltz in E flat which is familiar to concert audiences. Next comes 'Aurore', a solo dance with a colourful and expressive moderato introduction followed by a light but not very distinguished Allegretto non troppo . 'La Prière' is an expressive little piece, a $\frac{6}{8}$ Andante in E flat: in 'Le Travail', representing the mid-day hours, a melody in thirds is accompanied by a ceaseless 'spinning-wheel' type of figure. There follows 'L'Hymen', a betrothal dance. The next piece, 'La Paix', is now performed as a pas de deux for Swanilda and Franz. Its viola melody, Andante espressivo , is as near to romantic nobility as Delibes ever attained. The next dance, originally the 'Marche des Guerrières', is now performed as a variation for Franz: it is a brilliant, if slightly crude, piece of martial music. Then comes Swanilda's variation, originally the 'Danse de Fête', an Allegretto in G. The ballet ends with a final 'Galop', originally the 'Dance of the Evening Hours', which is an effective piece with plenty of vivacity.

It will be seen that some changes from the original have been made in the latter part of the third act, and in fact most modern ballet companies make their own alterations to *Coppélia*. The version described above is that performed at present by the Royal Ballet. This derives, not from the original choreography of St. Léon, but from the version prepared for the Maryinsky Theatre by Ivanov, and reproduced in later years by Sergeyev and Cecchetti. In addition Dame Ninette de Valois revised the whole production in 1954, and this version is now used by both the Royal Ballet companies. The Royal Danish Ballet presents a rather different version in which there is very much more mime and less dancing. This is also used by the Festival Ballet in England. The score of *Coppélia* is for normal symphony orchestra, with double woodwind, four horns, two cornets, two trumpets, three trombones, tuba, percussion, harp, and strings. The scoring is in no way unusual, but is rather more symphonic in style than was usual in Paris then.

In spite of the success of *Coppélia* Delibes did not wish to write nothing but ballet music, and his next stage work was the opera *Le Roi l'a Dit*, which however was little more than a *succès d'estime* when produced at the Opéra-Comique in 1873. However he returned to the Opéra three years later with the mythological ballet *Sylvia,* which was first produced on 14 June 1876. The book was by Jules Barbier and de Reinach, and the choreography was by Mérante. Again the music was a great success, and *L'Opinion* wrote on the day after the first performance: 'M. Léo Delibes has written a score which reveals the hand of a master symphonist. The picturesque

[64]

choice of themes, the highly-coloured orchestration make this ballet to my mind an exquisite work, perhaps too refined and delicate for the glare of the footlights.' To-day we find the music light and tuneful rather than symphonic, but it was clearly a cut above the other ballet scores of the time, and a good deal of the music is familiar from concert performance. The ballet itself has never been quite so successful as *Coppélia*, but a good many modern companies have performed it at one time or another. The present Royal Ballet production at Covent Garden dates from 1952 and has new and very effective choreography by Frederick Ashton. As in *Coppélia*, about half the music accompanies the dramatic story—the mime music is indeed more emotional in quality than that of *Coppélia*, and at times achieves an almost Wagnerian flavour—while the rest is dance music which is fully capable of standing on its own, with its considerable melodic appeal, even if it does not pretend to any great depth of expression, and it fits the stylized plot to perfection. The orchestra is the same as for *Coppélia*, plus an additional harp.

Like *Coppélia*, *Sylvia* is in three acts. Before the first act there is a Prelude; then the curtain rises on a scherzo-like dance in quick tempo for the fauns, dryads and woodland folk. In the next dance, a pastorale called 'Le Berger', Amyntas dreams of the nymph he has seen in the forest: this is followed by 'Les Chasseresses', hunting music of no particular distinction—Sylvia and her nymphs appear. After a short 'Intermezzo' comes the 'Valse lente', with its unusual melody very much in the French style. It somehow combines aristocratic distinction with popular appeal. There follow a 'scene' and a 'Cortège Rustique', and the act ends with a dramatic scene portraying the capture of Sylvia by Orion. An entr'acte, which again makes use of the 'Valse lente', prefaces the second act, in which we see Sylvia as Orion's captive. After the opening 'Scene' comes the 'Pas des Ethiopiens', a violent dance in which piccolo and percussion play a prominent part. Then in the 'Chant Bacchique' Sylvia begins to make Orion drunk in order to effect her escape. This followed by the 'Scene' and 'Dance of the Bacchante', during which two dancers play tambours de Basque on stage, and in the final 'Scene', Sylvia escapes through the help of Eros.

The last act, as in *Coppélia,* is mainly a divertissement, and contains much of the music which is well known from the concert suite. It begins with the famous 'Marche et Cortège de Bacchus', an extended and brilliant march in the best theatrical style, to which the villagers honour the god of wine. In the following 'Scene' Amyntas returns, and in the ensuing barcarolle discovers Sylvia among the slaves of Eros. This barcarolle, as well as the later 'Pas des Esclaves', contains and important part for alto saxophone—an early example of its use. Now follows the divertissement proper, beginning with the famous pizzicato movement which has made Delibes' name universally known. Next come a number of dances for the various principals: an Andante with a prominent part for violin solo; a variation for Amyntas; a pas de cinq; a 'pas des Esclaves'; a dance for the Muses and Apollo; a valse-variation for Sylvia; and a final 'Stretto-Galop'. The ballet ends with an apotheosis at the temple of Diana and the appearance of Endymion. Some of the dances in the divertissement in the Royal Ballet production are taken from Delibes' earlier ballet *La Source*: these include Amyntas's variation and the dance of the Muses. The Andante with violin solo is a pas de deux, the 'Pas des Esclaves' is used for a dance of two goats, and the valse-variation is omitted (at one time it was used in *Coppélia*): in addition several of these dances have been specially rescored for the Royal Ballet production. As a whole *Sylvia* is an extremely effective score, and it is perhaps surprising that the ballet has not had the wide appeal of *Coppélia,* especially as so much of its music has become well known. Probably the stronger dramatic story of *Coppélia* has been found more interesting than the somewhat stylized classical myth of *Sylvia*.

After *Sylvia* Delibes wrote no more full-length ballets, but turned his attention mainly in the direction of opera, producing *Jean de Nivelle* in 1880 and his best-known work, *Lakmé*, in 1883. Between these two operas he also wrote the incidental music for *Le Roi s'Amuse*, the Victor Hugo play on which the libretto of Verdi's *Rigoletto* is based. Delibes' music includes a set of dances 'in the olden style', a kind of pastiche of seventeenth-century French dance music, but extremely well done in their way. This suite is also familiar to concert audiences. (The passepied, incidentally, makes use of the same theme from the sixteenth-century Arbeau's *Orchésographie* which Peter Warlock used as the second movement of his *Capriol Suite*.) It is a pity that Delibes did not concentrate more on ballet, for his other works, with the possible exception of *Lakmé*, have never been greatly successful, whereas his two full-length ballets justify his claim to be regarded as the father of modern ballet music.

As we have seen, the first school of dancing in Russia was founded in 1735: the first director of it, however, was a Frenchman, and most of the dancers were foreigners to start with, though gradually Russian dancers began to take a larger and larger part in the ballet companies of Moscow and St. Petersburg. After a succession of French directors, there arrived in St. Petersburg in 1847 yet another Frenchman, Marius Petipa from Marseilles. He controlled the destinies of dancing in Russia for over fifty years, and was responsible for raising the standard of Russian dancing to the level we know to-day. In fact by the end of the century the Russian dancers were the finest in the world; and Petipa also improved the standards of choreography. He was the real creator of the ballet d'action, and was also the first to insist that the leading dancers should be recruited from the corps de ballet, which of course meant that every member of the company had to be technically first-class. Petipa composed fifty-four new ballets besides reviving a number of old ones, and his work prepared the way for the modern ballet.

But even with Petipa's reforms a good deal of conventionality remained in the ballet. The choreographer, composer, designer, and librettist all tended to work in watertight compartments without any preliminary collaboration. Often the composer knew nothing about the subject of the ballet, but was simply ordered to turn out so many variations, entrées, marches, etc. As a result most of the ballets produced during this period have not survived in the repertoire, and it says much for Tchaikovsky's feeling for the medium that he was able to rise above the handicaps imposed on him and produce three masterpieces of ballet music.

Tchaikovsky may be justly described as the ballet composer *par excellence*: he had an extraordinary gift for catching the exact atmosphere needed in a particular dance, and his almost unfailing gift of melody and his feeling for orchestral colour ensured that he would be able to convey this feeling to the audience. Curiously enough his dramatic gifts, so evident in his later symphonies, failed to work so well when he applied them to opera, and though there are many fine and moving dramatic moments in *Eugene Onegin* and *The Queen of Spades*, for instance, the music somehow lacks the inevitable rightness of his ballet scores. Yet Tchaikovsky had comparatively little success as a ballet composer in his lifetime. The reasons for this are uncertain, but it would seem that his ballet music, immediately appealing as it is to us to-day, was thought complicated and obscure by those of his contemporaries who could not see beyond the conventionalities of composers like Minkus.

Le Lac des Cygnes, perhaps the most famous of Tchaikovsky's three full-length ballets, began life as a small ballet written for the children of his sister Alexandra Davidov. They performed it during a summer holiday at Kamenka in 1871 when their uncle was on a visit to them. Four years later, when Tchaikovsky was commissioned to write the music for the *Le Lac des Cygnes* ballet, he used some material from this score. The first production took place at the Bolshoi Theatre, Moscow, on 20 February/4 March 1877, with choreography by Reisinger, an Austrian of mediocre talent. About a third of Tchaikovsky's score was omitted as being too complicated to dance to. This production was a failure, as one can well imagine. Tchaikovsky, always self-critical, attributed this failure to the poverty of the music, and resolved to rewrite it. But in the end he never did. The ballet was revived in Moscow in 1880 and again in 1882, with new choreography by Hansen, but it was still not a success, and it was not until after Tchaikovsky's death that *Le Lac des Cygnes* came into his own.

This was due to the enterprise of the veteran choreographer Petipa, who sent for the score and became enthusiastic about the music. He determined to mount the ballet in a new production, in collaboration with Ivanov, who was responsible for the more romantic and legendary parts of the ballet while Petipa himself looked after the more brilliant and realistic sections—though exact details of the collaboration are not known. The second act was given in 1894 at the Maryinsky Theatre in St. Petersburg in a memorial programme of Tchaikovsky's works—he had died in the previous year—and the whole ballet was mounted at the same theatre on 15/27 January 1895. In spite of the contradictory elements caused by the collaboration of the two choreographers—which many modern ballet companies further complicate by altering the sequence of dances and making numerous cuts—*Swan Lake* has remained the epitome of the romantic ballet ever since that day, and has increased in strength and popularity with the passage of time. The story has a powerful, romantic and lyrical atmosphere, and also allows of the introduction of both purely classical and character dances.

The underlying unity of the ballet is strengthened by the music, which is not only effective throughout but also emphasizes the poetry and romance of the subject. It does, in fact, make one believe in fairy tales, and this is where Tchaikovsky's genius as a ballet composer lies.

The music consists mostly of self-contained numbers. Although Tchaikovsky does not follow the story dramatically in quite such a detailed way as the music of earlier ballets like *Giselle* or *Coppélia* does, he expresses its general mood much more closely, and this can be felt even in the indifferent performances of the ballet to which we are sometimes subjected. The ballet is in four acts and consists of some thirty-six separate numbers. As various different versions of the music can be found in productions by different companies to-day, it will be as well to describe these numbers in detail, in the order given in the piano score published in 1949 by the Tchaikovsky Foundation in New York. This conforms to the Petipa production of 1895.

The first act begins with an introduction in the mood of the poetical and romantic 'Swan music' which is to dominate the lake scene in the second act. The curtain rises on dance No. 1, a brilliant 'Scene' in quick tempo for the celebrations of Prince Siegfried's coming of age. Then, in the 1895 version, follows a pas de trois in which light and charming solos for the two girls in $\frac{2}{4}$ time alternate with a vigorous $\frac{6}{8}$ for the man. All three join in a brilliant, quick Coda in $\frac{4}{4}$ time. (In the 1877 version the waltz (No. 4) came at this point.) No. 3 is again a 'Scene', for the entrance of the Princess-Mother, and No. 4 in this version is the well-known waltz, which rises to a great climax. No. 5 is a pas d'action, a comedy scene between Wolfgang and one of the girls. This replaces a pas de deux in the 1877 version which is now usually transferred to Act III, where it provides the material for Odile's famous solos. No. 6 is a short introduction leading to No. 7, the 'Danse des Coupes', an excellent polacca of symphonic stature. In the

Tchaikovsky in 1889—a photograph presented by him to Chekhov, with
the inscription 'From an ardent admirer'

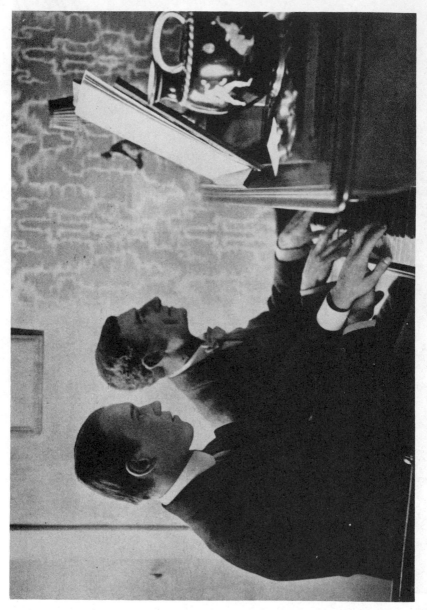

Nijinsky and Ravel playing *Daphnis and Chloë*

'Finale', No. 8, the Swan theme itself is heard for the first time. This haunting oboe melody acts as a unifying element throughout the ballet.

The second act, the scene by the lake, has often been given as a separate ballet: indeed this is the only part of *Swan Lake* which most ballet companies have in their repertoire, and the Royal Ballet was the first company outside Russia to perform the ballet complete. It begins with the well-known introduction based on the Swan theme. Then No. 10, an Allegro scene, shows the arrival of the Huntsmen and the discovery of the Swan Maidens and Odette. The music of the mime scene between Odette and the Prince is marvellously expressive, and the harsh brass chords which herald the arrival of the sinister Rothbart are extremely striking. As chords they are nothing out of the ordinary, being the diminished sevenths which were so dear to every romantic composer throughout the nineteenth century, but it is the way in which they are introduced which is novel and arresting. Then comes the entry of the Swan Maidens and their waltz. After this woodwind chords and harp cadenzas lead to the famous pas de deux, one of the best-known pieces in all ballet music. This begins with a violin solo accompanied by harp chords—what could be simpler and yet more effective?—and later the solo cello takes over the theme while the violin weaves a poignant countermelody. (Incidentally, this pas de deux and the preceding waltz came just before the end of the act in the 1877 version, but they are now invariably placed in the middle, as in Petipa's version.) Next comes the equally well-known 'Dance of the Cygnets', with its chirpy four-square rhythm, followed by a new and more brilliant version of the waltz. Then comes a solo for Odette, and finally in this group of dances is the Coda , a vigorous $\frac{6}{8}$ dance, simple in style but brilliant both musically and choreographically. Then the mood changes back to that of the beginning of the act, and the swan music returns as Odette and the Swan Maidens disappear, leaving the Prince and his huntsmen gazing forlornly after them.

The third act, the brilliant ballroom scene, begins with the entry of the guests, followed by general dances. Then a fanfare heralds the appearance of Odile, followed by the mime of choosing the Prince's bride. None of the girls please the Prince, who believes Odile to be Odette. (In the Royal Ballet production Odile does not appear till after the mime of choosing the bride, at the second fanfare.) The next number was a pas de six, but this was never performed outside Russia, and the present Bolshoi ballet production does not include it either. Then comes a series of of characteristic national dances —Spanish (which includes castanets and good deal of national colour), Neapolitan, with an agile trumpet solo which strikes quite a 'modern' note, csárdás, and a mazurka. The order of these dances is sometimes varied. The 1877 version began with the csárdás, and this is followed by the present-day Royal Ballet production. After the characteristic dances comes a pas de deux for Odile and the Prince in the form of a waltz, with a lush string melody which leads to another of Tchaikovsky's superb solo violin passages. Next come two solos with music interpolated from other sources: first one for Odile, to an orchestrated version of Tchaikovsky's piano piece Op. 72, No. 12, and then a vigorous dance for the Prince to music composed by Drigo. Finally we reach the Coda, which is brassy, noisy and brilliant: in this occur the famous thirty-two fouettés with which Odile dazzles both the Prince and the audience. The music of the Allegro which ends the act returns to that of the earlier mime of choosing the bride. The Prince chooses Odile, but then discovers that he has been deceived and that she is not Odette. The curtain falls on his disillusionment.

In the fourth act we are back by the lakeside. Both the 1877 and the Petipa versions begin the act with an entr'acte, and Petipa follows this with another interpolation, an orchestration of Tchaikovsky's Waltz in E flat, Op. 72, No. 11. Then comes a mournful dance for the Swans who await the return of Odette, followed by a dance for the cygnets, a lovely and nostalgic little movement in B flat minor which is almost reminiscent of Chopin. (The Royal Ballet version slightly alters the order of these numbers. It uses the music of the cygnets' dance as an entr'acte, and then leads from part of the original entr'acte and the final part of the swans' mournful dance to the interpolated waltz in E flat.) Then an agitated passage heralds the return of Odette, followed by storm music, which in the Royal Ballet version is somewhat cut. Next comes the music of the Prince's arrival, and after this Petipa interpolated another of Tchaikovsky's piano pieces, Op. 72, No. 15. The final section of the act, an Allegro agitato , is a short symphonic development of the Swan music, in syncopated rhythm and working up to a stirring climax.

Such is the sequence of the music in Petipa's 1895 production of *Le Lac des Cygnes*. The Royal Ballet company follow the 1877 version for Act I and Petipa for Act II. The general dances for the corps de ballet at the beginning of Act III are omitted, and the changes in Act IV have already been noted. But the choreography remains based on the Petipa-Ivanov version, as reproduced by Sergeyev. The version shown in London in 1956 by the Bolshoi Theatre Ballet was based on a new choreography by Gorsky which is different to Petipa's in many respects, but the musical changes were less fundamental. Acts I and II were similar to the versions used by the Royal Ballet: in Act III the general dances for the corps de ballet are retained, while the order of the characteristic dances were varied—Petipa's interpolations were also retained. In Act IV Petipa's interpolation of the Waltz in E flat was omitted but other music was interpolated after the Prince's entry.

Tchaikovsky's second full-length ballet, *La Belle au Bois*

Dormant (*The Sleeping Beauty*) was first produced at the Mary-insky Theatre, St. Petersburg, on 2/14 January 1890. The production was of unusual splendour, but the ballet was not a great success at first. However it soon established itself as a favourite and has remained so ever since, though productions of the whole ballet outside Russia have not been common—here again the Royal Ballet has shown unusual enterprise, having added the ballet to their repertoire as long ago as 1939.

The ballet is in three acts and contains some twenty-nine numbers: before the first act comes a Prologue. This begins with a short introduction in which the music associated with the evil fairy Carabosse soon leads to the flowing $\frac{6}{8}$ melody which is characteristic of the Lilac Fairy. This in turn leads into the first number, a lively and attractive march which accompanies the entrance of the lords and ladies and the mime of Catalabutte. The music here is bright, gay and theatrical in the best sense of the word. Then follows a 'Dance Scene', a graceful slow waltz with divided strings. In the ensuing pas de six the fairies present their gifts. This is a set of six variations—in the ballet sense of a solo dance and not the musical one of variations on a theme—with an introduction and coda. The names given to these Fairy Dances in the present Royal Ballet production are: Fairy of the Crystal Fountain, a flowing $\frac{2}{4}$ dance in B flat major; Fairy of the Enchanted Garden, a staccato $\frac{6}{8}$ dance in G minor; Fairy of the Woodland Glades—this dance is remarkable for the sustained brass chords accompanying the melody on pizzicato strings; Fairy of the Song Birds, an agitated fluttering for piccolo solo; Fairy of the Golden Vine, a brilliant, lively movement; and finally The Lilac Fairy, a waltz in C major.

The original version had different titles for these dances, as may be seen in the piano score published by the Tchaikovsky Foundation. These are 'Candite', 'Coulante. Flour', 'Falling Crumbs', 'Singing Canary', 'Violente', and the 'Lilac Fairy'. After the six variations comes a coda, a lively allegro movement in $\frac{4}{4}$ which is begun by the men and works up to a splendid climax. Then comes the 'Finale of the Prologue'. A suave clarinet melody accompanies the Lilac Fairy as she approaches the cradle of the Princess Aurora to bestow her gift. She is interrupted by the entrance of Carabosse, whose music is written in a vigorous $\frac{4}{4}$ time. It is brilliantly scored and is developed symphonically as the dance progresses. Her derisive laughter and sneering are most effectively portrayed; again, as in Rothbart's music in *Le Lac des Cygnes*, Tchaikovsky uses only diminished seventh chords, but they are most ingeniously handled.

Act I begins with a 'Scene' allegro vivo in E major, which evokes an atmosphere of festivity: within this comes the incident of the spinners being discovered but pardoned by the King. Tchaikovsky takes this dramatic interlude in his stride, portraying it musically yet not destroying the symphonic shape of the music. Next comes the famous Waltz, well known in the concert hall, and one of Tchaikovsky's finest creations in this genre. The succeeding number consists of three short sections which act as an introduction to the 'Rose Adage', again one of the most famous movements in all ballet. Its spacious melody is developed into a movement of magnificent theatrical colour. After the more sprightly dance of the Maids of Honour and the Pages there is an expressive solo for Aurora in the style of a slow waltz, with the melody on a solo violin and a delicate accompaniment in which short harp glissandi are prominent. The coda of this number, described by Petipa in his notes as 'general excitement and dancing' begins with a $\frac{2}{4}$ allegro giusto in G major. Aurora returns with the recapitulation of the first theme, and an ingenious transition into the final number of the act is made by the superimposition on the music of the coda of the rhythm of the waltz which is to follow—as it were a presentiment of the tragedy to come. This waltz begins in E flat major, at the point where Aurora seizes the needle, but her dance is abruptly broken off when she pricks herself, and there follows a striking dramatic passage based on Carabosse's music. Her tiny dance of death, based with Bach-like economy on a single semiquaver figure, is extremely effective, and her metamorphosis into sleep is accompanied by a symphonic development of the Lilac Fairy theme, which rises to a great climax and then dies away.

The second act begins with a kind of divertissement. First comes the music of the hunt and then of the game of blind man's buff: then follow a 'Scene' and four dances, those of the Duchesses, Baronesses, Countesses and Marquises—the Baronesses' dance is often omitted. This little divertissement ends with a farandole, which curiously enough is in mazurka rhythm. Next comes the arrival of the huntsmen, with a repetition of the music heard at the beginning of the act, and leading into the Lilac Fairy music. Aurora enters with a strongly rhythmical allegro vivace, and this is linked to the next number, a pas d'action. This is one of Tchaikovsky's large-scale dramatic creations: it begins with a cello solo theme with many subtle changes between $\frac{6}{8}$ and $\frac{2}{4}$ time. There is a short melodious allegro comodo in B flat (a variation for Aurora) before the presto with its quick repeated notes, and rushing staccato scale passages effectively portray Aurora's disappearance.

Before the third act, as performed at Covent Garden, comes the 'Panorama' (andantino in G) which is well known from the concert suite. This is here played as an interlude, but originally accompanied a transformation scene on the stage. Next, in this version, comes the scene of the Prince's search for Aurora, which originally came in the second act. This leads to the real opening of the act, a lively allegro movement in D. A brilliant polacca with a Chopinesque flavour accompanies the entry of the fairy-tale characters, who now appear in procession, led by Puss-in-Boots and the White Cat. Then follows a pas de trois for Florestan and his sisters in the form of an intrada , four variations (in the ballet sense) and a Coda. The intrada, a flowing $\frac{6}{8}$ movement in B flat, is one of Tchaikovsky's loveliest melodic inspirations, the tune twisting and turning on itself while never losing the insistent rhythm nor becoming monotonous. The variations consist of the 'Silver Fairy Polka', a variation in $\frac{2}{4}$ time which is normally cut at Covent Garden, and the 'Diamond' variation. The 'Coda' uses some of the material of this last variation and develops it with rushing scale passages to an agitated ending.

Now comes a pas de caractère, 'Puss-in-Boots and the White Cat', one of the most successful examples of cat music ever written: Tchaikovsky has caught not only the sounds that cats make but also their feline essence. This is followed by the well-known 'Blue Birds' pas de deux, which is in several sections. Its first number, adagio in C, is chiefly an interchange between flute and clarinet. At first the clarinet echoes the flute phrases, but later the position is reversed. The two instrumental parts are similar and closely woven together throughout, to portray the unity between the Prince, changed by magic into a bird, and the Princess Florina. Next follows a virile waltz for the man, and then the girl's Andantino, with its delicate flute part adorned with grace notes. The Coda does not return to any of the previously heard music and is based on new material throughout.

The next pas de caractère, 'Red Riding-Hood and the Wolf', is a scurrying staccato movement in G minor, which admirably portrays its dramatic story. Then follow two further pas de caractère which are normally omitted in the Royal Ballet production, that of Hop o' my Thumb, his brothers, and the Ogre, and that of Cinderella and Prince Fortune. Next comes the great adagio in C for Aurora and the Prince, one of Tchaikovsky's most majestic and expansive movements, with its broadly flowing melody and rich orchestration. There follows a variation for the Prince—this is not used in the Royal Ballet production, one of the 'Florestan' variations being substituted—and then one for Aurora, the latter with a solo violin part, marked 'staccato e grazioso', which is very typical of Tchaikovsky. The Coda music of this pas de deux is used for the dance of the Three Ivans, a vigorous allegro vivace in E. The next dance, a sarabande, is normally cut, and the ballet ends with a 'Finale and Apotheosis' in the form of an extended mazurka, culminating in an 'andante molto maestoso' in G minor, the modal harmonies of which enhance the dignity of the ending.

The score of *La Belle au Bois Dormant* is slightly larger than that of some ballets, containing a piccolo in addition to two flutes, a cor anglais as well as two oboes, and two cornets as well as two trumpets. The ballet has always remained a favourite in Russia, and is a prominent feature of the Moscow Bolshoi Theatre Ballet's repertoire to-day. Its first important production outside Russia was that staged by Diaghilev at the Alhambra Theatre, London, on 2 November 1921, under the title of *The Sleeping Princess*. The choreography was based on notes made by Sergeyev, who had been a producer at the Maryinsky Theatre and knew the original production. In addition some dances were choreographed by Bronislava Nijinska, and Bakst and Stravinsky also co-operated in the production, which was on an extremely lavish scale. Unfortunately it was not greatly successful. Diaghilev had himself steered balletomanes' taste in the preceding years away from the old-fashioned romantic type of ballet and towards more experimental types of work, and the revival seemed a step backwards to many people. In this production, as in the present Royal Ballet version, the 'Hop o' my Thumb' and 'Cinderella' dances were omitted in the last act. Instead Diaghilev inserted some numbers from *Casse-Noisette* and elsewhere. The choreography of the Royal Ballet version is based, like Diaghilev's, on Sergeyev's reconstruction of Petipa's original production. It has been a continuous success, and was in fact used for the reopening night of Covent Garden after the war in 1946.

On the occasion of the 1921 production of *The Sleeping Princess* Stravinsky wrote in an open letter to Diaghilev: 'Tchaikovsky possessed the power of melody, centre of gravity in every symphony, opera, or ballet composed by him. It is absolutely indifferent to me that the quality of his melody was sometimes unequal. The fact is that he was a creator of melody, which is an extremely rare and precious gift. Among us Glinka too possessed it. And that is something which is not German. The Germans manufactured, and manufactured music with themes and leitmotive, which they substituted for melodies.' And certainly Tchaikovsky's outstanding gift of melody explains a great deal of his success as a ballet composer; for it is melody and rhythm which are essential to all ballet music, and no amount of ingenious contrapuntal development or devices of orchestration can make up for the lack of them.

Before leaving *La Belle au Bois Dormant* we should mention a one-act ballet, *Aurora's Wedding*, which is based on its music and contains some of its characters. This was danced in the 1930's by Colonel de Basil's Ballets Russes, a company which contained many dancers who had previously been with Diaghilev, and has since been taken up by other companies with some variants. The music is mainly taken from the last act of *La Belle au Bois Dormant*, though some numbers from *Casse-Noisette* are also interpolated. It begins with the andantino introduction from Act III of *La Belle au Bois Dormant*, followed by the polonaise from the same act. Then comes the pas de six from the Prologue , followed by the 'Sugar Plum Fairy' from *Casse-Noisette*. We then return to Act II of *La Belle au Bois Dormant* for the dances of the Duchesses and Countesses (and in some versions also the Marquises) and the farandole. Next comes a pas de quatre (or in some versions the pas de trois of Florestan and his sisters from Act III), followed by the pas de caractère of 'Red Riding Hood and the Wolf', and the 'Blue Bird' pas de deux. Next the 'Chinese Dance' from *Casse-Noisette* is interpolated, followed by the 'Three Ivans' from *La Belle au Bois Dormant,* Act III, and the ballet ends with the final pas de deux, mazurka, 'Finale and Apotheosis' from the same act. It will be seen that this ballet is somewhat of a hotchpotch, but it has proved effective in cases where it has not been possible to mount the full-length version of *La Belle au Bois Dormant.*

Tchaikovsky's last full-length ballet, *Casse-Noisette,* was written in 1891–2 in response to a commission from the Imperial Opera at St. Petersburg, and was produced at the Maryinsky Theatre on 5/17 December 1892 together with Tchaikovsky's one-act opera *Iolanthe,* which had been commissioned for the same occasion. *Casse-Noisette* is therefore really a two-act ballet, though on occasion it has been divided into three. The scenario is based on E. T. A. Hoffmann's 'Nutcracker and Mouse-King', from his *Serapionsbrüder.* The choreography was begun by Petipa, who later handed it over to Ivanov, and the latter's name is now universally quoted as the choreographer. The suite drawn from this ballet has become world-famous on the concert platform, and the 'Miniature Overture' with which the suite begins is also the overture to the ballet. Here the bass instruments are omitted and the cheerful atmosphere of a children's party is immediately evoked. Act I, which is divided into two tableaux, begins with a piece which accompanies the lighting and adorning of the Christmas tree. It is in D major, allegro non troppo with a more sustained middle section. This leads directly into the 'March', familiar from the concert suite. Next comes a 'Galop and Entrance of the New Guests', bringing presents for the Christmas Tree. There follows a 'Dance Scene' in which the music becomes more descriptive, here depicting the arrival of the Councillor Drosselmeyer who brings a number of gifts, including mechanical dolls and a little wooden nutcracker. The dolls dance. The following

'Scene' and 'Grossvatertanz' are again mainly descriptive. Clara wants the nutcracker for herself, but Fritz also wants it and breaks it in their struggle. The 'Grossvatertanz', familiar to us from Schumann's *Carnaval* and *Papillons,* is a solid German folk theme which is associated with family parties of this kind. Then follow two further 'Scenes' which are linked together; they depict the departure of the guests. Then Clara, who has been sent to bed, comes down in her nightgown to look for her nutcracker, but falls asleep among the toys. An army of mice appears, and there is a tremendous battle between them and the Ginger Cake soldiers, the former being led by their king and the latter by the nutcracker. Clara, in her dream, fears that the mice will be victorious, and throws her slipper at the Mouse King. His subjects disappear, and the nutcracker is transformed into a Prince. The music of these two scenes is dramatically developed, though at some length, and as a result they are often cut. They also need first-class orchestral playing. But they are worth preserving, as apart from their musical value they do provide the centre of the story of the ballet, such as it is.

The Prince now invites Clara to accompany him to the Kingdom of Sweets, and their journey is shown in the second tableau of Act I. First there is a 'Scene' in which the toys come down from the Christmas Tree to honour the Prince and Clara. The music is a continuation of that of the previous scene, in a somewhat similar style. Then comes the 'Waltz of the Snowflakes', a large-scale symphonic waltz in Tchaikovsky's best vein. It ends with a brilliant presto Coda in which much use is made of the semiquaver figure which is an integral part of the waltz itself.

The second act is set in the magic castle on the Sugar Mountain, otherwise the Kingdom of Sweets. First comes an overture, and then the entrance of Clara and the Nutcracker Prince together with the court of the Sugar Plum Fairy. Then follows a divertissement which contains many of the dances which

were included in the concert suite. The first is a Spanish dance
called 'Chocolate'—this is not in the concert suite—followed
by the 'Arab Dance', representing Coffee. Next comes the
'Chinese Dance', representing Tea, and then the exciting
'Russian Dance', or Trepak. The final pair of dances are the
'Dance of the Reed Pipes', with its delicious passages for three
flutes, and 'Mother Gigogne and the Clowns'—the latter is
normally omitted nowadays. Next comes the big 'Waltz of
the Flowers', which ends the concert suite, and then a pas de
deux for the Prince and the Sugar Plum Fairy which is perhaps the finest music in the whole ballet. This consists of an
intrada, andante maestoso , with a broad and flowing melody
richly scored and symphonically developed, and two variations
—a tarantella and the well-known 'Dance of the Sugar Plum
Fairy', with its ingenious passages for bass clarinet and celesta.
Tchaikovsky had heard the latter instrument in Paris in 1891,
and here introduced it into Russia for the first time: its limpid
tones are exactly right for the atmosphere which he wished
to evoke here. The last part of the pas de deux is a coda,
vivace assai, and the ballet ends with a waltz-finale and
apotheosis.

Though *Casse-Noisette* has never quite achieved the popularity of its two famous companions—perhaps its rather naïve
scenario and also the fact that it does not really fill an evening
are somewhat to blame for this—it contains a good deal of
Tchaikovsky's most delightful and skilful music, and it has
remained in the repertoire of many ballet companies, either
as a whole or as a one-act divertissement: the Sadler's Wells
Ballet produced it complete as long ago as 1934. Apart from
the dance numbers in his operas, which have been discussed in
the previous chapter, a good deal of Tchaikovsky's other
music has also of course been drawn upon by modern choreographers: some notable examples are his fifth symphony
(*Les Présages*—Massine), his second piano concerto (*Ballet
Imperial*—Balanchine), the variations from the Suite in G, the

Serenade for strings, and various smaller works (*Hamlet*—Helpmann). As we shall see later, Stravinsky also drew heavily on Tchaikovsky in his ballet *Le Baiser de la Fée*. The use of these other works of Tchaikovsky for ballet purposes has met with varying success. Certainly his large-scale symphonic works are not really suitable for ballet purposes. Although Tchaikovsky himself was worried about his methods of symphonic construction, his symphonies and concertos are in fact worked out in a broad symphonic style—even if this differs from those of Beethoven or Brahms—which is not very suitable to being cut up into individual dance numbers, and Massine, for instance, when preparing *Les Présages* was compelled to make very considerable cuts in the score. Tchaikovsky in fact differentiated quite strongly between his dance music and his symphonic works, and always tried to see that each was suitable for its intended purpose. Those works of his which are divided up into short sections, such as the Variations from the Suite in G, are naturally much more suitable for ballet, and a dramatic symphonic poem like *Hamlet* also lends itself fairly easily to balletic treatment: but the ballets based on concertos and symphonies have shown a somewhat uneasy alliance between dance and music—the natural forms of the one do not really correspond to those of the other.

As an example of the type of collaboration which existed between Tchaikovsky and his choreographer, we may append here Petipa's instructions for the first scene of *Casse-Noisette*. Petipa, as an experienced choreographer, knew exactly what he wanted in the way of music, and tried to ensure that his composers would produce this. He asked for:

1. Soft music. Sixty-four bars.
2. The lighting of the tree. Sparkling music, eight bars.
3. The entry of the children. Noisy and joyous music, twenty-four bars.

[83]

4. The moment of astonishment and admiration. A tremolo for some bars.
5. March, sixty-four bars.
6. Entry of the Incroyables. Sixteen bars rococo, minuet tempo.
7. Galop.
8. The entry of Drosselmeyer. The music slightly frightening and comic at the same time. A broad section, sixteen to twenty-four bars.

   The music gradually changes in character, twenty-four bars. It becomes less mournful, brighter and ends in gaiety.

   Fairly solemn music, eight bars and pause.

   Repeat the same eight bars and pause.

   Four bars with chords of astonishment.
9. Eight bars mazurka tempo.

   Eight different bars mazurka tempo.

   Sixteen bars mazurka.
10. Waltz, sharp, jerky and very rhythmic. Forty-eight bars.

This may appear to be putting the composer very much in a strait-jacket, and so in a way it is. On the other hand a good professional composer ought to be able to make something interesting even out of exact limits of this kind, as Tchaikovsky certainly did. It is always better if the choreographer, composer and designer can work together in close collaboration of this kind, and if the choreographer can indicate his exact wishes before the music is even written, it will clearly help the unity of the ballet. It is after all the choreographer who is the final creator of the ballet, and it is much better if his wishes can be realized as closely as possible, provided that he and his collaborators are temperamentally suited to each other and to the theme of the ballet. We shall return to this point later.

After the death of Tchaikovsky Petipa was forced to seek rather less distinguished composers for his ballets, the only one of any real importance being Alexander Glazounov, who lived from 1865 to 1936. Glazounov had been brought up very much in the nationalist Russian school of Rimsky-Korsakov and Borodin, and his earlier works, written before he was thirty, such as the symphonic poem *Stenka Razin*, have a definitely Russian flavour which contrasts with the more cosmopolitan style of Tchaikovsky. He was precociously brilliant at an early age—when only seventeen he wrote a symphony which won general commendation—but unfortunately his style became less distinguished and distinctive as he grew older, and his ballet music all dates from the period when this decline was beginning to set in. His ballet *Raymonda*, with choreography by Petipa, was first produced at the Maryinsky Theatre on 7/19 January 1898. The story is set in the Middle Ages and includes troubadours, a Saracen knight and a statue which descends from its pedestal and plays an important part in the action—together with lute playing, sword play, elves and goblins. These differing elements should have given Glazounov a good deal of scope for musical characterization, but he did not profit by them, and most of the music could fit any story and any age just as well. It is competent in the late nineteenth-century manner, opulent, pleasantly scored and completely undistinguished. However, *Raymonda* remains in the repertoire of the Bolshoi Theatre Ballet, and is mentioned here for that reason, and occasionally excerpts from it do appear in concert programmes.

Much the same may be said of Glazounov's other ballet scores, *Les Saisons* and *Les Ruses d'Amour*. The former was produced at the Maryinsky Theatre on 7/20 February 1900, again with choreography by Petipa. Here there is no story, and the seasons of the year are presented in the form of a straight divertissement. In the first scene Winter is shown with his friends Hoar-Frost, Ice, Hail, and Snow. In the second comes

Spring, with birds and flowers. Summer is enriched with Fauns, Satyrs, and Naiads, the latter wearing azure veils. Autumn is given over to the Bacchantes, and at the end the previous Seasons return for solo variations. Here again there is no attempt to give the atmosphere of the different scenes, and we are left with a string of more or less effective dances, some of which are heard from time to time in concert programmes. Music of this kind is much better used as a background to purely abstract dancing, and this has been excellently done by Frederick Ashton, who used music from Glazounov's ballets, as well as his Valse de Concert No. 1 and a piano mazurka orchestrated by Robert Irving, for his *Birthday Offering*, presented at Covent Garden on 5 May 1956 in honour of the twenty-fifth birthday of the Sadler's Wells Ballet. Here the series of solo dances fits admirably with the music: there is no story, and the only characterization is that inherent in the personalities of the solo dancers for whom the dances were created.

Stravinsky and Debussy at the latter's house

Diaghilev (right), with Cocteau, in 1924

IV

The Impact of Diaghilev, 1909–1929

AS we have seen, the Russian ballet still remained full of conventionalities even at the end of the nineteenth century, and it was not long before a new broom—or rather two—arrived to sweep away the cobwebs. The first was the young choreographer Michel Fokine, who had successfully passed through a severe course of academic training at the Imperial Ballet School in St. Petersburg and now, about 1904, began to formulate his ideas on the nature of ballet: in fact he drew up some notes for the reform of ballet which he submitted to the Director of the Maryinsky—needless to say, no notice was taken of them. Later he published his ideas in the form of five principles, of which the first states that 'Man can and should be expressive from head to foot'—in contrast to the old style of dancing in which the upper part of the body was hardly used at all. The fifth principle declares that 'the new ballet, refusing to be the slave either of music or of scenic decoration, and recognizing the alliance of the arts only on the condition of complete equality, allows perfect freedom both to the scenic artist and to the musician. In contradistinction to the older ballet it does not demand 'ballet music' of the composer as an accompaniment to dancing: it accepts music of every kind provided only that it is good and expressive.' These principles form the foundation of modern ballet and have been accepted all over the world to-day.

The second new broom was a wealthy young man of good family, great intelligence, and a passionate interest in the arts, Sergei Diaghilev, who was at the centre of a small group of *avant-garde* painters, musicians, and writers in St. Petersburg. He organized some art exhibitions in Paris, and then some concerts of Russian music. In 1908 he startled Paris with a season of Russian opera, including *Boris Godunov* with Chaliapine, and in 1909 he gave his first ballet season there. For this he commissioned Fokine to compose the ballet *Prince Igor*, to Borodin's 'Polovtsian Dances', together with *Les Sylphides*, a new version of a ballet *Chopiniana* which Fokine had already composed in Russia. Diaghilev had the means and the ability to put Fokine's ideas into practice, and their collaboration changed the whole face of modern ballet.

The starting point of this collaboration, as we have seen, was the idea of the artistic unity of the ballet. The choreographer, composer, designer, and librettist were each to express himself unhindered in his own way, but at the same time the results of their efforts were to be welded into an artistic whole. This is not always an easy ideal to achieve, but Diaghilev showed considerable insight in his choice of artists to collaborate in each particular ballet, and where a real fusion took place, as for instance in *Petrouchka* and *Le Tricorne*, the results have outstripped every other ballet since. In addition Diaghilev saw to it that the ballets were presented in the finest possible way: he had an unsurpassed company of dancers, headed by Nijinsky and Karsavina, and he managed to get the leading composers and painters of the day to work for him—both those of the middle generation like Debussy and Ravel, and also the young *avant-garde* experimenters of the time like Stravinsky and Picasso. The result was a sudden injection of life into the decaying framework of the old romantic ballet, with results that are now history.

From the technical point of view Diaghilev made two important innovations. Instead of the three-act ballet lasting the whole evening he concentrated on short one-act ballets which could be combined into a triple bill; and as well as commissioning composers to write new scores specially for the company, he encouraged his choreographers to look for music already written for other purposes which could be made into ballets—for this he often commissioned composers to arrange or orchestrate music written for other media, as in the Rossini-Respighi *Boutique Fantasque* or the Pergolesi-Stravinsky *Pulcinella*. Both these practices have been more or less universally adopted by all ballet companies outside Russia, where the three-act ballet is still preferred to this day. Some companies, like the Royal Ballet, combine both methods and stage three-act as well as one-act ballets.

The practice of taking music already written for some other purposes and making it into a ballet score can be extremely successful if tastefully done, as in *Les Sylphides,* for instance. It can also lead to deplorable results, as we shall see in the final chapter of this book. But before going any further, let us examine some of the principal ballets mounted by the Diaghilev company in the years immediately before the first world war. Apart from two ballets which Fokine had already mounted in Russia, *Le Pavillon d'Armide,* to music by Nicolas Tcherepnine, and *Cléopâtre,* by Arensky and Taneyev, the principal novelties of the 1909 season were *Les Sylphides* and *Prince Igor.*

The idea of making a ballet to Chopin's music first came to Fokine when he saw the score of four Chopin pieces orchestrated by Glazounov under the title *Chopiniana*: these were a Polonaise, a Nocturne, a Mazurka, and the Tarantella. Fokine added a waltz which Glazounov also orchestrated for him, and the ballet in this form was first produced on 8/21 March 1908 by artists of the Imperial Ballet in St. Petersburg. The only dance in classical style at this stage was the Waltz, danced by Pavlova and Obukhov. On 6 April 1908 another version was given with the dances now all in the classical style. The orchestration was by Maurice Keller, except for Glazounov's orchestration of the waltz.

Les Sylphides was first performed in the form that we now

know at the Théâtre du Châtelet, Paris, on 2 June 1909. Fokine described the idea of it as a 'romantic reverie', and it is indeed a purely romantic set of dances without any story. The Chopin pieces used in it are as follows:

Overture. Prelude Op. 28, No. 7, transposed down from A to A flat so as to lead into the next number, and played twice through.

Nocturne in A flat, Op. 32, No. 2. This is taken rather slower than one would play it on the piano, but the line of the dance maintains the rhythmic flow, and so the slow speed does not become disturbing to the listener.

Valse in G flat, Op. 70, No. 1.

Mazurka in D, Op. 33, No. 2.

Mazurka in C, Op. 67, No. 3. The man's solo is also taken slower than the normal pianistic speed so that his leaps need not be hurried.

Prelude—the same one which was heard as an Overture, but now played three times through.

Valse in C sharp minor, Op. 64, No. 2—a pas de deux.

Valse Op. 18—finale.

Les Sylphides is an extremely satisfactory example cf the art of building up a ballet score from a number of short pieces which were intended for quite different purposes— and it is one of the earliest of its kind. This practice has, of course, become common among modern choreographers, and many of them have tried it with varying degrees of success. It really needs someone with the sensitivity of a Fokine to do this kind of thing successfully, and there are very few other ballets which have achieved a similarly satisfactory result. The only drawback to *Les Sylphides* is the matter of orchestration. Innumerable arrangements of the music have been made by different musicians, but none are really satisfactory from the musical point of view. Probably Chopin's music is too wedded to the piano to fit properly into any other medium, and though the score always provides a perfectly adequate support for the dancing and indeed add a strongly poetical atmosphere to the ballet, one never feels that it is really orchestral music in the proper sense. However this is a small point. *Les Sylphides* has been immensely popular since its first production, and it is a *sine qua non* for every ballet company to have in its repertoire.

The *Prince Igor* ballet, based on the 'Polovtsian Dances' from Borodin's opera, was also produced during Diaghilev's first Paris season, at the Théâtre du Châtelet on 19 May 1909. The opera, we may recall, remained unfinished at Borodin's death, and the orchestration of it was undertaken by Rimsky-Korsakov and Glazounov. The second act, in which the dances come, was in fact orchestrated by Rimsky-Korsakov. At the first performance the original resources called for in the score, including a large chorus, were used for this ballet; but in many modern performances the orchestra is reduced in size and the choir omitted altogether, which of course considerably diminishes its effect. The ballet is made out of No. 8 in Borodin's score, the 'Dance of the Polovtsian Maidens', and No. 17, the 'Polovtsian Dances' themselves. Sometimes the 'Polovtsian March' is inserted as an overture. The music, well known from concert performances, is exotic, tender, barbaric, and exciting by turns: it is one of the finest examples of orientalism in Russian music, and the ballet took Paris by storm when it was first seen there. Fokine was perfectly justified in this case in making the music into a separate ballet, for *Prince Igor* is very rarely performed as a whole, and the ballet music in any case acts as a kind of divertissement within the opera. Diaghilev's action in putting this ballet on with his company has certainly served to popularize its music, and the ballet is now in the repertoire of a number of modern companies. What one would like to see of course, but very rarely does, is an operatic production of *Prince Igor* with a ballet company fully capable of carrying out the dances in the way Fokine intended them to be done.

Fokine followed up the success of the 'Polovtsian Dances' in Diaghilev's next Paris season by producing *Schéhérazade*, another oriental ballet based on Rimsky-Korsakov's well-known symphonic poem. This is an early example of the use for ballet of a score originally written for an entirely different purpose and Fokine's example has been followed by almost every modern choreographer. After the first performance, at the Paris Opéra on 4 June 1910, there was considerable discussion about the ballet, for Fokine had set only the second and fourth movements of Rimsky-Korsakov's score to dancing, using the first as an overture, and had completely changed the story indicated by the titles which the composer had given to the various movements of the work. These referred to four different tales taken from the *Thousand and One Nights*. Fokine based both the movements he selected on the first tale in the book, and bound them together into one story. This concerns the infidelities of the wives of the Sultan Shahriar. During his absence they abandon themselves in a wild orgy to the negro slaves of the court, but on the Sultan's return the orgy changes to a scene of slaughter as his soldiers fall on the revellers. This scenario gave Fokine plenty of scope for a lavish spectacle which is by no means out of keeping with the lush orientalism of the music, and only purists would object that the indications of programme given by Rimsky-Korsakov's titles have not been rigidly adhered to. Nevertheless the ballet has had an unfortunate effect as a precedent, for it has encouraged choreographers of less imagination and sensitivity to take almost any piece of music and fit any kind of balletic theme, suitable or unsuitable, to it—often with disastrous results, as we shall see in a later chapter. *Schéhérazade* is also one of the first ballets to be based on a full-length symphonic work. Admittedly Fokine took only half of it for dancing, and neither of the two movements is in the classical symphonic form—their sequence of moods is dramatic rather than symphonic, and therefore they are fairly easily adaptable to ballet purposes. But again this has opened the door to other choreographers who have attempted to base ballets on symphonies and concertos whose musical structure is completely at variance with anything in ballet. However we can enjoy *Schéhérazade* for its genuine excitement and power, and wish that more modern ballet companies had it in their repertoire.

At the same performance at the Paris Opéra on 4 June 1910, Fokine introduced to the western world another new ballet based on previously written music—Schumann's *Carnaval,* originally composed as a piano suite, but now orchestrated by K. Konstantinov. There had however previously been a 'collective' orchestration of the work in Russia. This project was launched by Glazounov, who was aided by a number of Russian composers, including Rimsky-Korsakov, Liadov, Tcherepnine, Arensky, Sokolov, Klenovsky, and Wihtol, and it may have given Fokine the idea for the ballet. This latter consists of Schumann's complete suite in the original order—though the little four-note 'Sphinxes' are of course omitted—and as the work is in a number of short movements of a fantastic type, including references to the characters of the Italian Commedia dell'Arte as well as to those of Schumann's own imagination, it is highly suitable to balletic treatment, and in fact makes an enchanting entertainment of a divertissement type which has remained highly popular ever since its first performance. The only trouble, as with *Les Sylphides,* has been the question of orchestration. Schumann's method of piano writing lends itself to orchestral transference rather more easily than Chopin's, being more solidly constructed from the harmonic point of view. Nevertheless there are many numbers in the suite which obstinately remain piano pieces, no matter how ingenious their orchestration may be. Most companies to-day use their own orchestral version of *Carnaval,* and there is no universally accepted orchestration of it.

Another ballet based on an orchestrated piano piece was

Le Spectre de la Rose, again with choreography by Fokine, produced at the Théâtre de Monte Carlo in 1911. This is a short pas de deux, originally danced by Karsavina and Nijinsky, to the music of Weber's 'Invitation to the Dance'. Here, however, there was a ready-made orchestration available made by a composer of genius. Berlioz had arranged the piece for orchestra in 1843, for a production of *Der Freischütz* at the Paris Opéra. A ballet was of course obligatory at the Opéra for all productions at that time, and the spoken dialogue had to be set as recitative. Berlioz, a great admirer of Weber, was entrusted with the task, and though he was against the introduction of a ballet where Weber had needed none, he thought that, *faute de mieux,* it would be better to make it up from music by Weber himself rather than risk the insertion of some hack dance tunes by another composer—it was even suggested that the ball movement from Berlioz' *Symphonie Fantastique,* and the fête scene from his *Romeo and Juliet* should be inserted into the ballet, but this Berlioz firmly refused to allow. In the end the ballet was made up of Berlioz' orchestration of the 'Invitation to the Dance' and some dance movements from *Oberon* and *Preciosa.* But Berlioz relates that the choreography was extremely poor, and it was not till *Le Spectre de la Rose* that the balletic possibilities of Weber's piece were fully realized. There have of course been several other orchestrations of this piece since, including a very ingenious one by Weingartner which combines some of the themes contrapuntally, but Berlioz' version has remained the most brilliant and effective.

Two further examples of 'oriental' ballets should be mentioned—apart, of course, from Richard Strauss' *La Légende de Joseph,* which has an oriental setting and shows some oriental characteristics in the music. *Thamar* was produced at the Théâtre du Châtelet on 20 May 1912, with choreography by Fokine. It is based on the symphonic poem by Balakirev which is one of the earliest examples of orientalism in Russian music.

Though begun before Rimsky-Korsakov's *Schéhérazade* it was not completed till later, Balakirev, as usual, taking many years over the work. But Rimsky-Korsakov had of course seen *Thamar* in manuscript and certainly learnt a good deal from it. In this case Fokine was able to make use of the original story attached to the music, of an Eastern Queen who attracts passing strangers, especially handsome young men, to her castle, and after an evening of feasting and love, stabs them. At the end she is seen waiting for the next passer-by. Balakirev's music, fairly well known from the concert hall, is lavish and atmospheric and suits the purpose of the ballet very well.

The other 'oriental' production was Rimsky-Korsakov's last opera *Coq d'Or,* put on at the Paris Opéra on 21 May 1914, again with choreography by Fokine. This was done in an unusual way in that the cast of singers stood round the back of the stage, while the dancers in front mimed their actions. In a fantastic work of this kind such treatment can come off, but it was not entirely successful, and in 1937 Fokine revived it in a shortened form for the de Basil company with the singing parts transferred to the orchestra: this worked very well, and was one of the most colourful items in that company's repertoire. But we must now turn to Diaghilev's principal discovery, the young Russian composer Igor Stravinsky.

Stravinsky's first ballet, *L'Oiseau de Feu,* was first produced by the Diaghilev company at the Paris Opéra on 25 June 1910, with choreography by Fokine and décor by Golovine: Karsavina danced the Firebird and Fokine himself Ivan Tsarevitch. The conductor was the well-known French composer Gabriel Pierné. The story is adapted from several Russian fairy tales. The score had originally been commissioned from Liadov, whose *Contes Russes* Massine produced as a ballet in 1919. However, the veteran composer was not able to produce it quickly enough for Diaghilev, who persuaded the young

Stravinsky to postpone work on his opera *Le Rossignol* and write the ballet instead. Stravinsky worked in very close collaboration with Fokine, who gave him every detail of the mimed scenes and also discussed with him the relationship of the music and dance at every stage in the composition of the score. In contrast to the majority of earlier ballets, the music is intended to be played without a break, though it still falls into a number of short scenes and dances in the normal ballet tradition; but its continuity has set an example to many modern one-act ballets. In the old type of ballet divided into self-contained numbers the breaks between them were liable to be filled by applause for the dancers, thereby breaking the dramatic continuity, and though this is not particularly serious in a divertissement or abstract ballet, it is bound to make any kind of dramatic scene less effective.

Although *L'Oiseau de Feu* is described as being in one act and two scenes, the second scene is of very short duration, only occupying the last few minutes of the ballet. The introduction with its mysterious quaver movements in the bass sets the atmosphere at once, and quite early on we reach the celebrated passage in glissando harmonics for violins, violas and cellos. Here the violins are supposed to tune their E string down to D, and all the instruments carry out the glissando on their D strings. In fact the music of this ballet in general is full of fantastic and impressionistic effects: Stravinsky took the imaginative ideas of his master Rimsky-Korsakov and developed them still further, and his music is also in the decorative and pictorial tradition of Glinka and Liadov, mingled with the discoveries of the French Impressionist school of Debussy, Dukas, and Ravel. As we shall see, these influences did not last long in Stravinsky's musical development, and even here they are interpreted in a far more radical manner than in the works on which Stravinsky modelled his style at the time. But the whole score is full of imagination, and it represents a very considerable achievement for a young man of under thirty. Stravinsky seems to have felt intuitively from the start what was needed in a ballet score, and this intuitive feeling remained with him all his life, in spite of his later superficial changes of style: in fact one can say that Tchaikovsky and Stravinsky are the greatest masters of ballet music who tower above all other composers for this medium.

The curtain rises on the enchanted garden of Kostchei, and soon the Firebird herself appears, pursued by Ivan Tsarevitch: then follows the Firebird's fantastic dance, her capture by Ivan Tsarevitch—purely descriptive music of great dramatic skill—and her pleadings, which take the shape of a more definite dance form, adagio—allegretto—adagio. After the moment when she plucks out her feather and gives it to Ivan the music again becomes freely descriptive. Then the thirteen enchanted Princesses appear and play with the golden apples, to a charming scherzo-like movement in G major, the middle section of which later appears in a more elaborate form during the dramatic 'Infernal Dance of the Subjects of Kostchei'. Ivan Tsarevitch appears suddenly. Then comes the 'Ronde des Princesses', a charming little piece which culminates pianissimo in the moment of the kiss—its main theme is a Russian folk song which Rimsky-Korsakov had previously used in the second movement of his Sinfonietta on Russian Themes. Diaghilev, incidentally, was unaware of this fact until it was pointed out to him by Edwin Evans: it is, however, a typical example of Stravinsky's borrowing process which he continued to carry out throughout his life. When at a loss for a melody of his own—and he never was a really great melodist—he either borrowed someone else's or used a folk theme: and in the case of a ballet based on Russian folk stories he certainly had some justification for using Russian folk music as well.

Next follows the scene of daybreak, when the Princesses disappear, and then the Magic Carillon, to which the monstrous guardians of Kostchei rush out of their subterranean home and capture Ivan. This is a brilliant and dramatic piece of orchestral writing which is extremely effective in performance. Kostchei himself now appears, and we have his dialogue in mime with Ivan and the intercession of the Princesses—here again the music provides a dramatic background —followed by the appearance of the Firebird, who casts a spell on Kostchei's subjects and makes them dance. This leads to the well-known 'Infernal Dance of the Subjects of Kostchei', an effective concert piece which comes off brilliantly on the stage and leads to an enormous climax. A short bridge passage leads to the Berceuse, in which Kostchei and his court are sent to sleep so that Ivan can seize the 'egg of the world' and thus bring about the death of Kostchei. The Berceuse is a simple folk-song-like melody, and when the scene changes after Kostchei's death, the music right up to the final climax is based on a traditional Russian chorale which had previously been used by Rimsky-Korsakov—but Stravinsky alters its accents by changing it from $\frac{6}{4}$ to $\frac{7}{4}$ time. It makes a majestic and triumphant ending to the ballet: and the final cadence, in which unrelated common chords appear in succession under a tonic pedal, has since been made use of by many other composers in different ways.

Stravinsky made a seven-movement suite from the ballet which is often heard in the concert hall. He realized, quite rightly, that most of the music only comes to life when it accompanies the dancing, and that to make the complete ballet into an orchestral work would be a mistake. This suite demands a large orchestra, including quadruple woodwind and an additional trumpet besides the usual brass: the score also calls for three harps, thirty-two violins, fourteen violas, eight cellos and six double basses. Needless to say, an orchestra of this size is not normally to be found in any theatre, even at Covent Garden, where the ballet was first performed in 1954 in a revived version of Fokine's original choreography made by Serge Grigoriev and Liubov Tchernicheva. It has since become one of the most popular works in the Royal Ballet repertoire. In 1949 Stravinsky made a slightly revised version of the score for rather smaller orchestra.

Stravinsky's second ballet, *Petrouchka,* was first produced at the Théâtre du Châtelet, Paris, on 13 June, 1911. The part of the Ballerina was danced by Karsavina, of Petrouchka by Nijinsky, and that of the Showman was taken by the veteran ballet master Cecchetti. Stravinsky had originally conceived the work as a piano concerto in which the piano represents the wild gestures of a malevolent puppet who is answered by the orchestra. It was Diaghilev who persuaded him to turn the work into a ballet, and the plot was evolved in collaboration between Stravinsky, Diaghilev and Benois, the designer. It is again a Russian folk theme, based on the annual Shrovetide Fair in St. Petersburg, the principal characters being the Showman and his three puppets, Petrouchka, the Ballerina, and the Moor. The ballet is in four tableaux which are played without a break. They are in fact connected by the very effective device of a persistent drum rhythm which keeps up the excitement of the atmosphere while the scenery is being changed. Stravinsky's first ideas for the work are to be found mostly at the end of the first tableau and in the second, and here we are reminded of the origin of the work as a piano concerto by the prominent piano part—after the second tableau the piano almost disappears from the score.

Petrouchka shows Stravinsky's imaginative powers at their highest. Here is real ballet music which successfully combines a number of disparate elements into a perfect and well-constructed whole. The carnival scenes, which act as a background to the dramatic action and were not of course part of Stravinsky's original scheme, are mainly based on popular tunes which Stravinsky culled from various sources. Thus, in the first scene, the barrel organ tune is a French popular song, '*Elle avait une jambe en bois*', and the musical box tune is a waltz by Lanner. Similarly in the final scene the 'Nursemaids'

[99]

Dance' is a Russian theme which Tchaikovsky had previously used, and the 'Coachmen's Dance' is based on a Moscow street song. Probably many of the other tunes are of similar origin, but this is of little importance compared with the skill with which Stravinsky uses them. The style here is more radical harmonically than that of *L'Oiseau de Feu*. The rhythms are much more complex and the orchestral writing more jagged and less romantic. The music for Petrouchka himself is based on an extension of Rimsky-Korsakov's style, but here handled far more radically. The passage in the second scene, for instance, in which Petrouchka curses his unhappy life is based on the simultaneous use of two common chords a tritone apart—here mainly C major and F sharp major. This was probably suggested by the well-known passage in the second movement of Rimsky-Korsakov's *Schéhérazade,* where these two chords are heard in alternation for some bars as the background to a melodic fragment, but it was Stravinsky who had the idea of telescoping them by sounding the two chords together. As a matter of fact he had been anticipated in this by Liszt, who used the same two chords simultaneously in his 'Malédiction' for piano and strings, written some time in the 1830's, and there is a curious coincidence here, for the passage in *Petrouchka* where this effect first appears is in fact called 'Les Malédictions de Petrouchka' in the score. But a coincidence it must be, for Liszt's work remained unpublished till 1915, four years after the first production of *Petrouchka*.

The principal musical features of the score may be briefly mentioned. Here there is no longer much question of set dances or numbers, for the music is completely continuous—though there are a few numbers, such as the 'Russian Dance' in the first scene, which can be extracted as separate entities. The opening scene, with its tremolos and ostinato figures, brilliantly creates the background of a big popular festival, and against this the various characters are represented by their own individual themes and figures: the music in fact follows the action in detail throughout, and can hardly be separated from it. Before the Russian dance comes the short dramatic passage in which the Showman brings his puppets to life. Petrouchka's chief theme, with its bitonal arpeggios, is mainly heard in the second scene—this theme, incidentally, is very similar to the Lord Chamberlain's theme in Stravinsky's early opera *Le Rossignol*. The piano cadenza at the end of this scene, as Petrouchka tears down the walls of his cell, is again based on this figure. In the third scene comes the Ballerina's dance, with its deliciously vulgar trumpet tune, and the pas de deux for her and the Moor. In the last scene we return to the fair music, with different dance themes running through the same tremolo background as in the first scene. The revels are momentarily interrupted as the bear crosses the stage to heavy, lurching chords, and then the dance themes return, sometimes combined together contrapuntally, and rise to a climax as the puppets rush out of the booth and tear round the stage. At the end of the ballet, after Petrouchka has been killed by the Moor, and after the Showman has shown the crowd that he is only a rag puppet, his ghost screams defiance from the top of the booth to the same bitonal arpeggios which were heard earlier.

Petrouchka is a masterly score—perhaps Stravinsky's greatest achievement in ballet music, for here not only are all the different musical elements integrated with each other, varied in style as many of them are, but the music itself is completely at one with the action. The collaboration between Stravinsky, Fokine, and Benois in fact was a model of what such work should be, and the result is a ballet which was created as a unity and remains to this day one of the masterpieces of the ballet repertoire. If the choreographer, composer, and designer worked so closely together in all ballets there would be far fewer unsuccessful productions nowadays. As the music is so closely bound to the dancing, it is natural that the ballet as a whole does not make effective concert music, though it is often played in this manner. However, Stravinsky extracted a concert suite from it which does make some sense without the visual element. This consists of the latter half of the first scene, from the moment of the appearance of the Showman down to the end of the 'Russian Dance'; the second scene, in Petrouchka's cell, more or less complete; and the first part of the final scene, with the carnival music and dances, up to the point where the puppets burst out of the booth. The original score was again for very large orchestra, including quadruple woodwind, two cornets as well as two trumpets, two harps, celesta, piano, and plenty of percussion, but this is normally reduced in most ballet theatres to-day, and indeed some companies perform it with a pitifully inadequate orchestra which gives nothing like the effect intended. Nevertheless the ballet's qualities still shine through.

Stravinsky's third, and perhaps his most famous ballet, *Le Sacre du Printemps* (*The Rite of Spring*), followed two years after *Petrouchka*: it was first performed at the Théâtre des Champs-Elysées in Paris on 29 May 1913, again by the Diaghilev company, with choreography by Nijinsky. The book, by Stravinsky and Roerich, is subtitled 'Scenes of pagan Russia, in two parts', the first taking place by day, and the second by night. On the conception of the work Stravinsky wrote: 'One day I unexpectedly saw before me the picture of a great pagan sacrificial ceremony: the old priests, sitting in a circle, watch the death-dance of a young girl, whom they are offering to the God of Spring, in order to placate him. . . . In the spring sacrifice I wished to represent the greatest up-surge of Nature, continually renewing herself. In the intro-duction I have shown in the orchestra the fear which overcomes every sensitive spirit before the might of the elements. . . .' This introduction in fact represents the birthpangs of spring: in the first part of the ballet young men and the chosen maiden dance in celebration of the coming of spring, ending in a climax with the Adoration of the Earth. In the second the

Serge Prokofiev

Danilova, Tchernicheva, Doubrovska, and Lifar in *Apollon Musagète*, 1928

sacrifice of the chosen maiden takes place—her body is lifted up to heaven and this symbolizes the eternal cycle of nature, birth, growth, death, and rebirth.

None of Stravinsky's other ballets caused such a sensation on its first performance as *Le Sacre du Printemps*. The scenes at the Paris première are too well known to need repetition here, but the important fact is that this was no mere *succès de scandale,* to be soon forgotten, for indeed *Le Sacre du Printemps* has become one of the landmarks in modern music. Curiously enough, it is hardly ever performed as a ballet nowadays. Possibly the original choreography was unsatisfactory— Nijinsky was no great musician, and Stravinsky had to teach the complex rhythms of this work to him and the dancers by banging them out on a tin tray—and the later choreographic version by Massine (1920) ignores many points in the original scenario. But the work has invariably been successful in the concert hall. This may of course argue that it is therefore not good ballet music, but in this particular case the usual rules do not apply, for *Le Sacre du Printemps* is an exception to every musical canon, and is that rare thing, a unique masterpiece without forbears or progeny. Stravinsky himself, as we shall see, never attempted to write anything of the kind again; although his next ballet, *Les Noces,* also deals with scenes of primitive Russian life, the completely uninhibited expression of *Le Sacre du Printemps* is absent, and we can already see in it the beginning of that process of formalization and stylization which Stravinsky pursued for most of the rest of his life. And though *Le Sacre du Printemps,* through its novel uses of colour, harmony, and rhythm, has had an immense influence on the whole of modern music, direct imitations of it have been rare and unsuccessful—the only piece of the kind which remains in the repertoire to-day is Prokofiev's 'Scythian Suite'.

The ballet is scored for a very large orchestra, containing quintuple woodwind, eight horns, five trumpets, three trombones, two tubas, and percussion and strings to match. As in Stravinsky's previous two ballets, the music is continuous, but each part falls into a number of sections. The first part, 'Adoration de la Terre', consists of: 'Danses des Adolescentes', 'Jeu du Rapt', 'Rondes Printanières', 'Jeux des Cités Rivales', 'Cortège du Sage', and the final 'Danse de la Terre'. In the second part, 'Le Sacrifice', we have 'Cercles Mystérieux des Adolescentes', 'Glorification de l'Élue', 'Évocation des Ancêtres', 'Action Rituelle des Ancêtres', and the 'Danse Sacrale'. The music hardly calls for detailed analysis; it makes its effect on the listener by a kind of hypnotic suggestion which is very far removed from the procedures of symphonic form or even of ballet music of a more normal kind. In fact one has to sit back and let the music pour over one, as it were. This may not be the best way to listen to music in general, but, as I have said, *Le Sacre du Printemps* is an exceptional work. The very opening, with its mysterious high bassoon notes—a sound previously unheard in the orchestra—sets the atmosphere at once, and thereafter tiny melodic fragments appear and combine with one another like the growth of plants or flowers. Later the stamping rhythms and crushing discords suggest the primitive rite, and the whole works up to a series of climaxes of orgiastic excitement. Admittedly this method of writing, if it does not come off, can produce barren results, and there are some passages in the middle of the second part where Stravinsky seems momentarily to have lost his inspiration, but they are redeemed by the overwhelming rhythmic power of the final 'Danse Sacrale'. The melodic fragments which provide some kind of a foundation for the music are mainly simple and modal, using only four or five notes, around which they revolve endlessly. They are combined with complex polytonal harmonies, violent and irregular rhythms and striking percussion effects which all combine to make *La Sacre du Printemps* a masterpiece of its kind.

One of Diaghilev's first acts after the arrival of his company in Paris in 1909 was to enquire about French composers from whom he might commission ballets, and he was soon put in touch with Ravel. Fokine suggested the theme of *Daphnis and Chloë*. Ravel was not too keen at first and suggested various alterations in the scenario, but eventually he set to work on the score. However, this work was interrupted by other compositions and by the first performance of *L'Heure Espagnole*, and it was not finished till 1912. Meanwhile Ravel had had two other ballets mounted, though neither score was written in the first place for the stage. In 1912 Rouché, the director of the Opéra, who was a warm admirer of Ravel, suggested putting on his suite *Ma Mère l'Oye*, originally written as children's pieces for piano duet, as a divertissement for the Théâtre des Arts. Ravel orchestrated the original suite, wrote his own scenario for the ballet, and added a Prelude, a 'Spinning Song' and four Interludes to link the original five movements. In this form it was put on at the Théâtre des Arts on 21 January 1912, and had a great success. The ballet contains much of Ravel's most charming music, beautifully scored, and the original suite is of course familiar from concert performances. It is extraordinary what a varied effect Ravel manages to draw from very small forces.

A few weeks later Ravel was asked by Trukhanova, a Russian dancer engaged at the Opéra, to allow her to dance his *Valses Nobles et Sentimentales*, a piano work composed in the previous year. Ravel scored the work in a fortnight in March, and the ballet was first performed on 22 April 1912 at the Théâtre du Chatelet. Ravel's suite takes its title from Schubert's piano-duet waltzes, and Ravel suggested to the dancer that the scene of the ballet should be laid in 1820, in the salon of a hard-hearted beauty in which the characters express their sentiments through the language of flowers. *Adélaïde, ou le langage des fleurs,* as the ballet was called, was first performed in the same programme as Dukas' *La Péri,* also a first performance, and together with danced versions of d'Indy's *Istar* and Florent Schmitt's *La Tragédie de Salomé*. Each composer conducted his own work. Ravel's waltzes are sophisticated versions of the popular dance form, especially from the point of view of harmony. They have a great deal of charm and wit, and are of course known to-day as purely orchestral pieces. One American ballet company has hit on the idea of making a half-hour ballet out of the *Valses Nobles et Sentimentales* added to Ravel's *La Valse*: but the style of the two waltz pieces are too different from them to coalesce properly. The earlier set of waltzes are brief, pithy and written in short phrases, in contrast to the long lines and dramatic effects of *La Valse*.

Meanwhile the score of *Daphnis and Chloë* was proceeding steadily. Parts of it had been tried out orchestrally in 1911, and eventually the first performance took place at the Châtelet on 8 June 1912, under the direction of Monteux. Nijinsky and Karsavina danced the principal rôles. Ravel had some difficulty in completing this score, and the final Bacchanale was revised several times. But it remains his biggest work and in some ways his greatest achievement outside his operas. It is scored for a large orchestra, and there is also a considerable part for a wordless chorus, which adds a great deal of colour to the work. Ravel wrote of the score: 'My intention was to compose a vast musical fresco, caring less about archaism than fidelity to the Greece of my dreams, which can be assimilated fairly easily to the Greece imagined and depicted by the French artists of the end of the eighteenth century. The work is symphonically constructed according to very rigorous tonal plan, by means of a small number of *motifs*, the developments of which ensure the homogeneity of the work.' Ravel's powers of construction are shown throughout the score and it is the architectural quality of the music which is most apparent. Although there is indeed plenty of sensuous colour and even impressionistic effects on occasion, these are subordinated to the musical design as a whole. The dramatic construction is simple. The ballet consists of three scenes, the first depicting the betrothal of Daphnis, interrupted by the invasion of the pirates who carry off Chloë; the second, showing Chloë in the pirates' camp and her rescue from there; and the third, her reunion with Daphnis, the pantomime of Pan and Syrinx, and the final general dance. Ravel uses modal scales on occasion, particularly the Dorian mode. These are not intended as archaic effects but were part of Ravel's natural style, and they are mainly used purely melodically and not harmonically. Most of the best of the music is contained in the two concert suites, which have become well known, particularly the second, which consists of the music of the final scene. The ballet itself was put on at the end of Diaghilev's 1912 season and had only two performances that year. It was repeated with success in 1913, but thereafter was dropped by the Diaghilev company. However the Opéra took it over, and it has had a number of performances there: in 1951 it was produced at Covent Garden by the Sadler's Wells Ballet with choreography by Frederick Ashton and a décor by John Craxton which is much more suitable to ancient Greece than the orientalisms of Bakst in the original production. It remained a popular item in the repertoire for many years.

Ravel wrote two more works intended for ballet, *La Valse* and the *Boléro*. The idea of a symphonic poem called *Vienna* was in Ravel's mind as early as 1906, but it was not till 1919–20 that *La Valse* was actually written. Ravel had been in poor health and had not felt like composing, but Diaghilev offered to commission a ballet from him, and this gave him the opportunity of carrying out his long-delayed plan. He wrote of it: 'I conceived this work as a kind of apotheosis of the Viennese waltz, in which, according to my feeling, is mingled the impression of a fantastic and fatal whirling dance. I place this waltz in the framework of an Imperial Court, about 1855.' And in effect *La Valse* is an immense Viennese waltz, beginning mysteriously: 'Billowing clouds let one just see glimpses of dancing couples. The clouds gradually dissipate: one sees an enormous hall filled with a whirling crowd.' The work consists of two enormous crescendos. In the first one fragments of themes, with a distinctly Viennese character, flit across the stage, as it were, until the lights go up in full blaze. In the second part of the work these phrases and the various waltz rhythms are pitted against one another, and towards the end a more menacing note creeps in, as if the dancing had gone mad and the whole company were doomed to destruction. It is a most dramatic and exciting work, and has won great success in the concert hall all over the world. It was in fact first performed at a Lamoureux concert in Paris on 8 January 1920, Diaghilev having decided after all not to put it on as a ballet. However, it has also achieved great success on the ballet stage, both at the Paris Opéra with choreography by Nijinska and in various productions by other companies, including the American one mentioned above.

Ravel's *Boléro* has a rather curious history. In 1928 he was asked by Ida Rubinstein to write a ballet for her. Feeling, as he often did, somewhat lazy about fulfilling this commission, he decided instead of writing an original work to orchestrate some of Albéniz's piano pieces. It then transpired that Albéniz's heirs had conferred the sole rights of arrangement for Albéniz's works on the conductor Arbós: and though Arbós gladly offered to waive this right in Ravel's favour, time was now getting short before the date of the first performance of the new work. 'After all,' Ravel said to his friends, 'I should be quicker at scoring my own music than somebody else's.' So he embarked on the work which he later described as 'Fifteen minutes of orchestra without music,' the *Boléro*. And indeed the piece consists simply of two alternating tunes over a steady rhythmical accompaniment, without change of key until just before the end. The whole interest lies in the orchestration and in the way in which the piece grows in a steady crescendo from beginning to end. It is an orchestral *tour de force,* which invariably comes off successfully when properly performed. in spite of the extreme thinness of the musical material. It was first performed in Ida Rubinstein's ballet season at the Opéra on 20 November 1928, together with *La Valse.* It has since become universally famous as a concert piece and has even been made into a piece of popular dance music. It shows, at any rate, that Ravel, always a supreme craftsman, could make something out of even the simplest musical idea.

Among the other chief French composers of the middle generation the leading figure was, of course, Claude Debussy: his ballet *Jeux* was produced by Diaghilev in 1913, with choreography by Nijinsky. *Jeux* is one of Debussy's most remarkable scores: it was written at the time when he was turning from the pure impressionism of works like *La Mer* to the more 'classical' approach which we can see in his late instrumental sonatas. The score of *Jeux* contains many colourful and beautiful passages, certainly, but the impressionistic effects are there as part of the structure of the work and are not just added for effect. The ballet is in the form of a continuous symphonic poem, divided into several subsections, with many changes of mood in spite of an underlying unity of feeling. The main musical element is a $\frac{3}{8}$ waltz-like theme, but this is frequently varied and interrupted by passing changes, following the course of the action. It is thus genuine ballet music, and is another proof of Debussy's skill in writing for the stage, as well as being a beautiful work in its own right. Unfortunately it is very infrequently performed, even in the concert hall. The ballet scenario is also not very effective, the principal male dancer having to wear tennis clothes throughout—it was originally designed as a pas de trois. But it is a ballet which is well worth presenting on the stage, especially with a new and more suitable scenario. Debussy's other music has of course been drawn on since for ballets by various companies, including *Children's Corner* and *Ile des Sirènes* at

Sadler's Wells: but *Jeux* remains his real contribution to the art. It was given a new Paris production in 1920 by the enterprising Ballets Suédois, as well as Debussy's charming *Boîte à Joujoux*.

As we have seen, Dukas' *La Péri* was given its first performance on 22 April 1912, in the same programme as Ravel's *Adélaïde* and works by d'Indy and Florent Schmitt. *La Péri* was conceived as a pas de deux: an oriental prince has travelled far into the desert to seek the flower of immortality which is guarded by a péri (or fairy), but instead of being content with the flower he desires the péri as well and so is doomed to die. Dukas' score is in the later French romantic tradition, lavishly orchestrated and with oriental overtones. It is effectively carried out and makes a good background for the dance, but it is music that is curiously hard to remember in itself, and it has never kept a very secure place in the concert repertoire— it has certainly never attained the popularity of Dukas's *L'Apprenti Sorcier*. Nevertheless it has been revived as a ballet on several occasions, the most recent being on 15 February 1956 at Covent Garden, with choreography by Frederick Ashton, and danced by Margot Fonteyn and Michael Somes. This production was extremely successful.

Of the other two works in the 1912 performance, Florent Schmitt's *La Tragédie de Salomé* had been written five years earlier, and was first performed on 9 November 1907 at the Théâtre des Arts, danced by Loie Fuller. This is also a work in the French romantic tradition, and it is the only one which has made Schmitt's name known outside France. It has indeed maintained its place in the concert repertoire, though ballet performances of it are rare. The other work, d'Indy's *Istar* variations, was originally written as a concert piece for the Concerts Ysaye in Brussels, where it was first performed in 1896. It is, however, suitable for balletic treatment in that the theme is somewhat similar to that of Salome's 'Dance of the

Seven Veils'. The music, which is a set of variations, begins with the most elaborate one and gradually becomes more simple until finally the theme is heard in complete nakedness.

Another French composer of this middle generation who won fame on the ballet stage at this period was Albert Roussel. The first of Roussel's three ballets, *Le Festin de l'Araignée,* (or *The Spider's Banquet*), was first produced on 3 April 1913, at the Théâtre des Arts, Paris. The scenario, based on Henri Fabre's *Souvenirs Entomologiques,* was by Count Gilbert de Voisins, and the décor by Maxime Dethomas. The plot is a simple one: a spider, settled in its web, is disturbed by giant ants who come to carry away a rose-petal. A worm appears, and then a butterfly which the spider captures—there is a dance in celebration of this. Then the ants and some mantises fight over an apple, and the spider ensnares both in its web. Next the mayfly appears, greeted by an ironic waltz. She too is captured by the spider. The scene is now set for the spider's banquet; but the butterfly is killed by a mantis, and meanwhile the other insects regain their freedom and prepare a funeral for the mayfly. In the end all the insects have either been killed or have disappeared, and the curtain falls on a deserted garden.

Roussel's music is mainly atmospheric and impressionistic, with a vein of delicate fantasy, and yet at times a robustness which reminds us that the composer came from the northern town of Tourcoing and had also served as a sailor for some years. The themes, if not memorable, are always effective, and the orchestral writing is subtle, with many pluckings and flutterings. In fact the music has a strength which is not usually to be found in impressionist works of this period, and there is even a certain squareness of rhythm which is typical of Roussel in other works. The mayfly's dance has the elegance of Berlioz's 'Danse des Sylphes', and in the funeral march Roussel refuses to give way to sentiment. The work has remained as a successful item in the concert repertoire, though it is hardly ever mounted as a ballet to-day.

Stravinsky's next ballet after *Le Sacre du Printemps* was *Les Noces*. This was begun as early as July 1914, but it was not ready for performance until nine years later, by which time Stravinsky had of course completed several other works. In fact *Les Noces* gave him a great deal of trouble. He originally thought of it as a 'grand divertissement, or rather a cantata, depicting peasant nuptials', and on his last visit to Russia shortly before the outbreak of the first world war he obtained the literary material for the text. By the following spring the first two of the four tableaux were sketched out but not orchestrated, and Stravinsky played these over to Diaghilev, who was on a visit to him in Switzerland at the time. Diaghilev was so enthusiastic about the work that Stravinsky felt bound to dedicate it to him. However, the composition was interrupted by a commission from the Princesse de Polignac to produce *Renard,* and after that was completed Diaghilev asked for the symphonic poem *Le Chant du Rossignol,* based on themes from Stravinsky's opera *Le Rossignol,* which he intended to use as a ballet. As a result *Les Noces* was not finished in short score till 1917, and as Diaghilev was unable to produce it at that time because of wartime conditions, Stravinsky did not hurry to orchestrate it. The orchestration in fact proved extremely troublesome: Stravinsky first scored part of it for a large orchestra including two separate string orchestras. He then got the idea of scoring it for a strange assortment of instruments consisting of an electrical pianola, a harmonium, two cimbaloms, and percussion. He actually orchestrated the first two tableaux for this combination, and then rejected the idea on practical grounds—cimbalom players are rare outside Hungary, and electrical pianolas are also hardly easy to obtain. Finally he decided on the combination which we know to-day, an ensemble of four pianos and percussion.

The four tableaux of *Les Noces* are played without a break.

In the first we see the bride having her hair combed and tied with ribbons by her girl friends. In the second, similarly, the bridegroom is being prepared for the ceremony and is asking for his parents' blessing on the match. The third shows the departure of the bride for the wedding. The fourth and longest tableau is the wedding feast itself. This contains a long story told by a drunken guest and ends with the bride and bridegroom being escorted to their bed, and their love song. The music, which makes use of a liturgical chant and also a popular Russian folk song, is intensely rhythmical and dramatic throughout. It is indeed one of Stravinsky's most original and exciting works. It is hardly a ballet in the normal sense, for the chorus sings almost continuously and there are several solo vocal parts as well. It is really a dramatic scene combining singing, dancing, and instrumental music, but its rhythmical and percussive character gives it a balletic feeling throughout. It is in fact the rustic wedding to end all rustic weddings, and Stravinsky, by basing it on the type of wedding ceremony which, though of ancient and traditional origin, is still practised in Russia and many Eastern European countries to this day, ensured that the feeling and atmosphere of the work would be entirely authentic and not a mere succession of clever tricks. One of the most impressive parts is the ending, where the pianos and bells die away quietly when the feast is over. It makes a superb contrast to the barbaric rhythms which have dominated the rest of the work. *Les Noces* presents some difficulties from the point of view of staging, but if these can be overcome it is an extremely effective work.

As early as 1909, while working on his opera *Le Rossignol,* Stravinsky had begun to feel that 'he could write music to words or music to action, but that the co-operation of music with both words and action was daily becoming more inadmissible to his mind.' Later he wrote regarding the sonorities of *Les Noces*: 'I recognized that the vocal element of my work, that is to say that which is founded on breathing, is best supported by an orchestra consisting only of instruments whose notes are obtained percussively. So I found my solution : the ensemble I chose consisted of pianos, timpani, bells, xylophone—instruments with definite notes—and also drums of different timbres and pitches—instruments with no definite note. This combination of sonorities arose, as may be seen, necessarily and solely out of my music to *Les Noces* and did not spring from the desire to imitate the sounds of a popular festivity of this kind. In any case I have neither seen nor heard a festival of this kind in the whole of my life.' Thus his approach to *Les Noces* was to some extent one of stylization, in contrast to the direct expressionism of *Le Sacre du Printemps,* and this tendency was carried still further in his next ballet, *Renard.* But in spite of Stravinsky's remarks quoted above, *Les Noces* does evoke a genuinely Russian atmosphere. The text in fact is based on the cult of the Russian Eros, on which Christian ritual had been superimposed to some extent. Stravinsky's use of Russian folk music is more flexible than in *Le Sacre du Printemps.* Large structures are built out of small phrases, with the real musical content in the vocal parts and the percussion ensemble supplying an evocative rhythmic ostinato background.

Renard, produced in 1917, is a short ballet, again based on a Russian folk tale, but it was not intended for a large theatre —in fact, like *The Tale of the Soldier,* it is suitable for performance in a drawing-room, and was meant to be acted by clowns, dancers, or acrobats, preferably on a trestle table, with the orchestra behind: or if performed in a theatre, it should be given in front of a drop-curtain. Four singers, two tenors and two basses, are stationed with the orchestra and represent the actors' voices. The instrumental ensemble is a small group of solo players, with cimbalom and percussion predominating—in some modern performances the cimbalom has been replaced by a harpsichord, but the clearer tone of the latter instrument does not seem to represent the composer's intentions. The characters are all farmyard animals, and certain percussion effects are associated with them—for instance a drum roll each time the cock jumps down from his perch and is caught by the fox—and the music is full of crowings and other animal noises. It is a gay little piece, lasting a bare quarter of an hour. Here, as with *The Tale of the Soldier*, we have a stylized version of a Russian folk story, and these two works for small combinations of instruments mark the transition between the enormous expressionist orchestra of *Le Sacre du Printemps* and the neoclassicism of *Pulcinella* and Stravinsky's later ballets.

But before Stravinsky reached this latter stage, he still had one more ballet to complete, *Le Chant du Rossignol*. The history of this goes back as far as his early opera, *Le Rossignol*, of which the first act dates from 1908, before *L'Oiseau de Feu*, and is a pot-pourri of the styles of Rimsky-Korsakov, Glazounov, Scriabin, and Debussy. After finishing *Le Sacre du Printemps* Stravinsky completed the second and third acts, but his style had radically changed by now, and he was only able to ensure some kind of musical unity by quoting the fisherman's song from the first act at the end of each of the other two. The second act makes much use of the Chinese pentatonic scale, while the music of the last act leans towards Scriabin and even Schoenberg in its increasing avoidance of tonality. Stravinsky himself was not too happy about the result, and when Diaghilev visited him after the completion of *Renard* and suggested performing *Le Rossignol* as a ballet with the singers in the orchestra, Stravinsky replied with the proposal that he should turn the last two acts into a symphonic poem for orchestra alone, which could then be used as a ballet score. This he did under the title *Le Chant du Rossignol*, but the ballet when produced had no great success, in spite of Matisse's décor and costumes. It is divided into three parts: the 'Festival in the Palace of the Emperor of China', the 'Two Nightingales', and 'Illness and Recovery of the Emperor of China'.

[115]

(The story is based on that of Hans Andersen which was later used by the German composer Werner Egk for his ballet *The Chinese Nightingale*.) Stravinsky's chief problem in writing the symphonic poem was to find an instrumental equivalent for the original vocal parts. The song of the real nightingale in the opera was sometimes given to a flute, sometimes a solo violin, which naturally increased its range and led to some alterations in the orchestration. There are also some changes of key, and some cuts and repetitions. Though these changes certainly improved the symphonic structure of the music, its origin as an operatic vocal piece remains apparent, and in spite of the often fascinating chamber-music-like orchestral writing, *Le Chant du Rossignol* has never achieved real success.

Stravinsky's first neoclassical ballet, *Pulcinella,* was first performed at the Paris Opéra on 15 May 1920, under the direction of Ansermet. The choreography was by Massine, who also danced Pulcinella. Karsavina danced Pimpinella, and the décor and costumes were by Picasso—Stravinsky had insisted on this latter being commissioned to do this. The ballet was of course the idea of Diaghilev, who had noted the success of Tommasini's orchestrations of Scarlatti pieces in *Les Femmes de Bonne Humeur,* and also knew what Respighi was doing with the little Rossini pieces for *La Boutique Fantasque.* Indeed the immediate aftermath of the war had caused the ballet-going public to demand artificial comedies of the older type as a relief from their only too real sufferings of the last few years, and Diaghilev was astute enough to fulfil this demand. He had discovered in Italy some unpublished manuscripts which were thought to be by Pergolesi—though it now appears that they are not—and he suggested these to Stravinsky as the basis of his ballet. Stravinsky, who had just completed *The Tale of the Soldier* at the time and was now concerned with works like 'Rag-time' and 'Piano-Rag-music', was at first not too keen on the idea, but Diaghilev told him that he had also discovered in Naples a manuscript containing some ancient comedies including that of *Pulcinella,* a character who had something in common with *Petrouchka.* Stravinsky, now permanently exiled from his native Russia, was attracted by the idea of a Neapolitan counterpart to his Russian puppet figure, and agreed.

On getting to grips with the music, however, he saw that much more than mere orchestration was needed—the works were mainly trio sonatas, with no accompanying harmonies except a figured bass. Stravinsky added some of Pergolesi's arias, and made out of the eighteenth-century material a score for three singers and small orchestra consisting of eighteen numbers in his own recent style—that of *The Tale of the Soldier*—but based on Pergolesi's themes. The vocal numbers, arias, duets, and trios have nothing to do with the course of the action, and the singers are placed in the orchestra pit. The plot is a typical Neapolitan comedy, full of characters in disguises, mock deaths, and intrigues. The eighteenth-century music is given a twentieth-century twist, and if it can be arid to listen to merely as music, it is always extremely effective as an accompaniment to dancing. One can almost see in the course of the ballet how Stravinsky, at first approaching his work tentatively, as if in slight terror of playing about with music by a composer of another age, gradually increases in confidence until he finally reaches the ludicrous duet for trombone and double bass towards the end. It was Stravinsky's first experiment in basing his works on other composer's themes, and it was to have many successors in his later works. Whether one approves of this kind of process or not, there is no doubt that it is extremely well done here. *Pulcinella* is most frequently heard to-day in the form of the concert suite which Stravinsky extracted from the music, but occasionally concert performances of the whole ballet complete with singers are given, though stage performances of it are rare. At any rate it showed that Stravinsky had now finally reacted from the expressionism of his earlier ballets and had crystallized his style into the form in which it remained without essential alteration—except for the exigencies of certain specific works —until the mid-1950s.

Stravinsky's later ballets were not written in the first place for the Diaghilev company, and before discussing them we may first consider some of the important Diaghilev productions in the years immediately after the first world war. Of these one of the most famous is *La Boutique Fantasque,* with music by Rossini arranged by Respighi and choreography by Massine, first performed at the Alhambra Theatre, London, on 5 June 1919. The story is based on the scenario of an old German ballet which originally had music by one Bayer. It is concerned with a toyshop in which the toys come to life after the shopkeeper has closed the shutters for the night. Respighi selected the music from the large number of little piano pieces and songs which Rossini wrote in his later years, after his retirement from operatic composition. Some of the songs were published under the title *Serate Musicali* or *Soirées Musicales,* as we saw in an earlier chapter, but the piano pieces remained unpublished. Some of them, from an album called *Les Riens,* have fantastic titles, such as 'Four Hors d'Oeuvres', 'Radishes', 'Anchovies', 'Gherkins and Butter', 'Almonds', 'Abortive Polka', 'Castor Oil', and 'Capriccio Offenbachique' —this last became the can-can in the ballet. The score is divided into the following sections, all played without a break: Overture (Tempo di Marcia, Allegretto vivo); 'Tarantella'; 'Mazurka'; 'Danse Cosaque'; 'Can-Can'; 'Valse lente'; 'Nocturne'; and 'Galop'. The orchestra is fairly large, containing a piccolo as well as two flutes, a cor anglais as well as two oboes, three trumpets in addition to the usual horns and trombones, percussion, celesta, harp, and strings. Respighi has done his job of orchestration and arrangement extremely well. He really recreated the little pieces, and lifted them out of the genre of occasional salon music on to a far higher plane. As a result the score has a sparkle and gaiety

Drop-curtain by Picasso for *Parade*

Les Six in 1925. *Left to right:* Milhaud, Auric (here represented by a caricature by Cocteau) Honegger, Tailleferre, Poulenc, Durey. Cocteau at the piano

Les Six, with Cocteau, in 1952

which have ensured its permanent success, and the ballet is in the repertoire of many companies to-day—the present Covent Garden production was first staged there in 1947. Incidentally the 'Tarantella' is the well-known 'La Danza' from the *Serate Musicali*.

Another important new ballet was staged shortly after *La Boutique Fantasque*. This was *El Sombrero de Tres Picos*, or *The Three-Cornered Hat*, first produced at the Alhambra Theatre, London, on 22 July 1919. The music is by de Falla, the choreography by Massine, and the décor by Picasso—one of his finest designs for the theatre. In the first performance the Miller was danced by Massine and the Miller's Wife by Karsavina. This is one of the most successful ballets ever to be produced. As in *Petrouchka*, there is perfect harmony between music, choreography and décor, and the book by Martínez Sierra brilliantly expresses the atmosphere of life in a Spanish village. The music is not conventionally Spanish in the sense that much of Granados's or Albéniz's music is, but it gets deeper beneath the surface of the Spanish character, and when typically Spanish musical effects are introduced they are not there just for superficial local colour, but rather help to underline the drama and the feelings of the individual characters. It is in this that the subtlety and distinction of de Falla's mind is revealed. The story contains satire as well as passion and colour, and all these are admirably expressed in the music, which can convey the feminine capriciousness of the Miller's wife as well as the fury of the Miller when he thinks he has been deceived by her, and yet can mock at the doddering amorousness of the Corregidor: in fact the music grows out of the dramatic action and is always perfectly matched to it—although de Falla is still able to introduce a number of traditional Spanish dances which fit in perfectly naturally.

The Introduction has some unusual touches, including the sound of the dancers shouting behind the closed curtains, and also the voice of a mezzo-soprano singing. The score falls into a number of longish pieces, some of which are known from concert performances, but these are dramatically rather than symphonically constructed, and further the action at every point. The best known are the 'Dance of the Miller's Wife', with its mixture of $\frac{3}{4}$ and $\frac{6}{8}$ rhythms—a device which de Falla frequently uses in this ballet—'The Neighbours', the 'Miller's Dance' with its stamping crescendo, and final 'Jota' which works up to a magnificent climax. The orchestra is not large at the beginning—some of the brass do not enter until the finale—but piano and celesta are included, and Falla makes a masterly use of all his instruments. The score is not easy to perform properly, and often enough its effect is somewhat blurred in performance, but with a first-class orchestra it can make a magnificent sound. The ballet is in the repertoire of many companies to-day. Covent Garden had the advantage of a re-creation of it in 1947 by Massine, who was able to guide the company in their parts and also gave several guest performances in his original part of the Miller.

Falla's second ballet, *Love the Magician* (*El Amor Brujo*) was first produced at the de Lara Theatre, Madrid, in 1925. It is scored for a fairly small orchestra without trombones, but Falla's handling of his forces is masterly in its variety of colour. The scenario, adapted by Falla himself from a story of Martínez Sierra, concerns the ghost of a gipsy who returns to haunt his previous love whenever she is courted by a new suitor, and shows how finally the spectre is exorcized. The score is unusual in containing a part for a contralto singer who comments on the action from time to time: much of the music is extremely atmospheric, especially in the scenes connected with the gipsies and in the well-known 'Ritual Fire Dance'. The later sections, in which the exorcization of the ghost begins, are calmer in mood, and include a charming Pantomime in $\frac{7}{8}$ time, and the ballet ends with a scene of general rejoicing as day breaks. *Love the Magician* has maintained a place in the concert repertoire, but it is rarely performed as a ballet these days. This is a pity, as it is an extremely effective work with an interesting and unusual scenario.

The other young Russian composer who was considerably encouraged by Diaghilev was, of course, Sergei Prokofiev, who was born in 1891, nine years after Stravinsky. He started composing early, and by the time he was twenty had produced a good deal of piano music, a sinfonietta, a piano concerto and two short operas. In 1914 Diaghilev encouraged him to write the ballet *Ala and Lolly,* which is now known as his Scythian Suite, for owing to wartime difficulties it was never produced as a ballet, and to this day is heard only as an orchestral work. It clearly owes something to *Le Sacre du Printemps,* being also based on a story from the days of pagan Russia, and also being lavishly scored for an enormous orchestra: but Prokofiev was sufficient of an individualist not to imitate Stravinsky's musical style, and the music may be described as being more in the post-Rimsky-Korsakov impressionist tradition with many individual touches, and a strong element of Russian folk tradition in the background. It is a very brilliant and exciting work, and though it is not perhaps a regular member of the orchestral repertoire, it invariably makes a considerable impression in performance.

Prokofiev's first ballet to be staged by Diaghilev was *Chout (The Buffoon).* The music of this was written in 1915, but the stage production did not take place till 1921. Prokofiev by that time had left Russia temporarily and was living mainly in Paris. The story is based on a Russian folk tale from the Archangel region: this has been described as being 'drawn so directly from primitive art that it cannot belie its sources.' It is a farcical and somewhat savage tale in which Chout and his wife fool first seven other buffoons and then a rich merchant from whom they manage to extract a hundred roubles, which they then proceed to spend on a celebration with their friends. Prokofiev's music admirably reflects the humour and sarcasm of the story. Although it contains some impressionistic elements, as in the Scythian Suite, it is less complex in style than the former work. It is very Russian in feeling, and though in some ways it parallels *Petrouchka,* the music is less dissonant; it is mainly gay, vivid and folky, with a preponderance of $\frac{2}{4}$ rhythms. It is less sophisticated than Stravinsky's music of the period, and there are more native good spirits. The folky tunes are often surrounded by dissonant harmonies, and there is some grotesque woodwind writing and also some parody, for instance of a sentimental tune in a scene where Chout disguises himself as a young woman. The merchant is given a ponderous *motif* which accompanies him wherever he is present. There is some use of whole-tone harmony, and during the final celebration we hear the sound of an out-of-tune village fiddle. Altogether it is an amusing score, and much of it has been successful in the concert hall. The concert suite consists of twelve numbers, mostly from the later part of the ballet, though not all of these are always included. The ones most frequently heard are: 'Buffoon and Buffoon's Wife', 'Dance of Buffoons' Wives', 'Chout disguised as a young woman', 'Entr'acte 3', 'Dance of Buffoons' Daughters', 'Arrival of Merchant', 'Dance of Obeisance' and 'Choice of Fiancée', 'In the Merchant's Bedroom', 'Young woman becomes a Goat' and 'Final Dance'.

During his stay in Western Europe Prokofiev wrote three more ballets, *Le Pas d'Acier,* produced by Diaghilev in Paris on 7 June 1927, *L'Enfant Prodigue* (1928–9) and *On the Banks of the Borysthenes,* produced by Lifar at the Paris Opéra on 12 December 1932. *Le Pas d'Acier* was originally intended to be a portrayal of scenes of life in Soviet Russia, with a strongly industrial background: but the production was twisted almost to the point of caricature so as to provide 'Bolshevist exoticism' for the sophisticated Parisian audience, and the original simple design of Prokofiev and his librettist went somewhat astray. Nevertheless the ballet was a great success both in Paris and

London, and a good deal of this was due to Prokofiev's music, which, though harsh and strident at times, remained firmly rooted in its Russian background and in fact makes some use of Russian themes. But his next score, that for L'Enfant Prodigue, is of rather a different character. The scenario might be described as a sophisticated version of the Bible story in which the adventures of the Prodigal Son during his wanderings are somewhat enlarged on—among other things he meets some friends who make him drunk and rob him, and later he is attracted to a Beautiful Maiden: here the score achieves real warmth and feeling. Prokofiev's music is in a much simpler style than that for Le Pas d'Acier. It is somewhat stylized, and has a pale, autumnal quality which resembles some of the lyrical passages in his later ballet Romeo and Juliet. The best lyrical moments come in the parting of the son from his parents, in his first meeting with his friends, and in the scene with the Beautiful Maiden: in general the score is thin, economical, and ascetic. Prokofiev's last ballet written before returning to Russia, On the Banks of the Borysthenes, was not a great success. For one thing, the composer was given the sequence and character of the dances to write before any plot or theme had been thought out, and it was only much later that it was decided to set the scene on the banks of the Dnieper (for which Borysthenes is the old classical name): so any local colour in the score is more or less accidental. We shall return to Prokofiev's later ballets in the next chapter.

Diaghilev's collaboration with the French composers of the middle generation has already been discussed, and it was not long before he began to show interest in those of the younger generation too. The leader of the new movement in French music, which came into being during and immediately after the first world war, was not himself a young man. Erik Satie was born in 1866, nine years before Ravel, but as early as the 1880's his music had begun to show a revolt against the prevalent romanticism of the time. In those days most French composers were completely swamped by Wagner—even the gay Chabrier wrote a large Wagnerian opera called *Gwendoline*—and though the impressionism of Debussy did something to break the spell of Bayreuth in the first decade of the twentieth century, it was not till the first world war that romanticism was finally swept away and the new age of neoclassicism began. Satie's attitude may be roughly summed up in his famous warning to Jean Cocteau against Wagner: 'A property tree does not grimace because a character comes on the stage,' thus denying the whole principle of the Wagnerian *leit-motiv* which had ruled the theatre for so long. Satie was joined by the young composers who formed the group known as 'Les Six'—Milhaud, Poulenc, Honegger, Auric, Durey, and Tailleferre—in his stand against not only romanticism but impressionism too. The music of these composers in this period did not attempt to express what was happening on the stage, but was completely self-sufficient and took its style from popular music, jazz, music-hall and café songs parodied in a sophisticated way. The classical ballet of this type is Satie's *Parade*, first produced by Diaghilev in 1917, with its cast of Chinese conjurers, acrobats, circus managers and American girls, its décor by Picasso and its book by Cocteau, and its music based on rag-time themes. But Satie and his followers were not purely farceurs: they did express their revolt against romanticism and impressionism in a somewhat brash way, particularly in many works written in the twenties, but Milhaud, Poulenc, and Honegger went on to develop their own styles and become considerable composers in their own ways, and the direction in which music was launched at this time has continued to a very great extent. Stravinsky took up neoclassicism at an early stage, and to-day modern music has reacted on the whole against romanticism and even more so against impressionism; at any rate what Satie and 'Les Six' achieved was a healthy breath of air in the musty drawing-rooms of the late romantic period.

Parade is composed of a number of self-contained pieces, all fairly strict classical forms. The overture begins with a chorale and fugue, ending with a scale of bells. Then follows a somewhat monotonous march, which becomes pompous when the Chinese conjuror enters. The music quickens before the entry of the first Manager: then comes a lively two-step for the American girl, and a waltz for the Acrobats. The two Managers and the American girl dance to a rag-time, and the work ends with a reprise of the opening fugue. The score is ironic, fanciful and burlesque throughout—it is as far removed from, say, *Thamar* or *Daphnis and Chloë,* as it would be possible to imagine, and the only kind of representation is in incidentals, for instance, the American girl being accompanied by a typewriter or the acrobats by the hum of an aeroplane.

Satie's second ballet, *Mercure,* was produced at the Théâtre Cigale, Paris, on 15 June 1924, with choreography by Massine and décor by Picasso. This may be described as the adventures of Mercury in the form of 'poses plastiques', and it has often been referred to as a 'painter's ballet'. The score is simple, in contrast to Picasso's elaborate scenic constructions, and though fairground effects are not absent, it is mainly static and abstract in character. There is nothing approaching illustration, expect perhaps in one scene called 'Chaos'. As Constant Lambert has put it in *Music Ho!*: 'Instead of the harmonic and orchestral outburst and the avoidance of line that an impressionist composer would have brought to bear on the subject, Satie presents us with a clear pattern in two parts, a skilful blending of two previously heard movements, one the suave and sustained 'Nouvelle Danse', the other the robust and snappy 'Polka des Lettres'. These two tunes are so disparate in mood that the effect, mentally speaking, is one of complete chaos, yet it is achieved by strictly musical and even academic means, which consolidate the formal cohesion of the ballet as a whole.' This is typical of Satie's approach to his art, and it was to have a considerable influence on his successors.

Satie's third ballet, *Relâche,* was also produced in 1924, this time by the Ballets Suédois, an enterprising organization which gave four successive seasons in Paris at this time and included a number of *avant-garde* works in them. *Relâche* is described as a '*ballet instantanéiste*'. It had scenario and décor by the surrealist painter Picabia and a ludicrous cinematic entr'acte devised by René Clair, including characters crawling over the gargoyles of Notre Dame, and ending up with a funeral procession which gradually gets faster and faster until the coffin falls off the hearse and breaks open and the corpse comes to life and sits up. Even the title of this ballet contains a joke, for '*Relâche*' is the French for 'Theatre Closed', and there are various occurrences such as a dance without music for the prima ballerina—on her first entry she smokes a cigarette while the orchestra plays the music she is supposed to dance to —and some play with wheelbarrows. But in spite of these absurdities Satie's music remains cool, charming and not in the least funny. Milhaud spoke of its 'authenticity and perfection' in this ballet. This in fact was a characteristic of Satie's music in general, that the jokes in it were as it were stuck on the outside and do not affect the contents. In the cinematic entr'acte he makes no attempt to illustrate the images on the screen, but simply writes a series of phrases which are constantly repeated and juxtaposed, acting as a frame for the visual images, so to speak, and leaving the audience free to concentrate on them. Satie also completed another short ballet, *Jack in the Box,* which was orchestrated by Milhaud after his death.

Diaghilev, always an astute observer of the cultural climate of his time, was in on this new movement from the start, and the whole tendency of the Diaghilev ballets in the twenties was dominated by it. This period has been brilliantly described by Constant Lambert in *Music Ho!,* and it is unnecessary for me to repeat what he has said there, but we may profitably examine some of the more important ballets produced during this period. A good many of them, though effective choreographically or dramatically, were ephemeral musically, as we shall see, but Milhaud and Poulenc at least produced some excellent ballet scores which have survived to this day in concert performance, even if they are rarely or never seen as ballets.

Milhaud's first ballet, *L'Homme et son Désir,* dates from 1918. It was produced in 1921 by the Ballets Suédois. The book was by Paul Claudel, with whom Milhaud was later to collaborate in *Christophe Colomb* and other works, and the décor by Jean Parr. The theme of the ballet grew out of discussions which these three collaborators used to have in Rio de Janeiro in 1917, when Milhaud was stationed at the French Embassy there. It is a somewhat complex philosophical-astronomical idea, and the ballet has not survived into the modern repertoire, in spite of its highly original score.

Milhaud's second ballet score, *Le Boeuf sur le Toit,* or *The Nothing-doing Bar,* was originally written in 1919 as an accompaniment to a Chaplin film, but eventually Jean Cocteau wrote a pantomime scenario for it, and this was later produced in ballet form. The setting is an American bar during prohibition in the United States: a number of comically macabre events occur, including the decapitation of a policeman by an electric fan. Milhaud described it as a rondo-like assembly of popular tunes, tangos, maxixes, sambas, etc., some of them remembered from his day at the French Legation in Rio de Janeiro, and all joined together by a recurring theme. It is in fact real café music, spiced up with polytonal effects here and there. The main recurrent theme is on the banal side and tends to return too often, but the whole score is gay and amusing in a brittle twentyish kind of way. The rhythm throughout is a rather square $\frac{2}{4}$, speeding up each time the main tune returns, and the slow waltz which comes about two-thirds of the way through is a welcome relief from the rhythmical point of view. The influence of Latin America may be discerned not only in the use of maracas—in those days hardly a commonplace in the orchestra—but also in the melismatic turns of phrase. Often these give a distinctly romantic flavour to the music. In spite of its gaiety, the whole score is rather too long for what it has to say, each tune in itself being on the short side, and there is no development of the material. But the ballet is certainly interesting as a typical product of the period immediately after the first world war.

Apart from Milhaud's contribution to another farcical ballet, *Les Mariés de la Tour Eiffel,* a collaborative work by the members of 'Les Six', his next ballet was *La Création du Monde,* a more important work altogether, and one which has remained a landmark in the history of modern ballet music. In 1922 Milhaud visited the United States, and wrote of his experiences in a Harlem night club: 'This authentic music had its roots in the darkest corners of the negro soul, the vestigial traces of Africa, no doubt. Its effect on me was so overwhelming that I could not tear myself away. From then on I frequented other negro theatres and dance halls. In some of their shows the singers were accompanied by a flute, a clarinet, two trumpets, a trombone, a complicated percussion outfit played by one man, a piano, and a string quintet.' *La Création du Monde* is in fact scored for this combination plus an extra flute and trumpet, one oboe, and one horn, and with an alto saxophone replacing the viola.

La Création du Monde tells the story of creation as seen by a negro, and hence this enlarged jazz band is eminently suitable as its musical accompaniment: and the music itself is of course based on the kind of jazz which Milhaud heard in Harlem, but here stylized and often treated polytonally. The ballet begins with a calm overture in a D major-minor key, beautifully lyrical in mood. Then the first scene, the evolution of the world itself, is danced to a brisk, jazzy fugue. Scene 2, the

[128]

appearance of plants and animals, is a gentle, plaintive blues. Then a passage for flutes fluttertonguing leads to the third scene, a strongly rhythmical dance. The first part of the ballet has taken place at night. Now, as the dance dies down, day appears and man and woman are born—here the blues theme joins the dance music. The fourth scene begins with the 'Dance of Desire', led by the clarinet. This eventually calms down to the music already heard in the Overture, and then follows a great outburst of passion, in which the 'Dance of Desire' music is superimposed on the jazz fugue from Scene 1 —a most ingenious piece of writing which comes off brilliantly. In the fifth scene the music dies down to the strains of the blues tune, and finally the man and woman are left alone to the music of the overture. Nine remarkable closing bars sum up the whole score in a tender and lyrical passage.

La Création du Monde was first performed by the Ballets Suédois at the Théâtre des Champs-Elysées in Paris in October 1923. Though it is rarely performed as a ballet these days, its unique score, which successfully fuses the jazz idiom with a twentieth-century harmonic style, is heard from time to time in the concert hall, and it has served as a model to all those who wish to experiment in this direction.

Two other ballets by Milhaud were produced in 1924 by the Diaghilev company: *Salade*, based on a story from the Commedia dell' Arte, appeared at the Théâtre Cigale on 17 May, with choreography by Massine. It was also revived in 1935 at the Paris Opéra by Lifar and had a Budapest production in 1938, but it is not often seen nowadays. *Le Train Bleu* was produced on 20 June at the Champs-Elysées Theatre: this farcical piece had a book by Cocteau and a curtain by Picasso, with choreography by Nijinska. It may be described as 'a musical comedy danced instead of being sung.' The music, as in *Salade,* is light, gay and ephemeral, and the success of the ballet was chiefly due to the amusing scenario. Milhaud also arranged some music by Schubert and Liszt, including the

Grand Galop Chromatique, for Nijinska's ballet *La Bien Aimée*, produced at the Opéra on 22 November 1928.

Poulenc's best-known ballet, *Les Biches*, was first performed on 6 January 1924, at Monte Carlo by the Diaghilev company. There is no plot as such. The situation concerns the visit of three young men to a ménage of somewhat equivocal young ladies on a summer afternoon, and the atmosphere has a Firbankian quality. The ballet derived much of its charm from the delightful décor of Marie Laurencin as well as from Poulenc's attractive music, which was modelled to some extent on *Pulcinella*. Though there is no use of eighteenth-century themes here, *Les Biches* contained a few songs in addition to the dances, and the musical style is definitely neoclassical and takes its starting point from Stravinsky. There is quite a resemblance both in the harmonies and the orchestration; but the music is at once less frigid than Stravinsky and less brash than Milhaud's score for *Le Boeuf sur le Toit*, even if the music-hall influence may be felt here too. It is always pleasant and effective and is carried out with great taste. The ballet itself was recently revived at Covent Garden; a concert suite of five numbers from it is fairly frequently performed. This begins with the 'Rondeau' danced by the girls. This is not a classical rondo, but a simple structure with a cheerful opening theme leading later to a more 'cantabile' melody. Then a sustained passage for strings and brass leads to the restatement of the opening theme. Next comes the charming 'adagietto', well known as a piano piece, and then the 'Rag-Mazurka', danced by the Hostess and two of the men. This begins as a neo-Scarlattian $\frac{3}{8}$, but after various contrasting interludes it becomes increasingly syncopated in the manner of Stravinsky's rag-time music. Its coda leads into an andantino , a pas de deux. The Finale develops in the same way as the 'Rag-Mazurka'. Its innocently neo-classical opening leads by devious routes to a syncopated section in slower time, marked 'tragico'. *Les Biches* contains some of Poulenc's most delightful music,

and if the 'Rag-Mazurka' seems overlong for its content, the
the score as a whole has maintained its freshness after more
than thirty years of life.

We may now deal briefly with a few other of the most
important ballets of the twenties. All of these had in
common a certain brittle gaiety. Diaghilev was producing what the sophisticated audience of the time wanted,
and each new ballet had to have a new idea or 'gimmick'
to get itself talked about. Thus *Le Train Bleu* does not show us
any train but begins when we have arrived at its destination.
Within the Quota, produced in 1923 with music by Cole
Porter (in this case the production was by the Ballets Suédois)
was the first American jazz ballet to be shown in Paris, and
in *La Chatte*, produced in 1927 with choreography by Balanchine and not very distinguished music by Henri Sauguet,
the décor was mainly constructed of talc. Even in *The Triumph
of Neptune*, with music by Lord Berners—one of the two
English composers commissioned by Diaghilev to write a
score for him—the somewhat surrealist succession of scenes
was suggested by the old-fashioned 'penny plain, twopence
coloured' sheets of juvenile drama dear to Victorian youth.
But Berners' music, if not strikingly original, had a more
solid quality than most of the ephemeral scores of this period,
and extracts from it are still heard in the concert hall. The other
English composer to be commissioned by Diaghilev was
Constant Lambert, whose talent Diaghilev recognized before
he was twenty-one. The result was *Romeo and Juliet*, a somewhat sophisticated version of the story which Diaghilev
insisted on mounting with some highly unsuitable surrealist
décor, much to the composer's fury. However, Lambert's
score was remarkably successful, and led to his being asked to
compose a second ballet, *Pomona*, which was produced in
1927 with choreography by Nijinska: this, like *Romeo and
Juliet*, is in the cool, neoclassical manner of Lambert's earlier
style. Finally we should mention another ballet which was

more successful for its choreography than its music—*Les Matelots*, produced in 1925 with choreography by Massine and music by another member of 'Les Six', Georges Auric. The plot is a variant of that of *Cosí fan Tutte*, but in this case the girl remains faithful to her lover. The music is the usual potpourri of circus themes which we have already noted in the ballets of Satie and Milhaud, but here done with far less taste and skill.

To conclude this survey of the second and third decades of this century in Paris, we may mention two ballets written for the Diaghilev company by Italian composers: *La Jarre*, with music by Casella and book based on a Pirandello story (this was also successfully produced by Ninette de Valois at Sadler's Wells in 1934)—and *Barabau*, with music by Vittorio Rieti. This ballet remained in the repertoire for some time, but this was due more to the plot and to Utrillo's evocative décor than to Rieti's music, which is brassy and vulgarly ineffective. Also we may remember that the charming ballet, *The Gods Go A-Begging*, for which Sir Thomas Beecham selected and arranged music by Handel, was originally produced by Diaghilev. The concert suite from this has become a popular item.

Before dealing with developments in ballet outside France, we may briefly discuss two more Stravinsky ballets which fall within this period.

In 1927 Stravinsky was commissioned to write a ballet for a contemporary music festival held by the Library of Congress in Washington. His response to this was *Apollon Musagète*, a classical ballet scored for strings only. This was first performed as a purely orchestral piece, and was seen on the stage in London and Paris in the following year, produced by Diaghilev. Stravinsky's aim was to write a more or less abstract work—the scenario is of the simplest—which would base its musical style on the classical ballet of Lully's period. The first scene begins with a slow introduction which leads to a broad 'Olympian' theme—this latter is heard again at the end of the ballet. An accelerando leads to the scene of the birth of Apollo, followed by an allegro dance for the two presiding goddesses. Then the Olympian theme is heard again. The second scene, which constitutes the main part of the ballet, is a set of variations for different combinations of dancers. These include a dance for Apollo with solo violin accompaniment, followed by a concerted dance for Apollo and three Muses with a beautiful second subject and an ingenious contrapuntal stretto in quavers, crotchets, and minims simultaneously. The variation of Calliope, the Muse of Poetry, is headed by a quotation from the French classical writer Boileau, and the music is grouped throughout in sixes—an attempt to portray the alexandrine in music. Later comes an attractive solo dance for Apollo. The coda is one of Stravinsky's best allegro movements, and in the final Apotheosis the 'Olympian' theme returns and brings the ballet to a dignified end. Though some of the music is on the dry side, it is of course expertly done and does give the feeling of the old classical ballet in a modern form: and the final coda and Apotheosis are among Stravinsky's best pieces for the ballet stage.

In the following year Stravinsky brought out another ballet, *Le Baiser de la Fée*, commissioned by Ida Rubinstein. This was produced in Paris on 27 November 1928. It is dedicated to Tchaikovsky, in the same way that Stravinsky's earlier opera *Mavra* had borne a triple dedication to Pushkin, Glinka, and Tchaikovsky. But here Stravinsky went rather further and based several of the movements on actual themes by Tchaikovsky. Thus the long village fair scene in the second tableau is mostly based on Tchaikovsky's well-known Humoresque Op. 10, No. 2, the ensuing waltz comes from the Natha Waltz Op. 51, No. 4, the entry of the young man in the pas de deux from the Nocturne Op. 19, No. 4, the fiancée's variation and the opening of the third tableau from the Scherzo Humoristique Op. 19, No. 2, and the final scene of the third

[133]

tableau is based on the romance 'Ah! qui brûle d'amour', Op. 6, No. 6. Stravinsky has worked these themes into his own style much as he did those of Pergolesi in *Pulcinella*: *Le Baiser de la Fée* is one of the longest of his ballets, but the style throughout is clear and attractive, if a little on the thin side—many passages consist of a simple tune and accompaniment drawn out to great length. But the fairy-tale atmosphere of the story does not call for elaborate treatment, and the ballet has been one of Stravinsky's most successful stage works and has been taken up by several companies. The Sadler's Wells Ballet staged it as early as 1935, with choreography by Frederick Ashton. The original score was for small orchestra: later Stravinsky arranged some of the music to form a Divertimento for larger orchestra.

Though the main new developments in ballet in the second and third decades of the twentieth century took place in Paris, there were naturally also developments elsewhere, some of them influenced by Diaghilev's achievements and some of independent origin. There were old-established ballet companies in many cities in Germany, Central Europe and Scandinavia, and some of these began more experimental work during this period. In Germany, for instance, the young choreographer Kurt Jooss began creating a series of ballets for several theatres from 1924 onwards, but he did not found the company which bears his name until the thirties, and so discussion of this is better left to the next chapter. It should be said, however, that the Franco-Russian style of dancing was by no means universally followed in Central Europe, and many choreographers were more influenced by the athletic type of dance taught by Laban and Wigman, or some ballets showed a compromise between the two. The German composer Richard Strauss had been brought into the Diaghilev orbit as early as 1914, when his *Légende de Joseph,* with book by Hoffmansthal and Kessler, was produced at the Paris Opéra with choreography by Fokine. The name part was

[134]

Constant Lambert

Béla Bartók taking down the tune of a folk song from a recording

Ninette de Valois rehearsing *Job*

Balanchine rehearsing the New York City Ballet

taken by Massine—his first public appearance. Later this ballet was taken into the repertoire of the Vienna Opera with choreography by Kröller which was very much more in the Central European style than Fokine's. *La Légende de Joseph* has never been a very successful ballet. It is in fact a wordless play rather than a ballet, and though it contains a good many dances, these are a mere embroidery to the story. It is also very long for a one-act ballet—it lasts over an hour—and it is not one of Strauss' best scores, though indeed it has his usual lavishmess of orchestral writing. In fact Strauss' style is not really suited to ballet, for it depends on a solid symphonic texture of some complexity and richness and often with themes of some length, so that swift changes of mood to follow the dramatic action are not easy to achieve. Attempts have been made to turn other works of his into ballets, notably *Don Juan* and *Till Eulenspiegel,* but these have not been greatly successful, perhaps for the same reason. Strauss did write one further ballet, *Schlagobers (Whipped Cream),* which was produced at the Vienna Opera on 9 May 1924: this is a divertissement on the subject of confectionery of various kinds, and though its waltz was popular for a time, it has not held its place in the repertoire. Probably Strauss' most successful dance numbers—apart from the waltzes in *Der Rosenkavalier,* which are mainly not meant to be danced to—are the 'Dance of the Seven Veils' in *Salome* and the crazy dance of Elektra at the end of the opera of that name. But both these are meant to be danced by prime donne who need to have lungs of Wagnerian capacity—and therefore usually are of Wagnerian build as well—and the effect is often somewhat ludicrous unless the singer also happens to be a first-class actress. But as pieces of dance music they are both supremely effective.

In Budapest a ballet company had also been established at the Opera House for some years, and though many of the productions there were of no great musical interest, the existence of this company did lead to the composition of Béla Bartók's two ballets, *The Wooden Prince* and *The Miraculous Mandarin*. The former was written in 1917, and was produced in Budapest, thanks to the efforts of the Italian conductor Egisto Tango, who was in Budapest from 1912 to 1919. The story is a fable of a somewhat fantastic and symbolic kind: the moral, like that of *Beauty and the Beast*, being that man is held in thrall by appearances and cannot see the precious nature of people and things until he has made a sacrifice. The music is sharp and dramatic, with some influence of *Petrouchka*, and is in considerable contrast to the lyricism of Bartók's previous stage work, *Bluebeard's Castle*. Bartók could often express himself with considerable acerbity when dealing with the subject of human behaviour, and it is this side of him that is uppermost in *The Wooden Prince*. Neither the music nor the ballet itself is as well known as it should be, and it is to be hoped that this will soon be remedied, for *The Wooden Prince* is certainly one of Bartók's most interesting works.

His second ballet, *The Miraculous Mandarin*, is rather better known, if only because of the concert suite which Bartók made from the first half of the ballet and which has become a virtuoso concert item in the repertoire of many orchestras. Also there have recently been several stage productions of the ballet, including one by the Sadler's Wells Ballet in 1956, as well as others in Budapest, Munich and New York. But during Bartók's lifetime the ballet had little success, and it was not in fact performed in Budapest until after his death in 1945. Composed in 1919, it did get as far as a dress rehearsal at that time, but the production was vetoed because of the nature of the scenario, by Melchior Lengyel. This concerns three cutthroats and a girl who lure passers-by into their hovel and then kill them for their money—only the mandarin cannot be touched by them, for he is immortal as long as he does not feel love. At the end of the ballet his desire is at last satisfied by the girl, and his wounds now begin to bleed until he dies. Bartók has written a masterly dramatic score which expresses every facet of the story. Its rhythm and colour are most exciting, and it is full of effect throughout. It is indeed one of the finest scores in the whole ballet repertoire, and we can be glad that it seems at last to have come into its own on the international stage. Other works of Bartók have of course also been adapted for ballet, perhaps the most successful being the *Dance Suite* of 1925, a series of dances which is well suited to ballet purposes—and of course the well-known short set of 'Roumanian Dances' also provides suitable material for ballet. Other works which have been attempted with varying success include the 'Music for Strings, Percussion, and Celesta' and the 'Contrasts' for violin, clarinet, and the piano—the latter is certainly a most curious choice for a ballet, especially as in this particular case, *Caprichos*, the movements are played in the wrong order. In the next chapter we shall return to later developments in Central European ballet.

V

Ballet Music, 1930–1957

AFTER the death of Diaghilev his company split up, and a good many of his principal collaborators returned to their own countries, in many cases laying the foundations there of new ballet organizations based on the Diaghilev tradition. Serge Lifar became Director of Ballet at the Paris Opéra, Ninette de Valois founded the Sadler's Wells Ballet and Marie Rambert the Ballet Rambert in England, and Balanchine and Wilzak went to the United States where they helped to found the American School of Ballet. However, a number of Diaghilev's choreographers and dancers, headed by Massine and Nijinsky, remained together in Colonel de Basil's Ballets Russes de Monte Carlo, and this company may be regarded as the immediate successor of that of Diaghilev, for their repertoire included many of the ballets that Diaghilev had made famous, and for these de Basil's company in most cases retained the original décor and costumes. The more experimental ballets of Diaghilev's last period were mostly jettisoned, and the company concentrated on earlier ballets such as *Carnaval, Sylphides, L'Oiseau de Feu, Petrouchka,* and *La Boutique Fantasque.* And the new ballets which were produced for the de Basil company did not show any marked experimental tendencies on the whole: few scores were commissioned from composers, and the choreographers preferred to use music which had already been written for other purposes. Among these new ballets were *Cotillon,* produced in 1932, with choreography by Balanchine and décor by Christian Bérard. The music was chosen from various short orchestral and piano works by Chabrier, whose sparkling music is eminently suitable for dancing, and the whole provided a gay and successful entertainment. Another ballet of a somewhat similar type was *Le Beau Danube,* a work by Massine which is a brilliant evocation of the atmosphere of nineteenth-century Vienna: this had actually been produced for Etienne de Beaumont in 1923, but now appeared, ten years later, in a new form. The music was chosen from the waltzes, marches, polkas, and other dances of Johann Strauss, put together by the conductor Roger Désormière, and it too proved extremely successful. A ballet set to various pieces by Boccherini, *Scuola di Ballo,* was a comedy similar in style to *Les Femmes de Bonne Humeur,* but not quite so attractive.

Before discussing Massine's other new ballets for the de Basil company, we may briefly mention a few ballets by other choreographers. Nijinska produced *Les Cent Baisers* in 1935: the ballet is an attractive fairy-tale type of work, but the music, by Frederic d'Erlanger, is undistinguished, in the old romantic tradition. David Lichine, de Basil's principal male dancer, made a very theatrical ballet to Tchaikovsky's *Francesca da Rimini,* which was reasonably successful, and Fokine, as we have seen in an earlier chapter, successfully revived Gluck's *Don Juan* in 1936 and put on Rimsky-Korsakov's *Le Coq d'Or* as a ballet in 1937, as well as staging *L'Épreuve d'Amour,* whose music is rather doubtfully ascribed to Mozart.

But the principal novelties of the de Basil company in these years were Massine's four symphonic ballets, in which he attempted balletic treatment of symphonies well known in the orchestral repertoire. The first of these was *Les Présages* (1933) to Tchaikovsky's fifth symphony: here there is possibly a slight justification for dramatic treatment in that the work contains a 'motif of Fate' which appears in all four movements often in a quasi-dramatic manner—as in the slow movement, for example, where it twice interrupts lyrical passages with a crashing fortissimo. Massine accompanies every appearance of this theme with the entry of a diabolical figure in white, who appears to be casting a blight over the proceedings. But, as Constant Lambert pointed out in an essay on 'Music and Action' in 1936: 'There seems to be a growing theory that dancing which represents visually the formal devices and texture of the music must of necessity be pleasing to the musical mind. Nothing could be further from the truth. I am sure there must be innumerable musicians beside myself who experience the same feeling of exasperation when the choreographer turns the stage into a vast lecturer's blackboard and, by associating certain dancers with certain themes, proceeds to underline obvious formal devices in the music which anyone of average intelligence can appreciate with half an ear. Literal translations from one language to another are always unsatisfactory and usually ridiculous. "Symphonic" ballets are no exception to this rule.' And Dyneley Hussey put it even more concisely when he wrote in Grove's Dictionary: 'It would not be unfair to say that by the end of the exposition of a symphonic first movement the choreographer has done all he can do: but the music continues to soar upwards, leaving the dancers earthbound.' And in fact Massine was compelled to make a large cut in the finale of Tchaikovsky's Fifth Symphony in his ballet version of it. His second symphonic ballet, *Choreartium* (1933), to Brahms' Fourth Symphony, did not attempt to fit any kind of story of music, but here again the choreographic invention was not strong enough to match the flow of ideas in the music. And in his ballet to Beethoven's Seventh Symphony (1938) he not only repeated choreographic ideas from his earlier symphonic ballets, but he also introduced a highly unsuitable plot.

The only one of his symphonic ballets in which the music was already based on a detailed programme was *Symphonie Fantastique* (1936), where he was able to use Berlioz' original scenario: but even here there was no proper fusion between dancing and music, partly because of the tendency towards surrealism of the décor—surrealism was of course the fashion of the time—and partly because Berlioz' music is not really suitable for dancing to, apart perhaps from the Ball movement and some parts of the finale. The melodic lines are too long and each section is too symphonic in style to be split up into short dance movements. So the symphonic ballet has died a natural death since those days: and such choreographers as still use symphonies for ballet music tend to limit themselves to light-weight works like Bizet's Symphony in C, where the symphonic structure does not overweight their ideas.

A more successful Massine ballet was *Nobilissima Visione,* based on episodes in the life of St. Francis of Assisi, and produced in 1938. Hindemith's music, though a little more in the symphonic style than the average ballet score, is nevertheless dramatic and full of colour and feeling, and the production as a whole worked very well. Though the ballet itself is not often seen on the stage nowadays, an orchestral suite from the music, including the noble Passacaglia, has become one of Hindemith's best-known works.

During the second world war the majority of the members of the de Basil company were in America, and their subsequent history is linked with that of the growth of the American ballet, to which we shall return later. Meanwhile let us consider the important developments which took place in England during this period.

The Sadler's Wells Ballet was in the first place the creation of Ninette de Valois, who had been a dancer in Diaghilev's company. As early as 1926 she was asked by Lilian Baylis to supervise the ballets in the operatic productions at the Old Vic Theatre, and the ballet company later began to give performances there on its own. After the death of Diaghilev some ballet performances were also given by the Camargo

Society on Sunday evenings at the Cambridge Theatre: their new productions included two important works, Vaughan Williams' *Job* and Walton's *Façade*. When the Sadler's Wells Theatre was reopened in 1931 Lilian Baylis established a school of ballet there with Ninette de Valois as Director and a complete company was recruited, with Constant Lambert as musical director. Some of the more important productions of the Camargo Society were taken over by the Vic-Wells Ballet, as it was then called, and on 5 May 1931, the new company gave its first performance at the Old Vic. It had the advantage of considerable experience of the Diaghilev tradition: apart from Ninette de Valois and Constant Lambert, who had both worked with Diaghilev, some of his leading dancers, among them Lydia Lopokova, Alicia Markova, and Anton Dolin joined the company from the beginning. At the same time Marie Rambert, who had also been in Diaghilev's company, was carrying on her valuable work of training young dancers at the Ballet Club in Notting Hill Gate, and the Ballet Rambert has put on a number of productions on its own during the last forty years, which, though normally on a small scale, have always shown originality and enterprise: one of Marie Rambert's pupils, Frederick Ashton, soon joined the Vic-Wells company as assistant choreographer and maître de ballet, and remained as Associate Director till 1963, when he became Director; he retired in 1970.

From these two organizations the growth of English ballet began. Naturally the Sadler's Wells ballet, with its larger resources, has taken the leading rôle in this development: but it began in a fairly small way, with short ballets to music by Debussy, Bach, Schubert, Grétry, and others. Here the choice of Constant Lambert as musical director proved very wise, for with his wide knowledge and experience he was always able to suggest music suitable for dancing which was also good in its own right, and the high musical standard which the Sadler's Wells Ballet has kept up over the years was due in the first place to him. These smaller ballets were followed in September 1931 by Vaughan Williams' *Job,* which set a new standard in English ballet and also struck a note that was characteristically English, as opposed to the Franco-Russian style of most of the Diaghilev productions. The décor was based on Blake's illustrations to the Book of Job, and Vaughan Williams described his score not as a ballet but 'a masque for dancing'—a link with the old English form of the masque—but here, of course, without singing, and cast in a thoroughly modern idiom. Ninette de Valois' choreography also reflects the more stylized form of the masque, at any rate in some of the dances, rather than any continental models, and the whole work is a remarkably successful example of a ballet on a moral and religious theme which also provides dramatic stage action. The score is one of Vaughan Williams' most colourful works and is full of ingenious touches of orchestration, such as the saxophone solo for Job's comforters and the brilliant depiction of Satan in his moment of power. In fact it is so much linked to the stage action that it is ineffective when heard in the concert hall. *Job* has not had any direct successors—from its very nature it could hardly expect to—but it has shown that a serious and important theme can be treated in terms of the dance without any loss of dignity, and its success may have emboldened Massine to treat the life of St. Francis as a subject for ballet in his *Nobilissima Visione.*

During the next few years the company mainly concentrated on building up a repertoire, at first of shorter works specially created for it—many of these have not survived into the present-day repertoire—but also including a number of the more successful Diaghilev ballets such as *Sylphides* and *Carnaval.* Constant Lambert's *Pomona* was produced by the company in 1933, and two years later the experiment was made of staging his *Rio Grande*: this of course is a choral work, with an important solo piano part, and it overstepped the limits of ballet to some extent, brilliant though the music is in itself. Meanwhile the company had begun to include full-length ballets in their repertoire, such as *Giselle, Casse-Noisette,* and *Le Lac des Cygnes*—the last was the first complete production of the ballet outside Russia. In 1934 came *The Haunted Ballroom,* with music by Geoffrey Toye, of which the nostalgic waltz has survived in the present-day orchestral repertoire, and in the following year *The Rake's Progress* was first produced. Based on Hogarth's drawings, this is one of the most successful of all the Sadler's Wells productions, and it maintains its life to this day, both because of Ninette de Valois' brilliant choreography, and also to no little extent because of Gavin Gordon's music: this is to some degree a pastiche of eighteenth-century mannerisms, but it is carried out with such gusto and verve that it achieves independent life. It is not great music by itself, perhaps, but with the ballet it admirably achieves its purpose.

Another successful production of 1935 was *Façade,* with choreography by Frederick Ashton. Walton's music was, in fact, written in the first place as an accompaniment to Edith Sitwell's poems, recited by speakers through a megaphone, and it was scored for only seven instruments: however, the composer had arranged two suites from the music for full orchestra, with the rhythm of the speaking part adapted to instruments in some cases, and these served as the basis of the ballet.* The choreographer naturally took little notice of the poems which the music was originally designed to accompany—in any case they are evocations of atmosphere and associations of ideas and make little grammatical sense—and invented his own visual equivalents for the dances. These, as we all know, are mainly witty parodies of popular music, and in its ballet form the form has remained fresh and amusing ever since its first production. Later in 1935 Ashton also

* The order of the dancing is: Overture (Fanfare), Scotch Rhapsody, Nocturne Peruvienne, Yodelling Song, Polka, Foxtrot, Waltz, Popular Song, Tango, and Tarantella.

mounted Stravinsky's *Baiser de la Fée*, discussed in the previous chapter, with new choreography.

The year 1936 saw the première of another important Ashton ballet, *Apparitions*. The music for this was chosen by Constant Lambert from the lesser-known piano works of Liszt—that year was the fiftieth anniversary of Liszt's death—and these were scored by Gordon Jacob. The theme is adapted from Berlioz' programme for his Symphonie Fantastique: as the curtain rises we see a poet in his Gothic study attempting to finish a sonnet, 'L'Amour Suprême'. Inspiration eludes him, but he sees visions of a hussar, a monk, and a woman in ball dress: he takes laudanum, and the main part of the ballet represents his dreams. The music for this first scene begins with the well-known Consolation No. 3, which breaks off as the visions appear and changes into the first Valse Oubliée. As the poet takes laudanum we hear 'Schlaflos' (Sleepless), a rather gloomy late piece with a semi-religious ending. The first scene of the poet's dream takes place in a ballroom: the music begins with three pieces from Liszt's late collection called 'The Christmas Tree'. A rather sinister little march, called 'Hungarian', originally acted as an interlude, but is now normally cut; then comes a Mazurka, called 'Polish', and afterwards a romantic waltz, 'Jadis'. The last dance in this scene, in which the poet is continually meeting and being separated from the woman in ball dress, is the Galop in A minor, a brilliant virtuoso piece which has been scored here with equal virtuosity.

In the next scene the poet, having finally lost the woman in ball dress to the hussar, as he thinks, is lying exhausted on a snow-covered plain. His gloomy mood is expressed by another late piece, the Second Elegy. Then the spirits of the bells which he hears in the distance appear and mock him: here the music again comes from the 'Christmas Tree' suite, consisting of 'Evening Bells', a little 'Scherzoso', and 'Carillon', a brilliant short piece. Then a sinister procession of monks is seen approaching: they carry a bier on which lies the woman in ball dress, apparently dead. The music is one of Liszt's last pieces, 'Sinistre', a masterly evocation of the macabre, with some remarkable harmonic effects, and an ending in religious style—the poet is left praying in the snow as the procession moves on. Now the scene changes to a cave, where some unholy rite appears to be taking place: the woman in ball dress enters at the height of the revels, but her face is covered by a fearsome mask, and the poet shrinks away from her as she rushes towards him. The music for the entire scene is the Third Mephisto Waltz, a much more sinister and violent work than the well-known First Mephisto Waltz, and it rises at the end to a violent climax as the poet again collapses.

In the epilogue we are back in the poet's study: he awakes from his laudanum-inspired dreams and looks in vain for the visions which had haunted him. Finally, in despair, he kills himself: the music here is 'R. W.-Venezia', a short elegiac piece which Liszt wrote on hearing of the death of Wagner. At the end the music of the Third Consolation returns: the woman in ball dress enters with her companions and they bear the poet's body away: 'L'Amour Suprême' is achieved at last.

I have discussed *Apparitions* in some detail, not only because of the interest of the music, but also because it is a first-class example of how a ballet can be based on music written for another purpose provided that it is carefully chosen. Here Constant Lambert and Frederick Ashton worked in close collaboration on all details of the relation between music and dancing, and the result has been a ballet which held its place in the repertoire successfully for over twenty years. But it needs a choreographer with great feeling for music and also an understanding and originally-minded musical director to achieve such a result, and for every success in this type of ballet there have been innumerable failures—not so much in the Sadler's Wells company, where the musical standard has always been high, but in attempts elsewhere.

Apart from *Apparitions,* 1936 also saw the production at Sadler's Wells of two former Diaghilev ballets, *The Gods Go A-Begging* and *Barabau,* which were discussed in our last chapter. More important was a new production of Beethoven's *Prometheus* ballet, with choreography by Ninette de Valois. At the end of the year came *Nocturne,* an Ashton ballet to Delius' symphonic poem, 'Paris': this proved very successful at the time, though it has not remained in the repertoire. Early in 1937 came the first performance of *Les Patineurs,* a gay divertissement by Ashton to music of Meyerbeer selected by Constant Lambert, mainly from the Skaters' Ballet in *Le Prophète*: this has remained in the repertoire to this day. Another new production was *A Wedding Bouquet,* with music by Lord Berners and a text by Gertrude Stein: the latter was originally written for chorus, but in some wartime productions and also on an American tour it was declaimed by Constant Lambert himself: this ballet was an amusing parody of a conventional wedding party, though the music in itself was not particularly distinguished. A more important work from the musical point of view was *Checkmate,* with music by Bliss and choreography by Ninette de Valois. This is an extremely successful piece of theatre which has held its place in the repertoire: Bliss' flamboyant and colourful music is exactly what is needed for the scenario—which is a symbolical game of chess between Love and Death—and some of the dances have become popular concert items. It is also an example of the Sadler's Wells Ballet's excellent practice of commissioning works from British composers, and in the last forty years a very large number of British ballet scores have been specially written for them, with beneficial results both for the ballet and for British music in general.

Up to the war the Sadler's Wells company continued to put on new productions in fairly large numbers, including *Horoscope* (1938), a new ballet with music by Constant Lambert, based on the subject of a couple separated and then united by their different signs of the Zodiac: this score contains several very effective dances, and some of them have remained in the concert repertoire. The Prelude, in the form of a palindrome, is one of Lambert's most original creations. The same year the company also put on *Le Roi Nu,* with music by the French composer Jean Françaix—a rather lightweight work—and *The Judgment of Paris,* with music by another British composer, Lennox Berkeley. In 1939 came the full-length production of the *Sleeping Beauty,* now a familiar item in the Covent Garden repertoire, and another short ballet with music by Lord Berners, *Cupid and Psyche.* In the early days of the war the company were still able to continue at Sadler's Wells for a time, and there in January 1940 they produced another important Ashton ballet to music by Liszt, *Dante Sonata.*

The music for this was again originally a piano piece, but this time it was an extended one, the Fantasia quasi Sonata, *Après une Lecture du Dante,* from the second book of Liszt's 'Années de Pélerinage'. This was a comparatively early piece of Liszt's, and it is written in a fiery virtuoso style which makes it almost too much for one pianist or even one piano to cope with. So Constant Lambert wisely arranged it for piano and orchestra, leaving the more brilliant and virtuosic passages in their original piano form, while the heavier 'orchestral' writing was transferred to the orchestra. This arrangement sounded extremely effective: to it Frederick Ashton devised a semi-abstract ballet, with costumes and décor in black and white only, and with a struggle between two opposing groups, the Children of Darkness and Children of Light, as theme. The atmosphere of Dante's Inferno, which Liszt was trying to portray in his music, comes out brilliantly in the ballet, which was one of Ashton's most effective creations, and highly relevant to the times in which it was first produced. Unfortunately the orchestral material had to be left behind in Holland at the time of the Sadler's Wells Ballet's hurried escape from there in May 1940: the work had however been recorded commercially in Constant Lambert's arrangement, and for a time this recording was used in stage performances—not a very satisfactory solution, but the only possible one at the time. After the war the original material again became available, having been hidden from the Germans by Dutch patriots, and the ballet was produced at Covent Garden in 1946. At present it is not in the repertoire, but it well merits revival.

Another production dating from early 1940 was *The Wise Virgins*, to music arranged by Walton from Bach's cantatas: this arrangement was tasteful but effective, successfully avoiding both archaism and over-modernity, and it provided an interesting score which is often heard in the concert hall to-day. (One of its best-known numbers is of course 'Sheep may safely graze'.) Later in 1940 Constant Lambert put together a score from music by an English eighteenth-century composer, William Boyce, in whom he had long been interested, and this formed a short ballet, *The Prospect Before Us*.

From 1941 onwards the Sadler's Wells Ballet was mainly centred on Burnley, from where it made tours of many parts of Britain. It had no orchestra at this time, and the music was played on two pianos by Hilda Gaunt and Constant Lambert. However, it was also able to give some seasons at the New Theatre in London, where it was possible to provide an orchestra, and a number of new productions were given there during the war years. These included Ashton's *The Wanderer*, to Schubert's Wanderer Fantasia in Liszt's arrangement of it for piano and orchestra: this was a semi-abstract ballet with some resemblance to *Dante Sonata*. Constant Lambert also arranged Purcell's *Comus* music to form a ballet, and this was produced in 1941 with choreography by Robert Helpmann, who also made an effective ballet to Tchaikovsky's symphonic poem *Hamlet*, the action being treated in a visionary, dream-like manner—as if Hamlet's past life were passing through

[149]

his fevered and dying brain. An original ballet by Walton, *The Quest*, after Edmund Spenser, was produced in 1943, but this was not greatly successful. In the following year Andrée Howard produced Roussel's *Le Festin de l'Araignée* with new choreography, and a second ballet by Bliss, *Miracle in the Gorbals*, was also produced. Though less well-known than *Checkmate*, this was a highly effective score which is often heard as a concert suite nowadays: it makes some use of natural sounds, such as the wailing of a ship's siren, and also of Scottish popular tunes.

After the end of the war the position of the ballet was completely altered by the reopening of Covent Garden as a permanent home for both opera and ballet. The Sadler's Wells Ballet became the resident company there, and they also formed a second company, the Sadler's Wells Theatre Ballet, which performed at Sadler's Wells itself. Both companies remained under the direction of Ninette de Valois, and ballets and dancers were exchanged between the two companies: generally those ballets which needed most dancers and were most suitable for a larger stage were performed at Covent Garden and those requiring smaller resources at Sadler's Wells, but several ballets were in the repertoire of both companies.

At first both companies somewhat naturally concentrated on building up their repertoire again after the wartime upheavals: the larger company had to adapt themselves to the larger stage space of Covent Garden, while the smaller company had a number of new dancers to train. However, some new productions were put on even during the first post-war season of 1946. At Covent Garden a new Bliss ballet, *Adam Zero*, was produced in April: based on a somewhat symbolic theme this did not prove to be a great popular success, though some of the music was very effective. Shortly afterwards Ashton produced *Symphonic Variations*, to Franck's well-known work for piano and orchestra: this is an extremely

Galina Ulanova as Giselle, in Act I

Margot Fonteyn as Giselle

well worked out abstract ballet, and has deservedly remained in the repertoire. Another new production was *Les Sirènes*, with music by Lord Berners. Meanwhile the smaller company had produced Celia Franca's *Khadra*, to music by Sibelius, and also *Mardi Gras*, with music by the young British composer Leonard Salzedo: this company has always made a point of commissioning works from some of the younger and less well-known native composers, often with very happy results. Salzedo certainly has a gift for dramatic composition, as could also be seen in his later ballet, *The Fugitive*.

The principal event of 1947 at Covent Garden was the visit of Leonide Massine, who staged his own ballets *Le Tricorne* and *La Boutique Fantasque* with the company, giving some performances himself as The Miller in the former ballet: he also created a new ballet for them, *Mam'zelle Angot*, to the tuneful music of Lecocq, chiefly taken from his operetta *La Fille de Madame Angot*, and rescored by Gordon Jacob. This is an effective comedy ballet which still remains in the repertoire, even though some of the rescoring has been done with a heavy hand. Meanwhile the Theatre Ballet had mounted *La Fête Étrange*, a dream-like ballet by Andrée Howard to music chosen from Fauré's works and scored by Lennox Berkeley— an eminently suitable choice for this work—and also *Adieu*, to music by Scarlatti, which marked the first appearance with the company of another young choreographer of brilliance, John Cranko.

In the following year Ashton presented Stravinsky's *Scènes de Ballet* at Covent Garden: this work had previously been produced in America, and we shall return to it later in connection with American ballet. Another foreign ballet presented with new choreography by Ashton was Prokofiev's full-length ballet *Cinderella*, originally produced in Russia in 1945, and to this we shall also return. Ashton and Massine also produced new ballets to Strauss' 'Don Juan' and Haydn's 'Clock' Symphony respectively, but neither of these was greatly successful. During this period the Theatre Ballet produced a number of new short works, none of them of great importance, except perhaps for Andreé Howard's amusing *Selina,* a Victorian pastiche to music by Rossini, and the next noteworthy event was the production at Covent Garden in 1950 of *Don Quixote,* with choreography by Ninette de Valois and music by Roberto Gerhard, a Spanish pupil of Schoenberg who had been living in England since before the war. Gerhard's brilliant and subtle score is one of the finest and most remarkable pieces of ballet music ever produced for the company, and he was one of the few modern composers who could really make an orchestra sound: he also composed another very effective and original ballet, *Pandora,* for the Ballet Jooss.

Two other Covent Garden productions of 1950 were Balanchine's *Ballet Imperial,* to Tchaikovsky's Second Piano Concerto—an effective piece of abstract ballet, if hardly expressing the varying moods of the music—and *Ballabile,* by the French choreographer Roland Petit, to music by Chabrier selected by Constant Lambert. Lambert had resigned from the musical direction of the company in 1947, but he remained as artistic adviser and guest conductor until his death in 1951: he was succeeded, first for a short period by Warwick Braithwaite, and then by Robert Irving, who held the position of musical director and adviser from 1949 till 1958, and admirably maintained the musical standards set by Constant Lambert. *Ballabile* has something in common with *Cotillon,* but the stage treatment is far more fantastic and even surrealist: the music comes partly from Chabrier's shorter orchestral works such as the Suite Pastorale and partly from orchestrated piano and two-piano works such as the Valses Romantiques and the Bourrée Fantasque.

The year 1951 saw the production at Sadler's Wells of *Pineapple Poll,* an amusing entertainment by John Cranko set to music of Sullivan arranged by Charles Mackerras: Sullivan's works had only just come out of copyright, and so this was the first opportunity of using his music for ballet purposes. *Pineapple Poll* remained one of the most successful items in the Theatre Ballet's repertoire. In July 1951 Covent Garden produced *Tiresias,* Constant Lambert's last ballet, with choreography by Frederick Ashton. The scenario, devised by Lambert himself, is a fairly straight treatment of the classical story of Tiresias' changes of sex in his earlier life: in the first and last scenes he appears as a man and in the intervening one as a woman. The music, scored for an unusual orchestra without upper strings but including a large assortment of wind, brass and percussion, is very effective at moments, particularly in the lyrical second scene and in some of the more dramatic parts of the last scene—the quarrel between Zeus and Hera: but there is some repetition in it, and the acoustics of the orchestra pit at Covent Garden failed to let it make its full effect.

Later in 1951 came a Massine ballet specially devised for Covent Garden, *Donald of the Burthens,* based on a Scottish legend. The music, by Ian Whyte, was partly based on Scottish folk tunes, including the very effective use of a piper on the stage in the final dance, and these sections of the music were the best: the dramatic parts tended to lack originality. Early in 1952 Covent Garden also staged *A Mirror for Witches,* a ballet by Andrée Howard on the theme of witch-hunting in New England in the seventeenth century: the music was the first ballet score by the Welsh composer Denis ApIvor, and very effective it proved to be. Using a thoroughly modern idiom, based to some extent on the twelve-tone technique, the music was dramatic and colourful throughout, and showed ApIvor's gift for stage writing. This was further shown in his score for *Blood Wedding,* produced at Sadler's Wells in the following year with choreography by Alfred Rodrigues: the story, based on Lorca's play, again gave ApIvor the opportunity for exciting and dramatic music. His third ballet score,

[153]

Saudades (1955), though interesting musically, was less successful in that it did not seem to fit well with the choreographer's ideas. ApIvor also rescored some of Donizetti's music for the ballet *Veneziana,* produced at Covent Garden in 1953 with choreography by Andrée Howard: this was mainly a divertissement with little dramatic action, and the music was chosen partly from music written by Donizetti for ballets in his operas, such as *La Favorita,* and partly from vocal excerpts from his operas, which of course needed to be rearranged so that they would sound effective on the orchestra alone. ApIvor did his work with skill, and the result was a pleasing ballet which is perhaps more effective on a smaller stage than in the large arena of Covent Garden.

Several other younger composers were commissioned to write scores during this period. Arthur Oldham provided some witty music for *Bonne Bouche,* a farcical ballet by John Cranko, produced at Covent Garden in 1952: most of it was extremely amusing, but the joke went on too long. Humorous music was also written by John Addison for *Carte Blanche,* produced by the Theatre Ballet in 1953, and by Anthony Hopkins for *Café des Sports,* given by the same company a year later. Scores in rather more serious vein were written by Richard Arnell for *Harlequin in April* and by John Gardner for *Reflection,* but neither of these are heavyweight dramatic ballets. At Covent Garden Malcolm Arnold was commissioned to write the music for the Coronation ballet in 1953, *Homage to the Queen,* with Frederick Ashton as choreographer. This was a divertissement ballet consisting of a large number of short dances: Arnold carried out his task with great effectiveness, providing a number of really danceable movements in contrasting characters which admirably fitted the choreographer's ideas. A second ballet by Malcolm Arnold, *Rinaldo and Armida* (1955), was in a more romantic and dramatic vein. Among the more established composers, Britten's Variations and Fugue on a theme of Purcell was used as the basis of another ballet by Frederick

Ashton in 1955, and in the same year Alan Rawsthorne wrote his first ballet score, *Madame Chrysanthème*, to a story by Pierre Loti which is very similar to the Belasco-Long play on which Puccini's *Madame Butterfly* was based: in the ballet Loti's original astringent ending was preserved.

Another ballet in which operatic music was used for the score was Cranko's *The Lady and the Fool*, produced at Sadler's Wells in 1954: the music was taken from the lesser-known operas of Verdi, particularly the earlier ones, and was rescored by Charles Mackerras. Here the rescoring was sometimes done with a heavy hand: but the ballet was extremely successful, and was taken over by the larger company, being more suitable to a big stage—in addition the fullblooded music needs a larger orchestra than the smaller company could comfortably provide. Two other ballets of importance were produced at Sadler's Wells in 1955, both with choreography by Kenneth MacMillan, a brilliant young choreographer who brought an original note into British ballet: these were *Danses Concertantes*, a ballet written by Stravinsky in America during the war but now produced for the first time in England, and *House of Birds*, a fantastic fairy story set to piano pieces by the modern Spanish composer Mompou. Some of these had been scored by the composer and the rest were orchestrated by the company's musical director, Jack Lanchbery: though somewhat Debussyan in flavour, these pieces have an astringent quality which fitted in well with the choreographer's ideas. In the following year MacMillan produced *Noctambules* at Covent Garden, and then *Solitaire*, based on Malcolm Arnold's *English Dances*, at Sadler's Wells.

Two further ballets, apart from Ashton's new version of Dukas' *La Péri*, complete the tale of productions at Covent Garden up to 1957. The first of these was *Birthday Offering*, a divertissement staged by Frederick Ashton on the occasion of the twenty-fifth birthday of the company in May 1956: the music was chosen from ballet and other music by Glazounov, some of it being scored by Robert Irving, and it made an extremely agreeable entertainment. The other ballet, produced on 1 January 1957, was Britten's *The Prince of the Pagodas,* with choreography by John Cranko—the first full-length ballet by an English composer to be staged at Covent Garden, and Britten's first score to be specially written for ballet. The music is brilliant and full of invention throughout, as one might expect: there are certain *longueurs,* chiefly due to the fact that the ballet contains two divertissements, one in the second and one in the third act, and there are also several dances in which the invention of the composer and choreographer are so different from each other in character that they make a somewhat uncomfortable effect. But the whole production is certainly a bold effort, and the brilliance of the décor and stage effects make it an entertainment which can well stand up to its length. The company then commissioned another full-length ballet, *Ondine,* from the young German composer Hans Werner Henze, and this was produced in 1958 (see pp. 173 and 188): Henze has written several ballets for Continental theatres, and is thoroughly experienced in dramatic work.

Since the beginning of 1957 some organizational changes have taken place in the Sadler's Wells Ballet: both companies are now grouped together under the title The Royal Ballet, and the smaller company has left its permanent home at Sadler's Wells to come under the direction of Covent Garden. Looking back over the first twenty-six years of its history one cannot fail to be struck by the enormous variety of ballet productions which it undertook, and its repertoire contained, side by side with all the major nineteenth-century full-length ballets, a large number of modern ballets, some of the most experimental kind. And in all cases a serious attempt was made to obtain the best possible music for the ballets, whether by commissioning scores or by choosing already existing music. Naturally not all their new productions were equally successful, but the status of ballet has been immeasurably increased in England—in fact it now draws a larger public than opera—and it is certainly amazing that so much has grown from such small beginnings in such a comparatively short time. Not even lack of any previous ballet tradition or the interruption of a major war have checked this steady growth, which has been mainly due to the untiring efforts of Ninette de Valois and Frederick Ashton, aided on the musical side by Constant Lambert and, later, Robert Irving.

The history of ballet in the United States has some points in common with that of English ballet: it, too, did not begin seriously till after the death of Diaghilev, and it has also enormously increased in achievement and in public appreciation during the last forty years. Up till 1933 ballets were only performed by visiting companies, such as those of Diaghilev and de Basil, but during the thirties native American ballet began to grow. A figure of primary importance here was Balanchine, who settled in America after the death of Diaghilev, and produced a number of ballets of great interest and importance. Another leading choreographer who came from abroad was the Englishman Antony Tudor, who went to America shortly before the second world war: he had already produced a number of interesting ballets in England such as *Jardin des Lilas* to Chausson's 'Poème', and *Dark Elegies* to Mahler's 'Kindertotenlieder'. The latter of course contains a part for a solo voice, and Tudor tended to enlarge the expressive power of ballet by introducing song, speech, pantomime, and anything else which seems suitable or necessary: this tendency has become a feature of ballets by other choreographers in America too. A third outside influence of importance was that of Stravinsky, whose *Jeu de Cartes* had its world première at the Metropolitan Opera House in 1937: in 1940

Stravinsky settled in America permanently, and he wrote several ballets specially for the American stage.

But this is not to say that American ballet is exclusively dominated by European influences—on the contrary, the native element in it is extremely strong. As Lincoln Kirstein wrote: 'American ballet style springs or should spring from our own training and environment, which was not in an Imperial School or a Parisian imitation of it. Ours is a style bred also from basket-ball courts, track and swimming meets and junior proms. Our style springs from the personal atmosphere of recognizable American types.' And it is certainly true that a salient feature of the American ballet style is its facility in giving the appearance that the dance movements are spontaneously improvised—in strong contrast to the polished mastery of the classical Russian style.

This more athletic and improvisatory approach to the choreographic style naturally has had some influence on the choice of music for American ballets. As in England, choreographers have used both the methods of commissioning scores, chiefly from native composers, and of using previously written music. Two ballets with music by Aaron Copland, *Billy the Kid,* produced at Chicago in 1938 with choreography by Eugene Loring, and *Rodeo,* first seen in New York in 1942 with choreography by Agnes de Mille, are typical of the native American creation. *Rodeo,* for instance, takes as its theme the Saturday afternoon Rodeo which is traditional throughout the American south-west: this is an exhibition of roping, riding, branding, and throwing carried out by the ranch hands, and followed by a Saturday night dance at the Ranch House. This is combined with the quest of the Cowgirl for her man—this part was danced by Agnes de Mille herself—and it can be seen that the whole atmosphere is as far away as possible from the sophisticated fairy-stories of many Franco-Russian ballets. This is naturally reflected in the music, which is simple, down-to-earth and effective: in the dance scene it is mainly based on folk tunes, the dance being of course a square dance. Another influence which is prominent in American ballet music is that of jazz: this can be seen, for instance, in another well-known ballet, *Fancy Free,* produced in New York in 1944, with choreography by Jerome Robbins and music by Leonard Bernstein. This satirical story of three sailors on a spree in town is naturally accompanied by brisk music with a jazzy flavour: but this is far removed from the sophisticated parodies of jazz which the French composers of the twenties put into their ballets for Diaghilev. Jazz is part of the American folk tradition, and an American composer would use it quite naturally as coming from his cultural background. Here the music admirably suits the broad comedy of the plot, though the fun is a bit too long drawn out.

However, a number of ballets more on the lines of the European tradition have also been produced in America, and noteworthy among these are several by Stravinsky. He was of course living in Paris up to the outbreak of the second world war, and there in 1934 he had produced *Perséphone* at the request of Ida Rubinstein, who had previously commissioned *Le Baiser de la Fée* from him. *Perséphone,* though sometimes described as a 'choreographic drama', is hardly a ballet in the normal sense: it is better thought of under its alternative title of 'melodrama for chorus, orchestra, tenor solo, and declamation', the words being partly declaimed by a speaker and partly sung by the tenor soloist and the chorus. Opinions differ very much about its quality: Stravinskians rave about it as being one of the master's finest works, but personally I have always found it somewhat arid, a view shared by many others. However, there are no such reservations about *Jeu de Cartes,* which is certainly one of his finest ballet scores and is also effective as a concert piece. The music throughout is dramatic and eminently danceable, and it has remained in the repertoire of American ballet companies ever since its first production in 1937. The plot is based on a game of poker, and the characteristics of the different cards are admirably expressed in the music.

Stravinsky's next American ballet, *Danses Concertantes,* was produced in New York in 1944 with choreography by Balanchine. This is a series of abstract dances scored for a small ensemble of twenty-four solo players, and is one of Stravinsky's more austere works. There is little in the way of melody, and the rhythms are subtle and varied. The music by itself is not particularly interesting to listen to, but with good choreography the ballet certainly makes its effect. That of Balanchine I have not seen, but the ballet was produced at Sadler's Wells in 1955 with choreography by Kenneth MacMillan, and there is no doubt that the dance movements made the score come alive in this version. And Balanchine's original choreography seems to have had a considerable effect on other choreographers in America. About the same time Stravinsky composed another abstract ballet, *Scènes de Ballet,* originally commissioned by Billy Rose for a revue; this is scored for normal-size orchestra including three trumpets and a piano. This was also given in New York with choreography by Balanchine, and appeared at Covent Garden in 1948 with choreography by Ashton. Stravinsky describes it as 'a classical ballet. . . . This music is patterned after the forms of the classical dance, free of any given literary or dramatic argument. The parts follow each other as in a sonata or in a symphony, in contrasts or similarities.' The score consists of eleven numbers in a somewhat angular style: there are no dramatic passages, and Stravinsky's aim is formal beauty throughout. The scoring is light, clear and cool. The ballet can make an attractive display of dancing, but it needs to be extremely well performed to make its effect.

Stravinsky followed this with *Orpheus,* a treatment of the classical legend in three scenes which are played without a break. Though the orchestra is small, the music is more dramatic than in either of Stravinsky's two previous ballets, especially, as might be expected, in the scene where Orpheus is torn to pieces by the Bacchantes. But on the whole the music is classical, dignified and restrained, and the final Apotheosis of Orpheus has the quality of *Apollon Musagète*. Here again is a score which is not particularly effective in the concert hall: but as soon as it is heard as a background to the dance it comes to life at once.

Stravinsky's next ballet was *Agon,* the score of which was completed in April 1957. Dedicated to Lincoln Kirstein and George Balanchine, it is written for twelve dancers, four men and eight girls, and consists of sixteen short dance movements. Although the ballet is scored for a normal-sized symphony orchestra, the orchestration is always very sparing, and a great deal of use is made of solo instruments. In his last years Stravinsky gradually adopted an extremely thin texture which is somewhat similar to that of Webern (a composer whom he admired greatly), and in this work many passages are actually based on the twelve-tone technique of Schoenberg, a method which Stravinsky had previously used in two movements of his *Canticum Sacrum* of 1955. In *Agon* the twelve-tone technique is not often used in the orthodox Schoenbergian manner, and the note-series is mostly split into groups of three or four notes which are then handled in an ostinato style; Stravinsky also preserved the essentially balletic character of the music by maintaining his customary flexibility of rhythm, and the work is eminently danceable in spite of its technical experimentation. Some of the movements are given the titles of seventeenth-century French dances such as saraband, galliard and bransle, but these dance forms are treated with some freedom: whereas the first bransle has the traditional aspect of a fast dance in $\frac{4}{4}$ time—though it begins with a canon for two solo trumpets—the second bransle is based on a regular $\frac{3}{8}$ rhythm for the castanets against which the other instruments have bars of $\frac{7}{16}$ and $\frac{5}{16}$. Canonic forms are used a good deal throughout the ballet—another tendency of Stravinsky's later music—and the orchestration varies constantly from one dance to another. The first production took place in New York on 27 November 1957.

Hindemith was also living in America during the war years, and he produced two ballet scores at this time, *Hérodiade* and *The Four Temperaments*. *Hérodiade,* scored for small orchestra, was written for Martha Graham, a dancer and choreographer who specializes in long solo dances: Hindemith's score is pleasant and effective without being anything more. *The Four Temperaments* has a more definite shape in being written in the form of a theme and four variations: and the theme and each variation are again subdivided into three parts, so that in spite of the limited resources—strings and solo piano only—there is a good deal of variety of mood and also the music falls into a number of short sections which are held together by the large framework. Each variation shows, as it were, how a person of each different temperament would react to the three sections of the theme: and this psychological approach gives an added interest to the music, which is one of the most successful of Hindemith's smaller-scale works.

Other composers who were living in America during that period have of course written ballet scores—Milhaud, for instance, wrote a not very successful score for a ballet based on Poe's *The Bells,* which was produced in 1946—but the most characteristic American ballets were those which had scores specially written by American composers. Apart from those already mentioned, *Fall River Legend,* produced in New York in 1948 with choreography by Agnes de Mille and music by Morton Gould, has been one of the most successful. The score is best in its quieter and more romantic passages, where Gould shows a real feeling for atmosphere: the style is somewhat eclectic, drawing both from popular dance music and from middle-period Stravinsky, but Gould undoubtedly has a feeling for ballet music, and though the more animated parts do not come off so well as the more lyrical passages, as a whole the score is very successful, and can mostly be listened to as music for its own sake. Another Gould score, *Interplay,* with choreography by Jerome Robbins, based on the theme of Dead End Kids from the sidewalks of New York, was also very successful on its first performance in New York in 1946, though it has not quite attained the reputation of *Fall River Legend.*

There are two further ballets with music by Copland: *Appalachian Spring* was written for Martha Graham, and is highly successful in its lyrical evocation of the country atmosphere. And Copland's clarinet concerto has been made into a ballet by Jerome Robbins on the theme of the Pied Piper: here the clarinettist sits on the stage, and the whole effect is original and good. A later ballet by Bernstein, *Facsimile,* has an effectively written score, containing many ingenious touches of orchestration such as the skilful use of a solo piano: it is a much more lyrical work than *Fancy Free,* and in fact its best moments come in the quieter sections—in the more strenuous passages the animation often seems forced. A less successful score was that by Alex North to a ballet based on Tennessee Williams' play *A Streetcar Named Desire*: here the use of jazzy elements did not help to underline the tragedy and pathos of the situation—nor did the somewhat ineffective staging. But the American Ballet Theatre, which has been responsible for most of the productions of new American ballets since the 1940s, has done admirable work in creating a genuinely American style of ballet: no company can expect successes every time, and most of what has been done is certainly worth while.

Before leaving American ballet I should mention a few ballets based on music originally written for other purposes which have achieved success in America. These include

Tudor's *Pillar of Fire,* to Schoenberg's early work 'Verklärte Nacht'—hardly a very balletic score, one would think—three works by Balanchine—*Symphony in C,* to Bizet's little symphony, *Divertimento No. 15,* to Mozart's music, and *Barocco,* to Bach's two-violin concerto. There have of course been many other such adaptations of music to ballet in America—too many, perhaps—and not all of them equally happy: one of the strangest ones was *Caprichos,* with the scenario based on Goya's extraordinary drawings—the somewhat enigmatic captions from them were printed in the programme—and set to Bartók's Contrasts for violin, clarinet and piano, with the movements in the wrong order. Seen in the vast spaces of Covent Garden, during the visit of an American ballet company, this seemed quite absurd. However, not all ballets in America go to such lengths, and if some of the experimentation is overdone, at least there are new ideas in plenty. Apart from the American Ballet Theatre and Martha Graham's company, the New York City Ballet has done excellent work in putting on new productions, and interest in the ballet is on the increase all over the United States. Foreign touring companies such as the Royal Ballet are invariably welcomed with enthusiasm, and there is no doubt that the cultural climate in America is healthy for the further development of ballet, even if, as we have seen, its main development is likely to be on native rather than European lines. As an agreeable mixture of American and foreign influences I may quote Samuel Barber's 'Souvenirs' (1952), originally written as a suite for piano duet, and scored at the request of the New York Ballet Society. Its six dances, waltz, schottische, pas de deux, two-step, hesitation tango, and galop, form a divertissement 'in a setting reminiscent of the Palm Court of the Hotel Plaza in New York about 1914', as the composer puts it in his note. The mood is of affectionate reminiscence: yet characteristically Barber relates his score to a particular part of the American scene rather than just leaving it as a set of dances imitating various European styles. Barber has also composed some effective music to a ballet on the subject of Medea: he certainly has a feeling for colour and effect which is highly suitable to the ballet.

Ballet in France, as we have seen, has had a long and continuous history. Side by side with the Paris seasons of the Diaghilev company, ballet of course continued to be performed at the Opéra and elsewhere, and the principal effect of Diaghilev's death was that Serge Lifar, one of his principal dancers, became director of ballet at the Opéra, a post he held till 1958. He was able to sweep away some of the cobwebs of tradition on his arrival there: as Arnold Haskell put it, 'He had to cut through a mass of red tape, some of which still clings, and to turn civil servants into artists. That he succeeded there can be no doubt: the names of the artists involved are the proof.' These include several who have now left the Opéra for work in independent companies, such as Yvette Chauviré, Renée Jeanmaire, and Jean Babilée. Lifar was able to bring to the Opéra the aims and traditions of Diaghilev, and to that extent he was able to give new life to a venerable tradition. But there are of course dangers in the complete control of a company by one man, and some of Lifar's choreography has been monotonous. He also tended to reduce the status of music and to make it purely the servant of dancing: this is taken to the extreme in the ballets *Icare* and *Chota Roustaveli*, which are accompanied by percussion rhythms only. Pure dancing of this kind needs a master choreographer with great musical sensitivity, and it is unlikely to become an important trend in the future history of ballet. At the other end of the scale the Opéra ballet mounted lavish productions of the opera-ballets of Lully and Rameau, with a spectacle equalling in splendour the operas of Meyerbeer a century earlier: but here the dances were confined to the formal styles of the seventeenth and eighteenth centuries, and there was no attempt to incorporate modern ballet movements.

This period was also notable for the production of two further ballets by Roussel. *Bacchus et Ariane,* a ballet in two acts, was produced at the Opéra on 22 May 1931: the libretto, by Abel Hermant, begins after the slaying of the Minotaur, and shows Theseus' desertion of Ariadne, who, desolate, leaps from a rock. She is caught by Bacchus, who makes her immortal. The music, more condensed and concise than that of *The Spiders' Banquet,* is vital and dramatic throughout; it is well suited to the stage action, and as a result does not make particularly good concert music, though two suites have been arranged from it, one from each act, and these are heard from time to time in the concert hall. Roussel's last ballet, *Aeneas,* was written in 1935, and was first performed in Brussels on 31 July of that year under Hermann Scherchen. The scenario, by Joseph Weterings, a Belgian admirer of Roussel, shows Aeneas consulting the Cumaean Sibyl: she foretells his adventures, his meeting with Dido and finally the foundation of Rome. These scenes are danced on the stage; and the ballet contains a part for a chorus of Aeneas' former companions, who beseech him not to deviate from his duty; so that here the chorus is not introduced just for colour, as in *Daphnis and Chloë,* but forms an integral part of the action. The music was written in a great hurry, and is somewhat patchy in consequence: but it does contain many fine moments, and there is an effectively percussive use of a solo piano.

But the most important event in modern French ballet was the foundation in 1944 of the Ballets des Champs-Elysées, which has definitely introduced a new note into the ballet of to-day. One of the directors of this company was Boris Kochno, who had been Diaghilev's right-hand man, but the

The Bolshoi Ballet production of *Le Lac des Cygnes*, Act III

1

leading spirit was the French choreographer Roland Petit, and it was he more than anyone else who was responsible for this new approach. His subjects were bizarre, fantastic, or macabre, with a strong emotional undercurrent: the influence both of surrealism and of Sartre's existentialism could be noted in some of his works—in France the ballet is as much the concern of poets, painters, and musicians as it is of the choreographer and dancer, and the French always enjoy novelties which express current artistic thought. Thus each new creation of Petit's was a novelty in one way or another: in one of his early ballets, *Les Forains,* the novelty was chiefly in the story, which concerns itinerant circus people, and in the scenery of Christian Bérard, which was actually constructed on the stage during the performance. The music, by Henri Sauguet, who wrote the score for the late Diaghilev ballet *La Chatte,* is adequate for its purpose but hardly more than that: Sauguet has never been a particularly inspired composer. Another composer of some experience, Jean Françaix, wrote the score for Petit's *Les Demoiselles de la Nuit*: this includes various 'effects' such as wailing-cat music: Petit has sometimes been prone to make the music somewhat subordinate and even crudely realistic in his ballets—in *L'Oeuf à la Coque* at the climax of the dance the chefs on stage add to the percussion department by beating on saucepan lids. But in general the scores for his ballets have a romantic, emotional flavour which is strong theatrically and full of imagination: a good example is the music for *Le Loup* by the young French composer Henri Dutilleux, which created a powerful atmosphere through its pulsating rhythms and considerably helped in putting the somewhat outré story across to the audience. In other ballets Petit has used rather more established French composers, such as Ibert in *Les Amours de Jupiter* and Auric in *La Chambre*: he has not so far been attracted to the younger French experimental composers. In regard to the relationship of dance to music in his ballets, Petit had sometimes been accused of being unmusical and of using the music merely as a background. It is truer to say that he prefers to follow the expression inherent in the music rather than to try to match every beat in detail. Even where the music is of little importance in itself it still has a definite theatrical purpose, and although normally only small orchestral forces are used, a good deal of variety of colour comes out of them. In cases where he has based his ballet on previously written music, his approach has sometimes been somewhat unusual. For instance *Le Jeune Homme et la Mort* was originally rehearsed to drum rhythms alone: various pieces were suggested to accompany the ballet, but finally André Girard, the musical director of the company, proposed Bach's Organ Passacaglia in C minor: the dancers did not even hear this music till the dress rehearsal! Here the noble music was deliberately chosen to provide a contrast, even a shocking one, to the sordid drama which takes place on the stage. In another ballet, *Carmen,* he has adapted Bizet's operatic score to form a ballet in five scenes. Certainly this is not what Bizet intended: but on the other hand it does make an effective ballet, and in some ways is nearer to Mérimée's original story than the opera is. One can sum up Petit's use of music in ballet by saying that what he principally aims for is a colourful effect made by a small combination of instruments, with much use of percussion: to this extent it resembles jazz or at any rate shows its influence.

A later development in France was that of musique concrète, and from the fifties onwards this has been used for balletic purposes. The method was invented about 1948 by Pierre Schaeffer and Pierre Henry, and they have been given technical assistance by the French Radio, who have provided them with the equipment to carry on their researches. Musique concrète consists in the first place of natural sounds, which may or may not be musical ones: these are recorded on tape and then played through an instrument called the Phonogène which can reproduce them at any given speed or pitch: they can also be played backwards, and the initial impact of a note, e.g. on a piano, can be cut off, while a short sharp sound like a string pizzicato can be prolonged indefinitely in duration by means of another machine called the Morphophone. All these sounds can be combined with each other by means of tape recordings, and it can be seen that the variety of effects which can be produced is clearly very great. The inventors of musique concrète do not wish it to be regarded purely as sound effects for background use but as a new kind of music which is an independent art: but it must be admitted that up to now they have hardly produced anything which can be regarded as a self-sufficient musical creation. However, this kind of music can be and has been very effectively used in conjunction with films, radio features and stage plays: and in 1953 *Orphée 53*, an 'opéra concret' with music by Pierre Henry, was produced at the Donaueschingen Festival in Germany. The musique concrète in this contains recorded speaking voices as well as effects which simulate choral singing: and this was used to accompany pantomimic movements on the stage. In addition Henry has provided music for two ballets for which Maurice Béjart has composed the choreography. The first of these, *Arcane*, 1955, is an abstract ballet based on pieces of musique concrète which Henry had previously composed: these consist of four short pieces called 'Musiques de Theâtre', another called 'Batterie Fugace' made from the sound of four drums, and the 'Séquences des Cataclysmes' from the film *Astrologie* for which Henry had composed musique concrète in 1952. In 1956 Henry wrote musique concrète for a dramatic ballet, *Haut Voltage*, which was first produced by the Janine Charrat Company in June 1957, again with choreography by Maurice Béjart. This concerns a woman endowed with supernatural power who dominates a young man and subjects him to the action of her magnetic force: when in a trance, he is charged with a powerful electric current, which eventually brings death to a young girl who loves him, disaster to the magical woman and madness to the young man. This power-fully dramatic subject is admirably suited by the extraordinary sounds of musique concrète, and the electronic effects are certainly in place here. It seems then that musique concrète may well have a part to play in the future of ballet, at any rate ballets of a certain kind. Musique concrète is extremely com-plicated and laborious to make, and its composition needs a considerable time: also the technical apparatus is very expensive and in general is only within the reach of radio stations and similar bodies. Electronic music, which has been extensively studied in Germany, may conceivably produce more fruitful results: but to this we shall return in the next chapter.

In other countries besides France ballet has developed con-siderably since 1930. In Italy ballet tended in the past to be regarded chiefly as an adjunct to opera, but it has now become more of an independent art, and a number of leading Italian composers have written ballets in recent years, apart from those mentioned in our last chapter as having composed scores for Diaghilev. Luigi Dallapiccola wrote a score for *Marsia* in 1939: the choreographer of this ballet, which is of course based on the classical legend of Apollo and Marsyas, was the Hungarian Aurel Milloss, who has settled in Italy and has done a great deal for the creation of a native school of Italian ballet. Dallapiccola's score is somewhat Ravelian—it dates from the days before he adopted the twelve-tone technique—but it is sensitively written and effective. Another leading Italian composer, Goffredo Petrassi, wrote the score of *Portrait of Don Quixote* in 1945: this was produced two years later by the Ballets des Champs Elysées in Paris, with Jean Babilée as Quixote and Natalie Philippart as Dulcinea. The book and choreography were again by Aurel Milloss. From the ballet the composer has made an orchestral suite consisting of the entire score minus two short interludes. After an introduction which begins with an important oboe theme, the first dance shows Quixote deciding on his mission of knight errantry, after reading a book of chevaleresque adventures: the music begins with a three-part invention for brass in a somewhat archaic style. After a quiet ending comes the second dance, in which Quixote starts off on his adventures. His obstinacy is expressed by an eight-note ostinato which is maintained throughout, and this leads to his first fall. An intermezzo, lyrical and skittish by turns, introduces Dulcinea: then we see Quixote at his religious exercises, accompanied by a mysterous 'adagio' movement which is full of colour and atmosphere. In the next dance, marked 'presto, drammatico e misterioso', Quixote fights his last battle, learns the truth about his ideas of chivalry and tears up the book of adventures which had inspired him. He dies disillusioned: in a slower interlude, in which the atmosphere is admirably sustained, Dulcinea appears and gives a violet to the ghost of Quixote. There is a final apotheosis of Quixote, in lightish mood and without any great climax. Petrassi's score is colourful throughout: it contains a good deal of writing for solo instruments and many dramatic effects.

Among the younger Italian composers Luigi Nono has written a ballet, *The Red Cloak*, which was first produced at the Berlin Festival in 1954. The scenario was based on Lorca's *Don Perlimplin and Belisa* by the choreographer Tatiana Gsovsky: the story concerns the love of the ageing Don Perlimplin for his young wife, Belisa, and her gradually awakening love for him, which comes too late to save him from committing suicide when he feels that he is not loved in return. Nono is certainly one of the most gifted of the younger European composers, and it is gratifying that he has been able to adapt his own somewhat extremist style to balletic purposes. In fact there is now a good deal of interest in ballet in Italy: several opera houses have permanent ballet companies, and that in Milan, for instance, was enterprising enough to put on

Britten's *The Prince of the Pagodas* within a few months of its first production in London in 1957.

The position in Germany has been somewhat more complex, though here too the position has been steadily improving. The tradition of Diaghilev and the Russian school of dancing did not really affect ballet there until after the Second World War, and ballet between the wars was mainly influenced by a style of dancing derived originally from Isadora Duncan, and of which Rudolf Laban and Mary Wigman were the principal exponents. This rather more athletic and expressionist style can be best seen in the well-known ballet *The Green Table* by Kurt Jooss, who was ballet master at the Münster and Essen operas in pre-Hitler days: this bitter satire on disarmament conferences was produced as long ago as 1926, but it is still, unfortunately, as topical as ever. Jooss had his own ballet school in Germany, which was transferred to Dartington Hall in England after Hitler's advent to power: after the war Jooss returned to Germany. However, apart from a few well-known ballets, Jooss' school has never had very much influence on the development of ballet in Western Europe, and few scores of note were written for him. One of the best was *Pandora,* by Roberto Gerhard: this shows all the subtlety and dramatic power which we expect from this composer.

After the war the Franco-Russian style of dancing began to have more influence in Germany, and ballet there now is far more comparable with that in other European countries. A number of German composers have written effective ballets, of which perhaps the best known is *Abraxas,* by Werner Egk: the theme is based on the Faust legend, but it has little in common with either part of Goethe's play. The music shows no great personality, but it is effective theatrical stuff, and the ballet has been generally successful. Egk has also written another ballet, *The Chinese Nightingale,* on the same Andersen story which Stravinsky used in *Le Chant du Rossignol.*

Another German composer of the same generation as Egk, Carl Orff, has written three works which he describes as *ludi scaenici* under the generic title of *Trionfi*: these consist of *Carmina Burana*, based on mediæval Latin poems, *Catulli Carmina*, and *Trionfo di Afrodite*. They consist mainly of solo and choral singing, and the dance movements in them are mainly incidental: Orff is an apostle of 'neo-primitivity', and the music chiefly consists of simple rhythms repeated *ad nauseam*. These works are certainly not ballets in the normal sense. Wolfgang Fortner has written a ballet, *The White Rose*, based on Oscar Wilde's *The Birthday of the Infanta*, produced in Berlin in 1950. His subtly written score combines the twelve-tone technique with elements of Spanish and Moorish colouring and even with boogie-woogie: it is a very successful blend of contrasting elements and is a considerable achievement, especially for a composer who has otherwise written little for the stage. Of the younger German composers the most talented is undoubtedly Hans Werner Henze, born in 1926: he has written several operas and ballets and even his symphonic music shows his dramatic gifts. He was musical director of the ballet at Wiesbaden for some years, and therefore has more practical experience of ballet than most other composers of his generation. He has written four ballets: *Jack Pudding, Labyrinth, Rosa Silber,* and *Maratona di Danza*—this last is for orchestra and two jazz combinations, and is an extremely successful piece of light music. He was later commissioned to write a full-length ballet, *Ondine,* for Covent Garden, with choreography by Frederick Ashton. His style is difficult to describe, as he tends to vary it according to whatever purpose he is writing for: it leans towards atonal and twelve-tone music, but Henze is not a doctrinaire composer, and his dramatic sense is sure enough to guide him in achieving the result he desires (see pp. 156 and 188).

Another development in Germany, which may at some

[173]

time have an effect on ballet—though up to now it is only in its infancy—is that of electronic music. This has been provided with technical facilities by the West German Radio in Cologne, and a group of young composers, under the leadership of Dr. Herbert Eimert, have been carrying on researches into this new medium for some years. Electronic music differs from musique concrète in that it is produced not from natural sounds but from an electronic oscillator: it is possible for the composer to indicate in his score, which he writes in the form of a graph in three parts, the exact frequency, duration and dynamics of each sound, and so this is a far more exact art than the more haphazard methods of musique concrète. Thus there is no reason why electronic scores for ballets should not be produced in the future, and they may well prove to be as effective as those made from musique concrète. At any rate this is a development which is well worth watching for the future: the most gifted composer of the group, Karlheinz Stockhausen, has already experimented in the use of the human voice in conjunction with electronic music.

Another interesting development in Germany has been the use of ballet in opera. In modern opera, ballet has somewhat naturally tended to become more and more integrated with the dramatic action, and the old idea of a divertissement interrupting the drama hardly exists to-day. Even the Paris Opéra no longer insists that all its operatic productions must contain a ballet! This process of the integration of the dance within the framework of the opera may be seen, for instance, in Busoni's *Doktor Faust,* written to the composer's own German text and first produced in Berlin in 1925. Here the main part of the action, set in the ducal park at Parma, begins with a Cortège in polacca rhythm which serves as a prelude: this is followed by a series of rustic dances in waltz rhythm with vocal parts, and then come sections in the style of a minuet and a march: in fact practically the whole scene is set in dance rhythms of one kind or another, and over these the vocal lines expressing the dramatic action go on continuously. And the intermezzo leading to the next scene is in the style of a sarabande.

Similarly in Berg's *Wozzeck*, which dates from about the same period, one highly effective scene is set in a café where a band on stage plays a Ländler continuously in the background with the main action in the foreground, as it were: this kind of thing has in fact become a commonplace in modern opera. A more elaborate scene which requires actual dancing may be found in the 'Dance Round the Golden Calf', which occupies the greater part of the second act of Schoenberg's opera *Moses and Aaron*, written in the early 1930's but not staged till 1957, at the Festival of the International Society for Contemporary Music in Zürich. This calls for solo singers, chorus, dancers, and orchestra, and all play their part in building up a violent and exciting scene which certainly shows that twelve-tone music is not incapable of expressing emotion! In fact a good deal of the music shows the most uncontrolled fury, and this scene made a great impression in the Zürich production of the opera. An interesting use of dancing can also be found in some scenes of Hans Werner Henze's opera *Boulevard Solitude*, a modern version of the Manon story: here dancing is sometimes used purely as a background decoration, without any effect on the main drama which proceeds at the front of the stage in the normal operatic way—but the presence of the dancers as it were behind the conversation gives these scenes an interesting and unusual atmosphere. Curiously enough it seems to be in Germany more than in other countries to-day that the most imaginative use of dancing in opera can be found, perhaps because of their tendency towards more experimental operatic productions.

As we have seen, ballet has a long history in the Scandinavian countries, particularly Denmark and Sweden, and in recent years modern composers have been encouraged to write new ballets to widen the old-established repertoires of the ballet companies. One of the most successful modern ballets performed by the Royal Danish Ballet is *Qarrtsiluni,* with music by Knudåge Riisager (*b.* 1897). This deals with a festival of the midnight sun in Greenland, and is in the form of an enormous crescendo, beginning on the percussion alone, and with the other instruments of the orchestra gradually joining in: similarly the stage action begins with static groups which break into movement one by one, until the whole company is in violent motion—a simple idea, but effectively carried out here. Norway has produced little in the way of actual ballet music, but one of the leading Norwegian composers, Harald Saeverud, has produced a number of orchestral works in the form of 'slåtten', folk dances inspired by the playing of Norwegian folk fiddlers. In his hands these have developed into extended works in dance forms which could well form the foundation of a national Norwegian style of ballet: some of them, such as the 'Kjempeviseslåtten' (or Ballad of Revolt) have a somewhat demoniac character. In Sweden, where the Royal Swedish Ballet is also a long-established organization, several modern composers have written ballets for it, including the leading composer Hilding Rosenberg and his younger colleague Karl-Birger Blomdahl (1916–1968), whose ballet *Sisyphus* was produced at the Stockholm Opera in 1957. Blomdahl was a very gifted and imaginative composer who absorbed the most interesting elements in modern experimental music and integrated them into his own style, as could be seen in his remarkable cantata *The Hall of the Mirrors.* He certainly had a gift for colour and effect which was very suitable for dramatic work.

Before discussing ballet in the U.S.S.R. we may briefly mention some developments in some of the other Eastern European countries. Yugoslavia has a fairly well-established tradition of ballet, as was made clear by the visit of the Yugoslav National Opera and Ballet to London in 1955: from two of the ballets they performed then one can see that the Yugoslavs have established a national style of their own. Both these ballets date in fact from the years between the two wars: The *Devil in the Village*, by Fran Lhotka, leans towards nineteenth-century harmonic effects to some extent, but the score also contains some more 'modern' passages such as a section for percussion accompanied by string and brass glissandi and another in 5 + 2 rhythm which is no doubt based on a folk dance. The folk element is also prominent in Kreshimir Baranovich's *The Gingerbread Heart*, though here the style is more reminiscent of Kodály. At any rate the chief aim of ballet music in Yugoslavia seems to be the synthesis of folk themes and rhythms with a modern orchestral technique, and this has been successfully carried out in many cases. The unusual rhythms and scales of Slavonic folk music add a touch of piquancy to the score, and there is every sign that this translation of folk dancing into an art form makes an excellent basis for a national style of ballet. Very much the same thing has happened in Hungary, where ballet has flourished for some time. Apart from the two Bartók ballets mentioned earlier, which are now a permanent feature of the Budapest Ballet's repertoire, a number of the younger Hungarian composers have also written ballets for the company. One of the most successful of these was *Förfangos Diákok* (*The Joking Students*) by Ferenc Farkas (*b*. 1908), produced in Budapest in 1950: the story is inspired by a comic folk story, and the action takes place in the university of Debrecen. The hero is a timid and bookish student who is made drunk by his fellow-students, and while in this state is led to commit the most fantastic eccentricities. Farkas' music is bright and effective, and the score contains traditional Hungarian dances such as the 'Recruiting Dance' (*Verbunkos*) and 'Tzigane Dance', as well as a scene at the fair at Debrecen. Another leading Hungarian composer, László Lajtha, also wrote two ballets for the Hungarian National Ballet.

In the other Eastern European countries, apart of course

from Russia, ballet does not appear to be so fully developed, at any rate so far as one can tell. There is however a great deal of official encouragement of ballet, and most of the national opera houses have a ballet company of some kind, which performs the dances in the operas and gives some independent performances as well. Where ballet has an independent existence it seems to be mainly based on folk music: and all these countries have State folk-song and dance ensembles of great technical efficiency, many of which have paid visits to the West in recent years. It would seem that such new ballets as are being written in Czechoslovakia, Rumania, and Bulgaria are mainly linked to the folk-song tradition: the same applies, but perhaps to a lesser extent in Poland, where experimentation has always been more in the air. And in the case of Poland there is an example of a fine pre-war Polish ballet in the shape of Szymanowski's *Harnasie*: this is described as a dance poem, and was inspired by the songs and dances, often barbaric in character, of the inhabitants of the Tatra mountains—Harnasie is the name of the legendary robbers who lived in those parts. This is a fine score which has been successfully performed both as a ballet and a concert piece.

Ballet in Russia has developed on rather different lines from that in the Western countries: the chief difference has been the absence of the influence of Diaghilev, whose main innovations were all made after his company had left Russia. This means that experimental tendencies have in general been avoided in Soviet ballet, and also that the staple entertainment has been the full-length ballet lasting the whole evening. Some one-act ballets have survived in the present-day Russian repertoire, including *Chopiniana* in its original version (cf. pp. 88–91), and in the 'twenties a certain number of new one-act ballets were produced: but it was found that the Russian public preferred a ballet with a dramatic story which was told at length and were not so much interested in dancing for its own sake. So it has come about that most of the pure dancing in Soviet ballets takes place in divertissements which interrupt the main action, and there are no abstract ballets as such. On the other hand the standard of dancing and also of mime have remained extremely high, and enormous attention is paid to details of production. Every member of the company is acting all the time that he or she is on the stage: the scenery is mostly realistic, and the whole ballet becomes more of a danced drama than a ballet as we know it here. This is not to say that there is no dancing as such: indeed the dance element remains of great importance, but it is always subordinated to the dramatic action.

Apart from the classical full-length ballets such as *Giselle, Le Lac des Cygnes, La Belle au Bois Dormant* and *Casse-Noisette,* which of course have remained in the repertoire, a number of the older full-length ballets have also been revived, such as Pugni's *Esmeralda,* Minkus' *Le Corsaire* and *La Bayadère,* and of later ballets, Glazounov's *Raymonda.* None of these, as we have seen, are of great importance musically, though Glazounov's score does provide an effective background to the choreographic action, even if he is inferior to Tchaikovsky in this particular romantic vein. Certainly the brief extracts from the Bolshoi Ballet's production of *Raymonda* shown in the Russian film *Concert of Stars* made one realize how effective this work can be if well produced and danced.

A very large number of new ballets have been produced in Russia during the last forty years, and I can only mention some of the most important. A difficulty of course is that very few of them have been performed outside Russia or the Eastern countries, and in many cases scores are not available: also a piano score of a ballet often gives a very misleading impression of the music. However, in some cases orchestral suites have been made out of the music which have won popularity in Western countries: this is the case with Shostakovitch's ballet *The Golden Age,* first produced at the Kirov Theatre, Leningrad—formerly the Maryinsky Theatre—in

1930, with the twenty-year-old Ulanova making her first appearance in a modern ballet. (She danced the part of the Young Communist Girl of a Western Country.) This satirical ballet 'dealt with the adventures and misadventures of a Soviet football team in a capitalist country, complete with detectives, shadowings, kidnappings, brawls, and changes of attire,' as V. Bogdanov Beresovsky puts it in his book on Ulanova. The orchestral suite from the ballet which has become a well-known concert item consists of four numbers: an introduction, in gay and cheerful mood, an elegiac adagio, an important feature of which is a long euphonium solo, a witty polka with many polytonal effects and showing Shostakovitch in his best parodistic mood, and the cheerful final dance which includes some imitations of accordion music. The whole score shows Shostakovitch in a fresh and gay mood similar to that of his first symphony and the concerto for piano, trumpet, and strings. Shostakovitch has composed several other ballets which are less well-known here: these include *The Bolt, Don Quixote,* and *The Limpid Brook*—the last-named was apparently received with disfavour by the Soviet authorities on its production in 1935.

Another composer who wrote a number of ballets, chiefly full-length ones, in the 1930's was Boris Asafiev: of these *The Flames of Paris,* a ballet about the French Revolution first produced at Leningrad in 1932, has become partially known in the West through the scenes from it which appear in the Russian film *Trio-Ballet.* It is certainly an exciting and dramatic scenario, and though the music is not particularly significant it is at any rate moderately effective. Two years later came his best-known ballet, *The Fountain of Bakhchisaray*: this was performed in London by the Bolshoi Ballet on their visit in 1956, and extracts from it are also included in the film *Trio-Ballet.* The story, taken from Pushkin, concerns the abduction of a young Polish girl, Maria, by a band of Tartars, who kill her fiancé and set her home on fire: imprisoned in the harem, she refuses the advances of the Khan Girei, but is herself murdered by the Khan's previous favourite, Zarema. Her death ennobles the wild and barbaric spirit of the Khan, and he mourns her for ever. The music attempts a certain formalism in that it tries to look back towards the period of Pushkin and Glinka without directly imitating that style. This is not a very easy thing to do: and when in addition the composer needs to bring in Polish dances for the early scenes and Oriental effects for the Tartars, one can see that the score is liable to become something of a hotchpotch. There are many effective moments in the ballet, notably the wild Tartar dance at the end of the first act, and also the important solo 'cello part in the third act where Maria is repulsing Girei's advances and Zarema's jealousy is becoming apparent: the use of the passionate upper register of the cello here certainly helps the dramatic action. But in general the music does not measure up to the highly effective and dramatic story and choreography, which is a pity; and even the device of 'framing' the story by quoting a setting of Pushkin's poem by his contemporary Guriliov at the beginning and end of the ballet fails to make its effect.

In 1936 Asafiev wrote the score for another ballet, *The Lost Illusions,* vaguely based on Balzac: here the hero is a composer, and an elaborate piano solo part represents his improvisations. This work has not been seen in the West, nor has another Asafiev ballet, *The Prisoner in the Caucasus* (1938). Another ballet of this period is *The Red Poppy* by the veteran composer Reinhold Glière (1875–1956): the concert suite from this has become well known, especially the 'Russian Sailors' Dance', which is an extremely popular and effective item.

A ballet with a similar theme to *The Fountain of Bakhchisaray,* though more direct dramatically and less full of poetical symbolism, is *Gayaneh,* with music by the Georgian composer Aram Khatchaturian. Here a village wedding is interrupted by the Oriental hordes, who carry off the bride and her bridesmaids and cast them into the Shah's harem: but here the girl stabs the Shah, and is saved from vengeance in the nick of time by the arrival of her menfolk, who rescue the girls, and all ends happily. The music for this ballet is extremely dramatic and effective: Khatchaturian, coming from Tiflis, knows Oriental folk music very well, and so his use of Eastern colour in certain scenes here is done with a sure hand and never degenerates into pastiche. Much of the music is well known from concert performance, and the 'Sabre Dance' in particular has become a popular number. (Excerpts from *Gayaneh* are also included in the film *Concert of Stars*.)

But the most important Soviet ballets to date, at any rate from the musical point of view, have been those with scores by Prokofiev. The two most famous Prokofiev ballets are of course *Romeo and Juliet,* and *Cinderella*: a third ballet, *The Stone Flower,* seems to have been less generally successful. Prokofiev returned to Russia in 1933 and lived there for the remaining twenty years of his life: he began writing the *Romeo and Juliet* music in 1935, and some orchestral excerpts were performed in Russia as early as 1936: however, the complete ballet was not staged till 1940 in Leningrad, with Ulanova as Juliet. This production was seen in London during the visit of the Bolshoi Ballet in 1956: a Soviet colour film has also been made of it, though in a slightly shortened form and with some scenic alterations to fit in with film technique. Nevertheless the film does give a good idea of at any rate the most important scenes of the ballet.

The main feature of the ballet is the portrait of Juliet herself, and for her music Prokofiev used predominantly slow tempi and mostly string and woodwind writing: seven themes altogether are associated with her, representing different aspects of her personality. After the noisy music of the opening street brawl we first meet Juliet as a high-spirited girl playing with her nurse: the music here is light and full of movement, with a series of rising and falling passages punctuated by quiet,

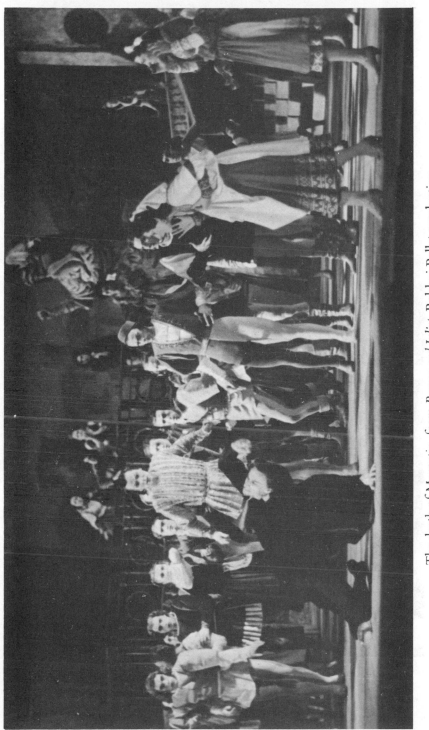

The death of Mercutio, from *Romeo and Juliet*, Bolshoi Ballet production

Igor
Stravinsky

Dame Ninette de Valois
and Sir Malcolm
Sargent addressing the
Royal Ballet Company
before their production
of *Petrouchka*

short chords 'like the clapping of hands in play' as Beresovsky puts it: but a warmer middle section suggests that she
will soon grow into a woman, and as her mother leads her
to the mirror to see her own maturity, the theme of doom
first appears in a fragmentary form on 'cello and cor anglais.
The scene of the Capulets' ball is accompanied by brilliant
orchestral colouring and powerful dance rhythms: a minuet
in 'rondo-like' form is heard behind the arrival of the guests.
When Juliet enters the music becomes lighter in texture,
though maintaining the $\frac{3}{4}$ rhythm. The climax of the scene
is the meeting between Juliet and Romeo. Prokofiev calls
this section a 'madrigal', by which he means a lyrical out-
pouring, a confession of love, with a cantabile theme for
violins and violas. Here Juliet's themes are heard lyrically and
tenderly: there is no hint of the playful girl. This leads to their
lyrical adagio . In the balcony scene Juliet's and Romeo's
themes are first exposed broadly and then interwoven poly-
phonically, but there is no real symphonic development. In
the betrothal scene in Friar Laurence's cell there is a flute
melody over an undulating accompaniment of violins,
clarinets, and harps which again seems to hint at a tragic
dénouement, as well as touches of ecclesiastical atmosphere.
After a rousing general dance in tarantella style, the duel
scene is brilliantly carried out, and one of the most striking
numbers is Mercutio's dance of death after he has been stabbed
by Tybalt: the music is based on the gay, jesting themes which
accompanied him in the scene of Capulet's ball, but here
coming hesitatingly, in fits and starts, as he tries to summon
his strength for a last brave effort of gaiety and defiance. It
is a most moving scene, especially when it is as well danced as
it was in the Bolshoi Theatre production. The finale of the
second act, in which the Capulets swear vengeance after
Tybalt's death at Romeo's hands, is a superb dramatic ensemble, accompanied by crashing chords for full orchestra.
    As a prelude to the third act Prokofiev repeats the music

which had originally accompanied the Prince's entry to quell the brawl in the first act: here it represents his sentence of banishment on Romeo, which we do not see enacted on the stage. Then comes the scene of the lovers' farewell: the music is reminiscent of that of the balcony scene. When the Nurse enters after Romeo has gone the music again reflects the playful phrases of Juliet's first scene with the Nurse, but only for a moment. After Juliet has returned from Friar Laurence with the potion a new theme appears on the bass instruments symbolizing her resolution to carry out the Friar's scheme. In her scene with Paris we are reminded of the formal quality of the minuet in her scene with him at Capulet's ball. In the tomb scene the main thematic material appears at first funereally, then more lightly: here comes the famous dance of Romeo with the seemingly dead Juliet in his arms. The music throughout this scene is lyrical and expressive, and its lightness of texture somehow underlines the tragedy more than heavier and more obviously mournful music would. Many people have criticized Prokofiev's score for *Romeo and Juliet* on the grounds of thinness, lack of drama, etc., but the point is that it was designed for the ballet and not for the concert hall. Like many ballet scores it is not always interesting to listen to by itself, but seen with the ballet it fulfils its purpose perfectly. It is naturally quite unlike Prokofiev's witty and percussive scores for the ballets which he wrote in the 'twenties for Diaghilev: if anything it has more in common with his score for *The Prodigal Son,* but it shows that Prokofiev was well capable of illustrating a lyrical and tragic story, and as presented by the Bolshoi company it is certainly one of the finest dramatic productions of our time: for this the choreographer, L. M. Lavrovsky, must take a great deal of the credit.

Cinderella was first produced at the Bolshoi Theatre in Moscow in November 1945, with choreography by Volkov: it was produced in 1948 at Covent Garden with new choreography by Frederick Ashton. As the original production is hardly known in the West, I shall deal mainly with the Sadler's Wells ballet production, which has become a firm favourite with the public ever since its first performance. The music was mostly written during the war, when the Kirov Theatre was evacuated to the town of Molotov: Prokofiev was also staying there, and so was able to work in close collaboration with the choreographer. The score is built up from a number of themes associated with the various characters: the principal one is the Midnight theme, which is associated both with Cinderella and the Fairy Queen—who is regarded to some extent as the embodiment of Cinderella's desires—and it appears both in the 'Dance of the Stars' and the famous 'Midnight Waltz'. The scoring is for large orchestra, with triple woodwind, three trumpets, four horns, four trombones, six percussion players, piano, harp, celesta, and strings: in addition there are two solo violins on stage and a brass band behind the scenes. The ballet is in three acts and consists of some fifty numbers. The music admirably succeeds in bringing the fairy tale to life, and is a successful blend of poetry and fantasy with some element of realism: so that one feels that all this could have happened, and this makes the story moving and not merely a superficial dream. Formally the score is well balanced and it is always alive and interesting rhythmically.

Act I begins with an overture, simple and direct, and stating Cinderella's theme and also that of her dream of the ball. Next comes the sewing scene with a dry jumpy rhythm which accentuates the comic character of the two Ugly Sisters: incidentally, these are usually played by men in England, following the pantomime tradition—in fact Frederick Ashton himself and his colleague Robert Helpmann have given riotous performances in these parts—but in the original Russian production they are played by women. Then Cinderella has a solo dance beginning with her own theme: this short and concise movement well expresses the pathos of her situation. Next comes the entries of the Father and the Fairy Beggar-woman—who is of course the Fairy Queen in disguise—and then the arrival of the dressmakers, hairdressers, etc., who are to fit out the two sisters for the ball. Now follows the comic scene of the dancing lesson, in which the sisters try to execute elaborate formal steps without any success; they are accompanied by two solo violinists on the stage. The sisters go off to the ball: Cinderella, left alone, dreams about the ball to the music which later becomes the main theme of the 'Midnight Waltz'. There follows a gavotte—ball-music—and then the Fairy Beggar-woman reappears. At her command the Fairies of Spring, Summer, Autumn, and Winter, together with the grasshoppers and dragonflies, appear and dance. Now the Fairy warns Cinderella that she must leave the ball before the clock strikes midnight: the music here anticipates the theme heard when the clock strikes in the next act. Cinderella goes off to the ball to the strains of a vigorous waltz which has one of the most striking melodies in the first act.

The second act begins with a kind of divertissement, with a Court dance enclosing several shorter dances: a mazurka and dance for four boys mark the arrival of the Prince, and after the entrance of Cinderella comes the big waltz, familiar as a concert piece, the themes of which have already been anticipated in the first act. After a short piece called 'A stroll' comes Cinderella's variation, with its beat constantly changing between $\frac{2}{4}$ and $\frac{3}{4}$: it is a short and very brilliant little number. After a variation for the Prince, the reception of the Guests and a duet for the two sisters comes the adagio , the pas de deux for Cinderella and the Prince, where their love is first really expressed. In the Coda-waltz which follows on from this, themes from the waltz which ends the first act are combined with those from the waltz heard earlier in the second act. Then follows the dramatic scene of the striking of midnight, admirably brought off as an orchestral effect, and Cinderella's hurried flight from the ball.

In the Soviet production the third act begins with a scene in lighter vein (this is omitted in the Royal Ballet version): it contains the entry of the Prince and the Bootmakers and three galops for the Prince with two other dances, one of them in Oriental style, sandwiched between them. The Prince has summoned all the Bootmakers in the kingdom to find out who made Cinderella's slipper: then he travels the world in search of her. Then comes the scene of Cinderella's awakening: it begins with her first dance from the first act, followed by the waltz from the end of the same act. Next is the scene of the Prince's visit to the Sisters' house, his meeting with Cinderella, a 'lingering waltz' and a final 'amoroso' which looks back to the music of Cinderella's dream of the ball in the first act. The whole score is beautifully carried out, and does exactly what is needed with both charm and mastery.

VI

Modern Developments, 1958-1972

SINCE 1958 the whole face of modern ballet has changed, a change which took place especially towards the end of the 1960s. The prettiness and artificiality of some of the older ballets has disappeared, and choreography, décor, and music have all become more forward-looking and more in keeping with modern conditions of life. This tendency has been reflected by the vast number of small experimental dance companies which have sprung up in recent years, and it is impossible to give a full description of them all. I can only note some of the most significant developments from the musical point of view.

The Royal Ballet at Covent Garden at first was not unduly experimental. Frederick Ashton remained the principal choreographer, taking over the directorship of the company when Ninette de Valois retired in 1963. His first important production in this period was *Ondine,* first given at Covent Garden on 27 October 1958. Here Ashton went back to the celebrated romantic story of the water-nymph who falls in love with a mortal, a story which had already been the subject of several operas and ballets in the nineteenth century. However, he did commission a score from a modern German composer, Hans Werner Henze, and though Henze's music was more in his earlier lyrical manner than in the more experimental style which he has adopted in recent years, it did inject a note of modernity into the romantic story while still providing a good deal of effective atmosphere. Particularly successful were the scene on board ship in the second act and the music for the entrance of the sea-creatures in the last act.

A more 'modern' ballet was *Antigone,* produced at Covent Garden on 19 October 1959, with choreography by John Cranko. Based on the classical legend, it makes a powerful plea for an individual stand against war. The choreography shows some influence of Jerome Robbins rather than the normal classical methods, and the music, by the Greek composer Mikis Theodorakis, is harsh and raw, quite unlike the popular music by which he is best known to-day. It is a very powerful and tragic piece.

MacMillan's next important ballet for the company was *The Invitation,* produced at the New Theatre, Oxford, on 10 November 1960. It is a ballet about sex, in which a young couple are involved with an older pair, the girl being savagely raped by the older man. For this MacMillan commissioned a score by Mátyás Seiber, the Hungarian-born composer who had lived in England since before the war. A former pupil of Kodály who had written some twelve-tone works, Seiber produced a score in a fairly modern idiom which suited the story well. Unfortunately he was tragically killed in a car crash a few months before the production.

After these two works in a modern idiom Covent Garden returned to more romantic themes in Ashton's next few ballets —*La Fille Mal Gardée* (1960), a new version of Dauberval's 1789 ballet set to music by Hérold; *The Two Pigeons* (1961) to André Messager's 1886 score; *Marguerite and Armand* (1963), a balletic version of Dumas' 'Dame aux Camélias' set to an orchestrated version of Liszt's B minor piano sonata; and *The Dream* (1964), based on Mendelssohn's music to Shakespeare's play. A more experimental work was Ashton's *Monotones* (1965–6), an abstract ballet to Satie's 'Gnossiennes' and 'Gymnopédies', orchestrated by Debussy and others, in which Ashton used the calm classical lines of the music to create a kind of ritual game of great beauty for the dancers, who wear starkly simple costumes on a bare stage.

Cranko had mainly been working in Stuttgart during this

period, and MacMillan, after producing an abstract ballet, *Symphony,* to Shostakovitch's First Symphony, for Covent Garden in 1963, and a pop-art version of Milhaud's *La Création du Monde* for the Royal Ballet touring company in 1964, was also mainly working in Germany. The work of both choreographers there will be discussed later. Meanwhile Ashton invited Antony Tudor back from America to create two ballets for his company. The earlier of these was *Shadowplay,* first produced at Covent Garden on 25 January 1967. In this the point of departure was the music by Charles Koechlin, a French composer of the older generation who wrote music of great originality which remained mostly unappreciated in his lifetime. The work which Tudor used was Koechlin's 'Le Livre de la Jungle' and in particular the sections called 'Les Bandar-Log' and 'La Course du Printemps', inspired by Kipling's 'Jungle Book': Koechlin saw the monkeys as symbols of anarchy and vulgarity as opposed to the order and mystery of the jungle and its 'noble' creatures and the boy Mowgli himself, and Tudor translated these symbols into balletic action. Tudor's second ballet for the company, *Knight Errant,* first produced at the Royal Opera House, Manchester, on 25 November 1968, is a bawdy comedy of amorous intrigue set to music from Strauss' *Le Bourgeois Gentilhomme* and *Ariadne auf Naxos.*

Ashton's next important ballet for the company was *Enigma Variations,* produced at Covent Garden on 25 October 1968. This is set to Elgar's famous score of the same name, using the shorter version of the finale, and is a skilful realization of the 'friends pictured within' of Elgar's dedication, but it is not just a collection of portraits: the loneliness and inner doubts of the artist are skilfully expressed by the choreography, which though restrained is always full of ideas.

Ashton retired as Director of the company in 1970. His place was taken by Kenneth MacMillan with Peter Wright as Assistant Director. Up to now there has been no major change in artistic policy. There have been some ballets with more progressive elements such as *Jazz Calendar* with its composed jazz score by the young British composer Richard Rodney Bennett and its pop-art designs, and *Sinfonietta* (Malcolm Arnold) with its psychedelic lighting effects. MacMillan's most recent full-length ballet for the company, *Anastasia* (1971), is a re-working of a ballet originally composed for Berlin. To the third act, set to Martinů's 'Symphonic Studies', MacMillan added two further acts set to Tchaikovsky's First and Third Symphonies, depicting various episodes in the life of the Russian Imperial family before the Revolution. The third act is not only quite different musically but is a dramatic exploration of the mind of the woman who claimed to be the only survivor of the family; it used a soundtrack as well as music and also incorporated films. The contrast between the realism of the first two acts—though even here the music and action do not always work well together—and the nightmare quality of the third act does not make a very well-balanced ballet. However, MacMillan is fertile in ideas and it will be interesting to see what the company does next under his direction. Meanwhile he has encouraged the work of the Royal Ballet Choreographic Group, which tries out experimental ballets with the purpose of adding the successful ones to the repertoire of either the main or the touring company. These have included such works as David Drew's *St. Thomas Wake,* set to Peter Maxwell Davies' absurd fantasy on 1920s fox-trots. A recent more experimental production for the main company was *Field Figures* by the American choreographer Glen Tetley to music by Stockhausen; Tetley's work is discussed in more detail below. MacMillan's latest ballet (1972) is *Triad,* to Prokofiev's First Violin Concerto.

The other British company of comparable age, the Ballet Rambert, though less well endowed financially and lacking the glamour of a theatre like Covent Garden, has nevertheless continued to act as a kind of gadfly to the Royal Ballet by producing works of a new and unusual kind. It was for the Rambert that Antony Tudor first produced *Jardin aux Lilas* and *Dark Elegies* before the war, and during the war the company continued to bring out new works in spite of wartime difficulties, such as Andrée Howard's *Fête Étrange* to Fauré's music, based on an episode in Alain Fournier's remarkable book 'Le Grand Meaulnes'; *Flamenco,* with music by the Spanish pupil of Schoenberg, Roberto Gerhard; and several works with commissioned scores by young British composers such as *The Fugitive* (Leonard Salzedo), *Mr. Punch* and *The Sailor's Return,* both by Arthur Oldham, and *Canterbury Prologue* (Peter Racine Fricker). Some of these ballets were produced in the immediate post-war years when the company mainly earned its living by touring, and provincial managements would only allow them to perform ballets they themselves had heard of, which rather inhibited experimentation. But from 1958 onwards the young choreographer Norman Morrice created one new ballet for them every year, usually with a modern score. *Hazaña* (1959) and *A Place in the Desert* (1961) both have music by the Latin-American composer Carlos Surinach, and after the reorganization of the company in 1966, made necessary by the increased costs of touring an orchestra and a corps de ballet, Morrice, as Associate Director of the company, was able to undertake more experimental works with his streamlined forces, which were now modelled closely on the Netherlands Dance Theatre. His *Hazard* of 1967 was a philosophical ballet on the nature of man, with a commissioned score by Leonard Salzedo, and in *1,2,3* (1968) and *Pastorale Variée* (1969) he used music by modern Israeli composers, Ben-Zim Orgad and Paul Ben-Haim respectively.

At the same time Morrice was keen to encourage new choreographers such as John Chesworth, whose *Pawn to King 5* with music by a pop group, The Pink Floyd, is a remarkable essay on the infectiousness of violence in society. The company also started a series of 'collaboration' programmes in which students from art and music colleges worked with young choreographers—a typical example is Geoff Moore's *Remembered Motion* with a score by a young student, Malcolm Fox—and other young choreographers who have produced ballets with modern scores are Amanda Knott (*Curiouser and Curiouser* to music by Elliott Carter) and Clover Roope (*Solo*—Alexander Goehr). Ballet Rambert is in a healthy condition at present, and has even found a place for experimental choreographers from abroad such as Glen Tetley, who in 1967 produced for them *Freefall*, a ballet to Max Schubel's Concerto for Five Instruments; this explores not only the physical act of falling, but also the idea of breaking loose from all conventional restraint. In the same year Tetley produced *Ziggurat* for the Ballet Rambert; based on ideas taken from Assyrian art, and using electronic scores by Karlheinz Stockhausen—'Gesang der Jünglinge' and part of 'Kontakte'—as well as projected colour film, it builds up a frightening picture of man suffering and disorientated, like an animal in his desperate frenzy. Tetley's third production for the Rambert was *Embrace Tiger and Return to Mountain* (1968), a title taken from one of the Chinese exercises of T'ai-Chi in which coolness of manner and reserve are important; for the score Tetley used an electronic work by the young American composer Morton Subotnick, 'The Silver Apples of the Moon'—cool and distant music.

Another British company which has carried out a good deal of experimental work is Western Theatre Ballet, founded in 1957. This was originally based on Bristol, and was an attempt to set up a regional ballet, but the company was soon forced on to the usual touring circuit. Director Peter Darrell's first programme in 1957 contained his ballet *The Prisoners* to Bartók's 'Music for Strings, Percussion and Celesta', and Darrell has used other Bartók scores in *A Wedding Present* (1962—Piano Concerto No. 3) and *Home* (1965—String Quartet No. 5). He also staged a new version of Debussy's *Jeux* in 1963 and his *Mods and Rockers* of the same year uses music by the Beatles. Darrell later commissioned the Australian-born composer Malcolm Williamson to write the score for a full-length ballet, *Sun into Darkness* (1966), about a village carnival turning almost accidentally into a ritual murder, a ballet which packed great theatrical punch. In 1967 Darrell asked the experienced choreographer Jack Carter to create the ballet *Cage of God* for the company. For this Carter chose music by Alan Rawsthorne, the Concerto for Ten Instruments and the Theme and Variations for Two Violins. The ballet interpreted the fall of man as a practical joke on the part of God. Carter, the resident choreographer of London's Festival Ballet (a company not noted for experimental work) had made his name in 1956 with *Witch Boy* to music by Leonard Salzedo, originally produced by the Ballet der Lage Landen in Amsterdam, where Carter worked from 1954 to 1957.

In 1969 Western Theatre Ballet moved to Glasgow and were renamed Scottish Theatre Ballet. They mainly tour Scotland and the north of England, with occasional London seasons. In 1970 Peter Darrell commissioned the Scottish composer Thea Musgrave to write a full-length ballet on the old fairy story of *Beauty and the Beast;* the result was a highly original score which contained a good deal of both sensitive and dramatic music. In 1971 Darrell produced a *Giselle* which threw out all the extra music which had crept in since the first performance and went back to Adam's complete original score.

Before leaving Britain I should mention the work of the London Contemporary Dance Company, which has several choreographic workshops, and while using the technique of Martha Graham, aims to find new choreographers of its own, such as Barry Moreland, whose *Summer Games,* set to Samuel Barber's music, is a nostalgic evocation of youthful summers. It has since continued on more and more experimental lines, and has already given two successful seasons.

In America Balanchine has remained in his dominant position as director of the New York City Ballet, but a number of new experimental companies have sprung up in recent years. In 1959 Balanchine actually tried to bridge the gulf between the classical tradition and modern dance by staging a ballet to all the works written by Webern for orchestra alone and inviting Martha Graham to undertake part of the choreography and bring her own company as guest artists. The resulting ballet, *Episodes*, was somewhat of a mixture: Martha Graham's part was a story ballet about Mary Queen of Scots, while Balanchine composed some austere classical dances and also a solo for Paul Taylor in the latter's own personal style. The ballet was later given without the modern dance sections, but the attempted collaboration was significant.

Meanwhile Robert Irving had left Covent Garden and joined the New York City Ballet as musical director, a post he still holds at the time of writing. In 1958 Balanchine staged *Stars and Stripes* to Sousa's music—one of the rare instances of his using music by an American composer—and in 1960 came *Liebeslieder Walzer,* set to both of Brahms' sets of dances for vocal quartet and piano duet; this makes a long ballet, lasting over an hour, and in spite of the ingenuity of the choreography the ear gets wearied by the perpetual ¾ rhythm—there are thirty-two waltzes in all! But Balanchine has always been catholic in his tastes, and he also created a short ballet to Stravinsky's *Movements* for orchestra, one of the master's most elliptical and Webernian works, and others to complex avant-garde works like *Metastasis* and *Pithoprakta* by the Greek-born pupil of Corbusier, Yannis Xenakis. Balanchine's *Ivesiana* uses music by the remarkable U.S. composer Charles Ives. As against this, in 1965 he mounted a full-length *Don Quixote* with a specially commissioned but undistinguished score by Nicolas Nabokov, and followed it with a new version of *Harlequinade* to music by the hack nineteenth-century composer Drigo, one of Petipa's favourite musicians. In 1967 Balanchine created the first full-length plotless ballet, *Jewels*. The first act, 'Emeralds', is danced to a selection of pieces from Fauré's music for 'Pelléas et Mélisande' and 'Shylock'; the second, 'Rubies', to Stravinsky's Concerto for Piano and Wind Instruments; and the third, 'Diamonds', to the last four movements of Tchaikovsky's Third Symphony. In this work Balanchine seems to aim at creating the atmosphere of the three countries he knows best—France in the first act, America in the second (for the music, though written by a Russian, is full of jazzy rhythms), and Russia in the third.

It would be impossible to list all of Balanchine's creations in detail; apart from works created for the New York City Ballet his ballets are in the repertoire of almost every dance company in the world, and he is without doubt the greatest classical choreographer of to-day. He does, however, sometimes invite guest choreographers to work with his own company. Jerome Robbins produced *The Afternoon of a Faun* for them in 1953 and *The Concert,* a very funny ballet danced to Chopin music orchestrated by Hershy Kay in 1956, and he returned in 1969 to create *Dances at a Gathering* for them. This is a long ballet, lasting over an hour, and again uses music by Chopin, this time in its original piano form; it has no plot, but evokes ideas of a lost European past. John Taras, who was assistant ballet master with the New York City Ballet, has re-staged Balanchine's ballets all over the world and has also created ballets for the NYCB itself, the chief being *Ebony Concerto* (1960) to the jazzy music which Stravinsky wrote for Woody Herman's band—this ballet was originally produced as part of a 'Jazz Concert'—and the more recent *Haydn Concerto.* He also reworked *Jeux* for the NYCB in 1966.

Of the other old-established American companies, Martha Graham has mainly used music by the more conservative American composers, such as William Schuman (*Night Journey*), Samuel Barber (*Cave of the Heart*), and Norman Dello Joio (*Seraphic Dialogue*). She has also turned to foreign composers on occasion—to the Mexican Carlos Chávez in *Dark Meadow* and the Israeli Halim El-Dabh in *Clytemnestra*. But on the whole the musical side of her ballets cannot be called experimental.

The same cannot be said of Martha Graham's pupil Merce Cunningham, who has had his own company since 1952. He has worked closely with John Cage and for a time with the painter Robert Rauschenberg, and he was one of the first choreographers to bring a definitely avant-garde element into ballet. Cage's theories of 'chance' music had an important influence on Cunningham's work. In *Variations V*, for instance, Cage's music was actually controlled in performance by the dancers' movements haphazardly affecting photoelectric cells arranged round the stage. But Cunningham also used composed scores—*Nocturnes* is set to music by Satie—and controlled noise: the first half of *Winterbranch* is danced in silence, while the second part is accompanied by chalk scratching on glass and a tam-tam being rubbed by a wooden stick, both amplified to an excruciating level of sound—these effects were arranged by LaMonte Young. John Cage has remained Merce Cunningham's musical director and they have continued to experiment with various types of ballet. In *How to Pass, Kick, Fall and Run* the 'score' consists of Cage sitting at the side of the stage and reading amusing extracts from one of his books to a stopwatch timing. Cunningham's solo *Collage* was set to an extract from Pierre Schaeffer's 'Symphonie pour un Homme Seul'—the first presentation of musique concrète in the United States. His *Suite by Chance* was the first work with a pure electronic sound score, commissioned from Christian Wolff.

Another Graham pupil who started his own company is Paul Taylor, but his style is completely different from Cunningham's. His *Piece Period* is a humorous period piece in reverse, with parodies of various affectations of style. His *3 Epitaphs* is a kind of surrealistic joke which sets vaudeville-style dances to music by the Laneville-Johnson Union Brass Band. Against this, *Aureole* is a purely lyrical ballet to music by Handel, and *Orbs,* set to late Beethoven string quartets, is basically a hymn of praise to man in spite of some comic episodes. Another modern dance company is that of Alvin Ailey, whose *Revelations* is a beautiful and moving suite of dances to spirituals.

Another old-established company is that of Robert Joffrey, which has had its summer residence in the New York City Center for some years. Joffrey studied both ballet and modern dance, and his early ballet *Pas des Déesses* is about the rivalry between three famous ballerinas of the past, to music by John Field. *Gamelan* (1963) creates the atmosphere of an exotic society in the form of eight 'choreographic essays'; the music by Lou Harrison imitates the sound of an Indonesian percussion ensemble and creates a mood of mysterious formality. *Viva Vivaldi!* is a display piece, while *Clowns,* to music by Hershy Kay, uses these beings as the characters for an allegory of man destroying himself through war. *Astarte* (1967) is a sensational multi-media work with music by a rock-raga group, the Crome Syrkus; it combines this with live performers, film projections, and blinding lights which make a fierce assault on the senses.

From 1962 Jerome Robbins had his own company, Ballets USA. For them he created three major works, *Moves,* a silent ballet 'about relationships', and two with symphonic jazz scores by Robert Prince—*NY Export, Opus Jazz* and *Events.* He also produced a revised version of *The Concert,* mentioned earlier, for his own company, bringing out even more clearly the humour of the contrast between the ordinary appearance of the concert-goers and their dream idealizations aroused by Chopin's music.

Like Joffrey, Glen Tetley studied both classical ballet and modern dance techniques, and he too appeared with Martha Graham, as well as American Ballet Theater and Ballets USA. In 1962 he created *Pierrot Lunaire* for his own company in New York; this subtle ballet to Schoenberg's well-known score has cross-references to *Petrouchka,* a work written in the same year as Schoenberg's, and develops the traditional struggle between the innocent white clown and the worldly-wise dark clown, mostly ignoring the Beardsleyesque imagery of Giraud's poems. Tetley then went to the Netherlands Dance Theatre (which is discussed below) but in 1966 he staged *Ricercare* for the American Ballet Theatre. This company, founded just before the war, had been temporarily disbanded owing to lack of funds, but was revived in time for a twenty-fifth anniversary season in 1964–5. For this Jerome Robbins did a new version of Stravinsky's *Les Noces*, transforming the original Russian folk dances into a universal treatment of a marriage rite. Later the company found a choreographer of their own, Eliot Feld, who created for them a Prokofiev ballet, *Harbinger*, a pure dance work, and *At Midnight*, to four of Mahler's five Rückert songs, expressing mainly the despair of love.

An extremely individual American company is that of Alwin Nikolais, who is choreographer, designer, and composer for his own works. He uses unusual tricks of lighting, so that a dancer can seem to appear and disappear, and his costumes often hide the shape of the dancer's body; the music is electronic and invariably effective. Nikolais has built up a new method which is exciting and very much his own. Among his principal ballets are *Tent*, *Tower*, *Somniloquy*, and *Sanctum*.

There are many other ballet companies of importance in America, including the Harkness Ballet, the enterprising University of Utah Repertory Dance Company, with whom Tetley has worked, and the Atlanta Ballet, for whom David Blair made some successful revivals of the classics. But it is time to turn to recent developments in Europe. In France Roland Petit has continued to produce a number of ballets for his own company, which he revived intermittently, but none of these had the success of his earlier ballets. In recent years he has created ballets to several large Romantic and post-Romantic musical works—Messiaen's *Turangalîla* symphony for the Paris

Opéra in 1968, Scriabin's *Poème de l'Extase* for La Scala, Milan, in the same year, and Schoenberg's *Pelléas and Mélisande* for Covent Garden in 1969. Unfortunately Petit's choreography often does not match his initial inspiration and ideas, and his mantle as an innovator has been taken over by another French-born choreographer, Maurice Béjart. After a period with his own company in Paris, for which he created some thirty ballets, including one to the musique concrète work by Schaeffer and Henry, *Symphonie pour un Homme Seul,* he was invited to direct the ballet at the Théâtre Royal de la Monnaie in Brussels and formed the Ballets du XXᵉ Siècle, which he still directs. For this company he has staged over forty ballets, beginning with a new version of the *Rite of Spring* which differs considerably from the original scenario—the first part is danced by men only, the second by women only, and both sexes come together only in the finale—but it is extremely effective in its own way. Béjart put on vast spectacles in large auditoria like the Royal Circus in Brussels, where he mounted ballets to Beethoven's Ninth Symphony, Berlioz' 'Romeo and Juliet', and a whole evening of Wagner. His daring as a producer is perhaps greater than his skill as an actual arranger of dances, but he has a large following. His *Sonate à Trois,* with a scenario based on Sartre's 'Huis Clos', is a claustrophobic ballet set to Bartók's Sonata for Two Pianos and Percussion. Béjart's latest full-length ballet, *Nijinsky Clown of God* (1971) mainly uses musique concrète by Pierre Henry, but also includes large sections of Tchaikovsky's *Pathétique Symphony* to represent Nijinsky's most famous dance roles.

Across the border in Holland a notable feature has been the emergence of the Nederlands Dans Theater. This was founded in 1959 by a small group headed by the American choreographer Ben Harkavy and the Dutch choreographer Hans van Manen. It aimed to use both classical and modern dance techniques and to develop a completely modern creative policy. They started with practically no resources, but were able to keep together and build up both a repertory and an audience. They aimed to put on ten new ballets a year, and have mainly succeeded in doing this. One of their early successes was *Carmina Burana,* to Orff's rumbustious score, with choreography by John Butler, an American unknown in Europe at that time. Glen Tetley put on *Pierrot Lunaire* for them, and in fact all their ballets were created by living choreographers. Tetley created *The Anatomy Lesson* for them in 1964 with music by Marcel Landowski; the scenario was inspired by Rembrandt's famous painting, showing man as victim of those who judge him—for his first ballet for the company Tetley wanted to make this a specifically Dutch work.

Tetley created seven more ballets for this company, including *Sargasso,* to music by Ernst Křenek, on the theme of woman becalmed in unhappy middle age; *Circles,* to Berio's ingenious score in which the performers play live against their own taped and distorted sounds; and *Arena,* again with a score by Morton Subotnick, set in a changing room where the pink-painted athletes' bodies suggest the bull-dancers of ancient Crete. Hans van Manen himself has also created several ballets for the company, including *Five Sketches* (1966), to Hindemith's work of that name, in which he, unusually, tries to emphasize the effort which goes into dancing, and *Solo for Voice 1* (1968), to John Cage's work of the same name. Here he put the singer on the stage and used her to inspire, incite, and provoke the dancers, who acted out a kind of mating ritual. The score is a kind of gibberish in the form of a free vocal cadenza. In another work, *Metaphors* (1966), van Manen noted that he was inspired by the vivid contrasts in the score, Daniel Lesur's Variations for Piano and String Orchestra; these generated in him a feeling of great tension which he tried to express in the contrasts between the dancers. Another member of the company, Jaap Flier, has created a ballet to György Ligeti's *Nouvelles Aventures* which represents a kind of conflict between man and the gods. Another American choreographer, Louis

Falco, mounted for the NDT in 1968 a work originally created for his own company, *Huescape,* to a collage of electronic music by Pierre Henry, Pierre Schaeffer, Lasry and Bachet. His most recent work for the NDT, *Journal* (1972), also uses a collage score, but in this case made by Burt Alcantara from the recorded voices of the dancers, and from time to time they make remarks or even just noises while they dance. The words were improvised in rehearsal sessions only very shortly before the première, and some of them are still ad-libbed in performance.

The other chief Dutch company, the Dutch National Ballet, has a different policy from the NDT: it is a large company with a big repertory ranging from the classics to the Fokine ballets, as well as revivals of famous modern works and creations by its own principal choreographer, Rudi van Dantzig, and others. Van Dantzig's most famous work, *Monument for a Dead Boy,* to music by the Dutch composer Jan Boerman, expresses in flashback the life of a boy who died young. His *Moments* of 1968 is a plotless ballet for seven dancers set to Webern's Six Bagatelles and Five Movements for String Quartet. Under his leadership the Dutch National Ballet is clearly assuming a more progressive appearance.

In Germany a great part has been played in recent years by British choreographers—if one includes the South African-born John Cranko. Since 1961 Cranko has been director of the ballet at the Stuttgart Opera House, and apart from mounting some of his earlier works there he has created a number of new ballets specially for the company. In January 1965 he staged a new version of Stravinsky's *Jeu de Cartes* there, and followed it in April with *Onegin,* a full-length ballet to music by Tchaikovsky, taken not from the opera itself but mainly from lesser-known works, though Pushkin's original story is preserved. On 7 November 1965 the Stuttgart Opera saw the première of two ballets, Cranko's *Opus 1* to Webern's early Passacaglia—a re-working of themes from his earlier ballets in a free choreographic style on the theme of the inevitability of death but the continuance of life itself—and MacMillan's *Song of the Earth*, to Mahler's mighty score, another and larger version of the same theme which is one of MacMillan's greatest ballets. MacMillan had previously created another ballet for the company in 1963, *Las Hermanas*, based on Lorca's highly dramatic play 'The House of Bernarda Alba', and set to Frank Martin's Concerto for Harpsichord and Small Orchestra. In 1968 Cranko created a more experimental ballet for the company, *Présence*, to music for piano trio by the avant-garde German composer Bernd Alois Zimmermann. This music had been written in 1961 and was intended for a ballet, but the composer had very different ideas from those of the classical ballet where the music 'carries' the dance: he wanted to juxtapose individual elements in a 'space-time structure', and the three instruments represent characters from literature—Don Quixote (violin), the idealist; Ubu Roi (piano), the earthly opportunist; and Molly Bloom (cello), the sex figure. The danced passages were set to Zimmermann's Trio and the pantomimes which precede or separate them to a mixture of taped sounds, speech, noises, and music. But Cranko returned to a more traditional approach in his two-act ballet *The Taming of the Shrew*, set to music by Kurt-Heinz Stolze after Scarlatti (1969). Peter Wright also worked with the Stuttgart company for some time and produced several ballets for them, including *The Great Peacock* in 1963; this was a reworking of a ballet originally produced by the short-lived Edinburgh International Ballet in 1958, in a season which also included the first performance of *The Night and Silence* by Walter Gore to music by Bach arranged by Charles Mackerras—the theme was the jealousy of a man for a woman which finally destroyed them both.

Kenneth MacMillan was director of the ballet at the Deutsche Oper, Berlin, from 1966 to 1969: while there he created a number of ballets, including the one-act *Anastasia* mentioned above. One of his earlier works there was *Concerto* (1966), to Shostakovitch's charming Second Piano Concerto, a work originally written for the composer's teen-age son to play with the Moscow Youth Orchestra. It is an abstract ballet of a very happy and light-weight kind. The Berlin ballet company was the only one in Germany which could present a serious challenge to Stuttgart, but at Wiesbaden the Hungarian-born choreographer and dancer Imre Keres has mounted a number of important works, including an hour-long *Romeo and Juliet* to the Berlioz score. At Hamburg, where under the direction of Rolf Liebermann the opera has long shown great enterprise in the commissioning of new works by composers from many countries, the ballet side has not yet become fully organized, but the present policy of inviting guest choreographers such as Glen Tetley and Marcel Marceau to create new works for the company looks like bearing important fruit in the near future.

The Royal Danish Ballet was taken over in 1965 by a new director, Flemming Flindt. His first ballet was a gripping adaptation of Ionesco's play *The Lesson,* about an apparently mild teacher who kills his pupil when carried away by the power he has obtained over her. The music for this ballet was by Georges Delerue, who also wrote the score for Flindt's *Three Musketeers,* a vigorous and brawling treatment of the Dumas story. Flindt also mounted his own version of Bartók's *Miraculous Mandarin,* a work which is well performed to-day by the Budapest Opera in a programme which also includes Bartók's other two stage works, *The Wooden Prince* and *Bluebeard's Castle.* Further east I should mention the work of the Batsheva Dance Company of Israel, who have mounted a number of enterprising productions. For them Tetley created *Mythical Hunters* to music by the leading Israeli composer Oedeon Partos. Here the dances are images of hunting, fight, and capture, in which each captured prey gives birth to a successor. In Czechoslovakia the Ballet Prague produced such enterprising works as Pavel Smok's *Frescoes,* to music by Martinů, and his *Gangrene,* to a score by Charlie Mingus.

In Russia ballet continued for some time in a fairly old-fashioned manner. In 1957, for instance, Vakhtang Chabukiani mounted an *Othello* in Tbilisi with music by Alexei Machavariani which gave an interesting account of the leading characters, but within the framework of the old heavy monumental style. But about the same time the young choreographer Yuri Grigorovitch staged a new version of Prokofiev's *The Stone Flower,* which had previously been unsuccessful in Lavrovsky's traditional production, and showed a new tendency in Soviet ballet: he rearranged the musical sequence, invented new choreography, and set the work as a series of dance episodes telling the story in dance terms without old-fashioned mime. This version was first staged by the Kirov Ballet in Leningrad and later by the Bolshoi in Moscow and at Novosibirsk.

The influence of foreign ballet companies had begun to infect Russian ballet, particularly the Paris Opéra Ballet, who took Balanchine's *Le Palais de Cristal,* to Bizet's Symphony in C, on a Russian tour, and also the New York City Ballet, who went to Moscow and Leningrad with the Webern ballet *Episodes* in 1962. In 1961 the young choreographer Igor Belsky made a highly dramatic ballet to the first movement of Shostakovitch's *Leningrad Symphony,* portraying the agony and ultimate triumph of the people of Leningrad during the war years when the Nazis were besieging the city; and in 1962 Kasyan Goleizovsky staged *Scriabiniana,* a suite of dances to Scriabin's music. Grigorovitch, now the director of the Bolshoi Ballet, has made a new version for them of the Khatchaturian ballet *Spartacus,* on the subject of a slaves' revolt in ancient Rome, and it is clear that choreographically, if not yet musically, Soviet ballet is adopting a more forward-looking attitude.

I would like to conclude this brief survey of modern ballet with a discussion of two tendencies which may become more marked in the future. Firstly, the use of ballet in television, especially now that colour television is becoming more widespread. Up to now little has been done except attempts to transfer already existing ballets to the television screen, but Peter Darrell, for instance, in two ballets specially created by Western Theatre Ballet for BBC Television, explored the idea that ordinary dancing on the small screen always looks out of place, and that what was wanted was simple movement based on a dancer's sense of rhythm and timing. He carried out these ideas in *House Party*, a new working of Poulenc's music to *Les Biches*, and *Orpheus*, to music by Raymond Leppard, with Orpheus seen as a pop star and Eurydice as a model girl. Clearly there is room for new ideas in television ballet which may well expand in the future. The other newish tendency is the increased use of vocal music, which has already been noted in several ballets, sometimes with orchestral accompaniment and sometimes on its own. This can certainly add a new dimension to ballet which is well worth exploring.

POSTSCRIPT

What is Ballet Music?

A S we have seen in the course of this short survey, ballets have been arranged to music of all kinds ranging from Vivaldi concertos to musique concrète. Can one then define the essentials of good ballet music? Obviously it must have rhythm and colour: melody, though desirable, is not so completely essential, as we can see in *Le Sacre du Printemps,* for instance. And it is best if the music is in short self-contained sections, each of which can be fitted to an individual dance: or if the ballet is based on a longer continuous work, such as a symphonic poem, for instance, it should contain a large number of short episodes or changes of mood which can be paralleled in the choreography. Franck's Symphonic Variations work well as a ballet score because each variation is comparatively short, whereas the symphonies of Beethoven and Brahms, and even those of Berlioz and Tchaikovsky, do not, because each movement is built up as a continuous whole and not as a number of short episodes loosely linked together. Two minutes is a long duration for a solo dance, and even a pas de deux or pas de cinq will rarely last more than four: how then can a symphonic movement lasting ten or twelve minutes make a satisfactory basis for dancing? And there is another point which Constant Lambert made in his essay on 'Music and Action' (in *Footnotes to the Ballet,* ed. Caryl Brahms, London, 1936): 'It cannot be emphasized too strongly,' he says, 'that although the composer is forced to adopt time as his medium he does not always approach time in the same way. Sometimes his themes succeed each other in dramatic sequence like the acts of a play, sometimes their sequence and their position in time are dictated by purely formal reasons. In a symphonic poem by Liszt or Strauss the former is the case. The triumphant apotheosis or pathetic death-scenes which end their works are definitely the last act of the play and represent the final word on the subject in hand. But this is not so in the case of a Mozart symphony. We have it on his own authority that Mozart conceived a symphony in its full form at one moment of time. It stands to reason, then, that the return of a theme in his works can have no narrative or dramatic significance. The recapitulation balances the exposition, much as a tree on one side of a picture might balance one on the other. We do not look at a picture "reading from left to right" as in a society photograph, but take in its design as a whole: and though we inevitably have to listen to a Mozart symphony from left to right, as it were, we should try as far as possible to banish this aspect of the work from our minds and try to see it as the composer conceived it, in one moment of time.'

That is the point: and choreography inevitably emphasizes the time-sequence of the music. This is the great weakness of symphonic ballets—apart perhaps from purely abstract ballets set to symphonic works of a fairly light calibre: and it is really best for the choreographer to choose a series of fairly short pieces for his individual dances or to have a score specially written which will carry out his ideas. In fact one can say that it is almost always better to have a score specially composed —certainly for any kind of dramatic or narrative ballet— unless for reasons of time or money this is impossible: there have been many successes in fitting choreography to previously written music, but they are far outnumbered by the failures.

How, then, is a ballet written? The king-pin is of course the choreographer: normally he starts out with a fairly clear idea of the kind of ballet he wishes to create: and if he is not lucky enough to find some previously written music which exactly

suits his ideas, he will ask a composer to write a score for
him. Here he has to be careful to choose a composer who will
write the kind of music he wants: and often the creation of a
ballet goes irreparably wrong at this stage. Though the choreographer will of course have a good intuitive feeling for music,
often he does not have a great knowledge of musical technique,
and he has to trust his intuition alone. He knows in his mind
the kind of music he wants, but he cannot express this in
words: his best method is to choose a composer whose work
he already knows and hope that he will get the results he
desires, and here there is always an element of chance.

The choreographer now furnishes the composer with a
detailed plan of the ballet, including not only the general
course of the dramatic action—if any—but also the details
of each individual section and dance: he will indicate the
approximate length each dance should be, as well as its speed
and character. The instructions given by Petipa to Tchaikovsky regarding Casse-Noisette (quoted on pp. 83-4) are typical
of this; except that nowadays the choreographer would indicate the duration of each section in minutes and seconds rather
than in bars—regular sequences of bars are not so common in
modern ballets. From this the composer will produce a piano
score of the ballet, and on this the choreographer bases his
dance movements. Here again there is a danger, as the piano
score of an orchestral work can often give an extremely
misleading impression, and often neither the choreographer
nor the dancers are able to hear the orchestral score of the
ballet until a few days before the first performance: by this
time all the movements have been worked out by the choreographer and rehearsed and learnt by the dancers, and it is too
late to make any changes if the piano score has given a false
impression of what the music sounds like on the orchestra.
And often the dancers are put off by the music at this stage:
they miss things in the orchestra which they were used to
hearing in the piano score, and may find that certain phrases

which they never heard in the piano score now suddenly emerge in the orchestra, to the detriment of what they were used to hearing at that particular point. This difficulty can be obviated to some extent nowadays by making a recording of the orchestral score—if it is ready in time and the orchestra is available—and rehearsing the dancers with that: but in general it is up to the composer to see that what will stand out prominently on the orchestra will also do so in the piano score, even if the latter thereby becomes somewhat unpianistic.

And what sort of music should he write? As we have seen, atmosphere and rhythm are the essentials: the dancers learn their movements by counting beats, so the rhythm must always be felt by them. The rhythms may be extremely complex—this is not so important provided that some rhythm is always there. And if it does not possess an atmosphere the music cannot help the choreographer in the creation of his dance movements: he has to interpret into visual action the effect the music makes on him, and then demonstrate these movements to the dancers so that they can copy and learn them. Various methods of choreographic notation have been worked out and are in use, but even so the movements have to be shown to the dancers in practice. So the creation of a ballet is an extremely complex affair in which the composer has to join and play his part in the best way he can: he should ideally be at the complete disposal of the choreographer for any necessary alterations or adjustments.

Ballet music must make its effect immediately: it is no use writing complex structures which require a great deal of intellectual effort to appreciate them. For this reason some of the severer classical forms, such as fugue, are not normally suitable to ballet: their structure is too self-contained to go well with the dance, and there may be a tendency to associate each entry of the fugue subject with a choreographic idea, which can lead to boring results. There are of course exceptions to this: Constant Lambert, in the essay mentioned above, quotes two examples from his own ballets of what he calls 'choreographic counterpoint', in which the choreographer is deliberately doing something which differs from the texture of the music. 'One', he says, 'was Ashton's treatment of a three-part fugato in *Pomona* as a lyrical dance for a *solo* dancer: the other was the astonishing choreographic fugue which Nijinska arranged to a purely homophonic passage in the finale of *Romeo and Juliet*.' But in general polyphonic complexity is best avoided in ballet music: one cannot hear all the themes simultaneously, and the result tends to be confused.

This is not to say that ballet music should be obvious and superficial: indeed it can be extremely subtle in its evocation of atmosphere. All one can say is that it should make its effect by simple means if possible, even if the effect aimed at is a complex one. And in the creation of atmosphere it is a great help if the composer collaborates not only with the choreographer but with the designer as well: he must know what the stage is going to look like while his music is being played, and similarly it helps the designer to know what kind of atmosphere will emerge from the music. If all three principals in the creation of a ballet can work closely together from the early stages onwards there is much more chance of it being a properly integrated whole, which the best ballets have always been. It is no use the composer turning out yards of score in a vacuum, and then letting the choreographer get on with it, so to speak: he is only likely to produce a lot of symphonic dances which are quite unsuitable for ballet. It is only through close collaboration, with the choreographer as the dominant partner, that there is any hope of a successful new creation.

DETAILS OF SOME
FIRST PERFORMANCES

Date	Title	Place
15 October 1581	BALLET COMIQUE DE LA REINE LOUISE	
23 February 1653	BALLET DE LA NUIT	Paris
14 February 1656	BALLET DE LA GALANTERIE DU TEMPS	Paris
17 January 1657	L'AMOUR MALADE	Paris
14 February 1658	BALLET D'ALCIDIANE	Paris
29 January 1664	LE MARIAGE FORCÉ	Le Louvre, Paris
14 October 1670	LE BOURGEOIS GENTILHOMME	Chambord
21 January 1681	LE TRIOMPHE DE L'AMOUR	Saint-Germain
23 August 1735	LES INDES GALANTES	Théâtre de l'Opéra, Paris
1761	DON JUAN	Burgtheater, Vienna
1775	BALLET ESPAGNOL	Vienna
11 June 1778	LES PETITS RIENS	Théâtre de l'Opéra, Paris
31 October 1786	THE WHIMS OF CUPID AND THE DANCING MASTER	Royal Theatre, Copenhagen
1791	RITTERBALLETT	Bonn
1794	LA FÊTE DE LA RAISON (LA ROSIÈRE RÉPUBLICAINE)	
28 March 1801	THE CREATIONS OF PROMETHEUS	Burgtheater, Vienna
14 May 1832	LA SYLPHIDE	Théâtre de l'Académie Royale de Musique, Paris
28 June 1841	GISELLE	Théâtre de l'Académie Royale de Musique, Paris
29 March 1842	NAPOLI	Royal Theatre, Copenhagen
22 June 1842	LA JOLIE FILLE DE GAND	Théâtre de l'Académie Royale de Musique, Paris
9 March 1844	LA ESMERALDA	Her Majesty's Theatre, London
20 March 1854	A FOLK TALE	Royal Theatre, Copenhagen
23 January 1856	LE CORSAIRE	Théâtre de l'Académie Royale de Musique, Paris
12 November 1866	LA SOURCE	Théâtre Impérial de l'Opéra, Paris
25 May 1870	COPPÉLIA, OU LA FILLE AUX YEUX D'EMAIL	Théâtre Impérial de l'Opéra, Paris
17 December 1872	CAMARGO	Maryinsky Theatre, St. Petersburg
14 June 1876	SYLVIA, OU LA NYMPHE DE DIANE	Théâtre de l'Opéra, Paris

Choreographer	Composer	Décor	Dancers
	Baltasar de Beaujoyculx		
Text by Benserade	Lully		Louis XIV
	Lully		
Text by Benserade	Lully		
Text by Benserade	Lully		
Text by Molière	Lully		
Text by Molière	Lully		
Quinault and Benserade	Lully		
	Rameau		
Angiolini	Gluck		
	Boccherini		
Noverre	Mozart		
Galeotti	Lolle		
	Beethoven		
	Grétry		
Vigano	Beethoven		
Taglioni	Scheitzhoeffer	Lami	Taglioni, M. Taglioni
Coralli and Perrot	Adam	Ciceri	Grisi, L. Petipa
Book by Bournonville	Paulli, E. Helsted, and Gade	Christensen	Bournonville, Fjelsted
Albert	Adam	Ciceri, Philastre, and Cambon	Grisi, Albert, Coralli, Petipa
Perrot	Pugni	Grieve	Grisi, Perrot
Bournonville	Gade and Hartmann	Christensen and Lund	Price, Hoppensach, Stramboe
Mazelier	Adam	Despléchin, Cambon, Thierry, and Martin	
Saint-Léon	Minkus and Delibes	Despléchin, Lavastre, Rubé, and Chaperon	Salvioni, Coralli
Saint-Léon	Delibes	Cambon, Despléchin, and Lavastre	Bozacchi, Fiocre
Petipa	Minkus	Roller	Grantzova, Gerdt
Mérante	Delibes	Chéret, Rubé, and Chaperon	Sangalli

Date	Title	Place
2 January 1890	LA BELLE AU BOIS DORMANT	Maryinsky Theatre, St. Petersburg
5 December 1892	CASSE-NOISETTE	Maryinsky Theatre, St. Petersburg
15 January 1895	LE LAC DES CYGNES	Maryinsky Theatre, St. Petersburg
7 January 1898	RAYMONDA	Maryinsky Theatre, St. Petersburg
7–20 February 1900	LES SAISONS	Hermitage Theatre, St. Petersburg
9 November 1907	LA TRAGÉDIE DE SALOMÉ	Théâtre des Arts, Paris
19 May 1909	PRINCE IGOR	Théâtre du Châtelet, Paris
2 June 1909	LES SYLPHIDES	Théâtre du Châtelet, Paris
20 May 1910	LE CARNAVAL (Standard Version) (Original version St. Petersburg, Lent 1910)	Theater des Westens, Berlin
4 June 1910	SCHÉHÉRAZADE	Théâtre Nationale de l'Opéra, Paris
25 June 1910	L'OISEAU DE FEU	Théâtre Nationale de l'Opéra, Paris
19 April 1911	LE SPECTRE DE LA ROSE	Théâtre de Monte Carlo
13 June 1911	PETROUCHKA	Théâtre du Châtelet, Paris
21 January 1912	MA MÈRE L'OYE	Théâtre des Arts, Paris
22 April 1912	ADÉLAÏDE, OU LE LANGAGE DES FLEURS	Théâtre du Châtelet, Paris
20 May 1912	THAMAR	Théâtre du Châtelet, Paris
29 May 1912	L'APRÈS–MIDI D'UN FAUNE	Théâtre du Châtelet, Paris
8 June 1912	DAPHNIS ET CHLOË	Théâtre du Châtelet, Paris
3 April 1913	LE FESTIN DE L'ARAIGNÉE (ballet pantomime)	Théâtre des Arts, Paris

Choreographer	Composer	Décor	Dancers
Petipa	Tchaikovsky	Levogt, Ivanov	Brianza, Oblakov
Ivanov	Tchaikovsky	Botcharov	Belinskaya, Del-Era
Petipa and Ivanov	Tchaikovsky	Botcharov and Levogt	Legnani, Gerdt
Petipa	Glazunov	Allegri, Ivanov, and Lambini	Legnani
Petipa	Glazunov	Lambini	Preobrazhenskaya Kshessinskaya, Legat
Guerra	Florent Schmitt		Fuller
Fokine	Borodin (cond. E. Cooper)	Roehrich	Smirnova, Fedorova, Bolm
Fokine	Chopin	Benois	Pavlova, Karsavina, Nijinsky
Fokine	Schumann (cond. Tcherepnine)	Bakst	Karsavina, Nijinsky, Bolm
Fokine	Rimsky-Korsakov	Bakst	Karsavina, Nijinsky, Cecchetti
Fokine	Stravinsky (cond. Pierné)	Golovine	Karsavina, Fokine, Cecchetti
Fokine	Weber	Bakst	Karsavina, Nijinsky
Fokine	Stravinsky (cond. P. Monteux)	Benois	Karsavina, Nijinsky
Jane Hugard	Ravel (cond. Grovlez)	Drésa	
Trukhanova	Ravel (*Valses Nobles et Sentimentales*) (cond. by composer)	Drésa	Trukhanova, Bekefi
Fokine	Balakirev (cond. P. Monteux)	Bakst	Karsavina, Bolm
Nijinsky	Debussy (cond. P. Monteux)	Bakst	Nijinsky, Nijinska
Fokine	Ravel (cond. P. Monteux)	Bakst	Karsavina, Nijinsky, Bolm
Author, de Voisins	Roussel		

Date	Title	Place
15 May 1913	JEUX (poème dansé)	Théâtre des Champs-Elysées, Paris
29 May 1913	LE SACRE DU PRINTEMPS	Théâtre des Champs-Elysées, Paris
17 May 1914	LA LÉGENDE DE JOSEPH	Théâtre Nationale de l'Opéra, Paris
24 May 1914	LE COQ D'OR (opera-ballet)	Théâtre Nationale de l'Opéra, Paris
12 April 1917	LES FEMMES DE BONNE HUMEUR	Teatro Costanza, Rome
12 May 1917	THE WOODEN PRINCE	Budapest
18 May 1917	PARADE	Théâtre du Châtelet, Paris
5 June 1919	LA BOUTIQUE FANTASQUE	Alhambra Theatre, London
22 July 1919	LE TRICORNE (EL SOMBRERO DE TRES PICOS)	Alhambra Theatre, London
2 February 1920	LE CHANT DU ROSSIGNOL	Théâtre de l'Opéra, Paris
21 February 1920	LE BŒUF SUR LE TOIT	Paris
15 May 1920	PULCINELLA	Théâtre de l'Opéra, Paris
8 November 1920	LE TOMBEAU DE COUPERIN	Paris
17 May 1921	CHOUT	Gaieté-Lyrique, Paris
6 June 1921	L'HOMME ET SON DÉSIR	Théâtre des Champs-Elysées, Paris
19 June 1921	LES MARIÉS DE LA TOUR EIFFEL	Théâtre des Champs-Elysées, Paris
2 November 1921	THE SLEEPING PRINCESS	Alhambra Theatre, London
18 May 1922	LE RENARD	Théâtre de l'Opéra, Paris
13 July 1923	LES NOCES	Gaieté-Lyrique, Paris
25 October 1923	WITHIN THE QUOTA	Théâtre des Champs-Elysées, Paris
25 October 1923	LA CRÉATION DU MONDE	Théâtre des Champs-Elysées, Paris

Choreographer	Composer	Décor	Dancers
Nijinsky	Debussy	Bakst	Karsavina, Schollar, Nijinsky
Nijinsky	Stravinsky (cond. P. Monteux)	Roehrich	Piltz, Goulok, Woronzow
Fokine	Richard Strauss (cond. by composer)	Sert, Bakst	Karsavina, Massine
Fokine	Rimsky-Korsakov	Gontcharova	Karsavina, Bulgakov, Cecchetti
Massine	Scarlatti– Tommasini	Bakst	Lopokova, Tcherni- cheva, Massine, Cec- chetti, Idzikovsky, Woizikovsky
Balázs	Bartók		
Massine	Satie	Picasso	Lopokova, Massine
Massine	Rossini– Respighi	Derain	Sokolova, Lopokova, Massine
Massine	de Falla	Picasso	Karsavina, Massine
Massine	Stravinsky (cond. Ansermet) Milhaud	Matisse	Karsavina, Sokolova, Grigoriev
Massine	Pergolesi– Stravinsky	Picasso	Karsavina, Tcherni- cheva, Massine
Jean Borlin	Ravel	Pierre Laprade	Borlin
Larionov and Slavinsky	Prokofiev	Larionov	Devillier, Slavinsky
Borlin	Milhaud	Andrée Parr	Borlin, Johanson
Borlin	Auric, Honegger, Milhaud, Pou- lenc, Tailleferre	Lagut	Witzansky Vahlander
Petipa and Nijinska	Tchaikovsky	Bakst	Spessivtzeva, Trefilova
Nijinska	Stravinsky (libretto & music)	Gontcharova	Nijinska, Idzikovsky
Nijinska	Stravinsky (libretto & music)	Gontcharova	Tchernicheva, Dou- brovska, Semenov
Borlin	Cole Porter	Murphy	Borlin, Bonsdorff
Borlin	Milhaud	Léger	Borlin, Strandin

[219]

Date	Title	Place
6 January 1924	Les Biches	Théâtre de Monte Carlo
9 May 1924	Schlagobers (Whipped Cream)	Operntheater, Vienna
17 May 1924	Salade	Théâtre Cigale, Paris
15 June 1924	Mercure	Théâtre Cigale, Paris
20 June 1924	Le Train Bleu	Théâtre des Champs-Elysées, Paris
19 November 1924	La Jarre	Théâtre des Champs-Elysées, Paris
29 November 1924	Relâche	Théâtre des Champs-Elysées, Paris
17 June 1925	Les Matelots	Gaieté-Lyrique, Paris
11 December 1925	Barabau	Coliseum, London
4 May 1926	Romeo and Juliet—A Rehearsal Without Scenery	Théâtre de Monte Carlo
3 July 1926	Jack in the Box	Théâtre Sarah Bernhardt, Paris
27 November 1926	The Miraculous Mandarin	Cologne
3 December 1926	The Triumph of Neptune	Lyceum Theatre, London
1927	Pomona	Buenos Aires
27 May 1927	La Chatte	Théâtre de Monte Carlo
7 June 1927	Le Pas d'Acier	Théâtre Sarah Bernhardt, Paris
16 April 1928	Rhapsody in Blue	Théâtre des Champs-Elysées, Paris
12 June 1928	Apollon Musagète	Théâtre Sarah Bernhardt, Paris
16 July 1928	The Gods Go A-Begging	His Majesty's Theatre, London
22 November 1928	Bolero	Théâtre de l'Opéra, Paris
22 November 1928	La Bien Aimée	Théâtre de l'Opéra, Paris
27 November 1928	Le Baiser de la Fée	Théâtre de l'Opéra, Paris
1929	La Valse	Théâtre de l'Opéra, Paris
12 May 1929	Le Fils Prodigue	Théâtre Sarah Bernhardt, Paris

Choreographer	Composer	Décor	Dancers
Nijinska	Poulenc	Laurencin	Nemchinova, Nijinska
Kröller	R. Strauss	Nigrin	Pichler, Losch
Massine	Milhaud	Braque	Massine
Massine	Satie	Picasso	
Nijinska	Milhaud	Laurens, Chanel; curtain by Picasso	Nijinska, Sokolova, Dolin
Borlin	Casella	Chirico	Friis, Borlin
Borlin and Picabia	Satie	Picabia	Borlin, Bonsdorff
Massine	Auric	Pruna	Sokolova, Nemchinova, Woizikovsky, Lifar, Slavinsky
Balanchine	Rieti	Utrillo	Woizikovsky, Lifar
Nijinska	Lambert	Ernst and Miro	Karsavina, Lifar
Balanchine (entr'acte)			
Balanchine	Satie Bartók	Derain	Danilova, Idzikovsky
Balanchine	Berners	Prince Shervachidze	Danilova, Lifar, Balanchine
Nijinska	Lambert		
Balanchine	Saguet	Gabo and Pevsner	Nikitina, Lifar
Massine	Prokofiev	Yakoulov	Tchernicheva, Danilova, Lifar, Massine
Dolin	Gershwin	Gladys Spencer-Curling	Nemchinova, Dolin
Balanchine	Stravinsky	Beauchant	Danilova, Tchernicheva, Doubrovska, Lifar
Balanchine	Handel–Beecham (cond. Beecham)	Bakst, Gris	Danilova, Tchernicheva
Nijinska	Ravel		Rubinstein
Nijinska	Schubert, Liszt, Milhaud	Benois	Rubinstein, Vilzak
Nijinska	Stravinsky (cond. by composer)		Rubinstein
Nijinska	Ravel	Benois	Rubinstein, Vilzak
Balanchine	Prokofiev	Rouault	Doubrovska, Lifar, Dolin

[221]

Date	Title	Place
26 October 1930	THE GOLDEN AGE	Kirov Theatre, Leningrad
26 April 1931	FAÇADE	Cambridge Theatre, London
5 July 1931	JOB	Cambridge Theatre, London
12 April 1932	COTILLON	Théâtre de Monte Carlo
3 July 1932	THE GREEN TABLE	Théâtre des Champs-Elysées, Paris
7–20 November 1932	THE FLAMES OF PARIS	Kirov Theatre, Leningrad
12 December 1932	ON THE BANKS OF THE BORYSTHENES	Théâtre de l'Opéra, Paris
19 February 1933	GLI UCCELLI	Casino Municipale di San Remo
13 April 1933	LES PRÉSAGES	Théâtre de Monte Carlo
24 October 1933	CHOREARTIUM	Alhambra Theatre, London
5 December 1933	LES RENDEZVOUS	Sadler's Wells Theatre, London
22 September 1934	THE FOUNTAIN OF BAKHCHISARAY	Kirov Theatre, Leningrad
20 May 1935	THE RAKE'S PROGRESS	Sadler's Wells Theatre, London
9 July 1935	ICARE	Théâtre de l'Opéra, Paris
11 February 1936	APPARITIONS	Sadler's Wells Theatre, London
4 April 1936	L'EPREUVE D'AMOUR	Monte Carlo
25 June 1936	DON JUAN	Alhambra Theatre, London
24 July 1936	SYMPHONIE FANTASTIQUE	Royal Opera House, London
10 November 1936	NOCTURNE	Sadler's Wells Theatre, London
16 February 1937	LES PATINEURS	Sadler's Wells Theatre, London
27 April 1937	THE CARD PARTY (later JEU DE CARTES)	Metropolitan Opera House, New York
27 April 1937	A WEDDING BOUQUET	Sadler's Wells Theatre, London
1 June 1937	CHECKMATE	Théâtre des Champs-Elysées, Paris
27 January 1938	HOROSCOPE	Sadler's Wells Theatre, London
October 1938	BILLY THE KID	Chicago
11 January 1940	ROMEO AND JULIET	Kirov Theatre, Leningrad
23 January 1940	DANTE SONATA	Sadler's Wells Theatre, London
24 April 1940	THE WISE VIRGINS	Sadler's Wells Theatre, London
27 January 1941	THE WANDERER	New Theatre, London

Choreographer	Composer	Décor	Dancers
Vynonen and Yakobson	Shostakovitch	Khodasevitch	Ulanova, Jordan
Ashton	Walton	Armstrong	Markova, Lopokova, Ashton
de Valois	Vaughan Williams	Raverat	Dolin
Balanchine	Chabrier	Bérard	Toumanova, Lichine
Kurt Jooss	Cohen	Heckroth	Jooss
Vynonen	Asafiev	Dmitriev	Ulanova
Lifar	Prokofiev	Larionov	Lifar
Fornaroli	Respighi		
Massine	Tchaikovsky (Fifth Symphony)	Masson	Riabouchinska, Lichine
Massine	Brahms (Fourth Symphony)	Terechkovich and Lourie	Baronova, Riabouchinska, Lichine
Ashton	Auber–Lambert	Chappell	
Zakharov	Asafiev	Khodasevich	Ulanova
de Valois	Gavin Gordon	Rex Whistler	Markova, Gore
Lifar	Rhythms by Lifar, orch. Szyfer	Larthe	Lifar
Ashton	Liszt–Jacob	Cecil Beaton	Fonteyn, Helpmann
Fokine	Mozart	Derain	Nemchinova, Eglevsky
Fokine	Gluck	Andreù	Vilzak, Lauret
Massine	Berlioz	Bérard	Toumanova, Massine
Ashton	Delius	Fedorovitch	Fonteyn, Helpmann
Ashton	Meyerbeer–Lambert	Chappell	Fonteyn, Helpmann
Balanchine	Stravinsky		William Dollar
Ashton	Berners	Berners	Honer, Fonteyn, Farron de Valois, Helpmann
de Valois	Bliss	Kauffer	Brae, May, Helpmann, Turner
Ashton	Lambert	Fedorovitch	Fonteyn, Somes
Loring	Copland	French	Loring
Lavrovsky	Prokofiev	P. Williams	Ulanova, Sergeyev
Ashton	Liszt–Lambert	Fedorovitch	Fonteyn, Somes
Ashton	Bach–Walton	Rex Whistler	Fonteyn, Somes
Ashton	Schubert–Liszt	Sutherland	Helpmann

Date	Title	Place
1941	BALLET IMPERIAL	American Ballet Caravan in South America
11 February 1941	THREE VIRGINS AND A DEVIL	New York
April 1942	PILLAR OF FIRE	Metropolitan Opera House, New York
19 May 1942	HAMLET	New Theatre, London
26 October 1942	RODEO	Metropolitan Opera House, New York
April 1944	FANCY FREE	Metropolitan Opera House, New York
September 1944	DANSES CONCERTANTES	City Center, New York
26 October 1944	MIRACLE IN THE GORBALS	Princes Theatre, London
2 March 1945	LES FORAINS	Théâtre des Champs-Elysées, Paris
21 November 1945	CINDERELLA	Bolshoi Theatre, Moscow
24 April 1946	SYMPHONIC VARIATIONS	Royal Opera House, London
25 June 1946	LE JEUNE HOMME ET LA MORT	Théâtre des Champs-Elysées, Paris
July 1947	LE PALAIS DE CRISTAL	Théâtre de l'Opéra, Paris
26 November 1947	MAM'ZELLE ANGOT	Royal Opera House, London
15 January 1948	ETUDES	Royal Theatre, Copenhagen
11 February 1948	SCÈNES DE BALLET	Royal Opera House, London
28 April 1948	ORPHEUS	City Center, New York
6 April 1948	CHILDREN'S CORNER	Sadler's Wells Theatre, London
22 April 1948	FALL RIVER LEGEND	Metropolitan Opera House, New York
22 May 1948	LES DEMOISELLES DE LA NUIT	Théâtre Marigny, Paris
21 October 1949	ABRAXAS	Städtische Oper, Berlin
20 February 1950	DON QUIXOTE	Royal Opera House, London
5 May 1950	BALLABILE	Royal Opera House, London
13 March 1951	PINEAPPLE POLL	Sadler's Wells Theatre, London

Choreographer	Composer	Décor	Dancers
Balanchine	Tchaikovsky (*Second Piano Concerto*)	Dobujinski	Marie-Jeanne
de Mille	Respighi	Motley	de Mille, Loring
Tudor	Schoenberg	Mielzinev	Kaye, Laing, Tudor
Helpmann	Tchaikovsky	Hurry	Fonteyn, Rassine, Helpmann
de Mille	Copland	Oliver Smith	de Mille, Miladova, Franklin
Robbins	Bernstein (cond. by composer)	Oliver Smith	Laing, Kriza
Balanchine	Stravinsky	Berman	Danilova, Danielian
Helpmann	Bliss	Burra	Shearer, Helpmann
Petit	Henri Sauguet	Bérard	Pagava, Petit
Zakharov	Prokofiev	P. Williams	Lepeshinskaya, Preobrazhensky
Ashton	Franck	Fedorovitch	Fonteyn, Somes, Shearer, Shaw, May, Danton
Petit	Bach (*Organ Passacaglia*)	Wakhewitch	Philippart, Babilée
Balanchine	Bizet (*Symphony in C*)	Fini	Toumanova
Massine	Lecocq–Jacob	Derain	Fonteyn, Somes
H. Lander	Czerny–Riisager	Nordgren	M. Lander, Bronaa, Jensen
Ashton	Stravinsky	Beaurepaire	Fonteyn, Somes
Balanchine	Stravinsky	Noguchi	Maria Tallchief, Magallanes
Cranko	Debussy	le Witt	Shore, Miller, Page Poole, MacMillan
de Mille	Gould	Oliver Smith	Alonso, Krupska
Petit	Françaix	Fini	Fonteyn, Petit
Charrat	Egk	Fenneker	Charrat, Orben
de Valois	Gerhard	Burra	Fonteyn, Helpmann, Grant
Petit	Chabrier–Lambert	Clavé	Elvin, Grant
Cranko	Sullivan–Mackerras	Lancaster	Fifield, Blair

Date	Title	Place
9 July 1951	TIRESIAS	Royal Opera House, London
12 December 1951	DONALD OF THE BURTHENS	Royal Opera House, London
4 March 1952	A MIRROR FOR WITCHES	Royal Opera House, London
17 March 1953	LE LOUP	Théâtre de l'Empire, Paris
9 April 1953	VENEZIANA	Royal Opera House, London
2 June 1953	HOMAGE TO THE QUEEN (Coronation ballet)	Royal Opera House, London
5 June 1953	BLOOD WEDDING	Sadler's Wells Theatre, London
25 February 1954	THE LADY AND THE FOOL	New Theatre, Oxford
1 April 1955	MADAME CHRYSANTHÈME	Royal Opera House, London
26 May 1955	HOUSE OF BIRDS	Sadler's Wells Theatre, London
1 March 1956	NOCTAMBULES	Royal Opera House, London
5 April 1956	BIRTHDAY OFFERING (pièce d'occasion)	Royal Opera House, London
29 May 1956	SOMNAMBULISM	Sadler's Wells Theatre, London
7 June 1956	SOLITAIRE	Sadler's Wells Theatre, London
1 January 1957	THE PRINCE OF THE PAGODAS	Royal Opera House, London

Choreographer	Composer	Décor	Dancers
Ashton	Lambert	Isabel Lambert	Fonteyn, Somes
Massine	Whyte	Colquhoun and McBryde	Grey, Grant
Howard	ApIvor	Adams and Howard	Heaton, Hart
Petit	Dutilleux	Carzou	Verdy, Petit
Howard	Donizetti–ApIvor	Fedorovitch	Elvin, Shaw
Ashton	Arnold	Messel	Fonteyn, Somes
Rodrigues	ApIvor	Isabel Lambert	Fifield, Poole, Trecu
Cranko	Verdi–Mackerras	Beer	Miller, MacMillan
Ashton	Rawsthorne	Isabel Lambert	Fifield, Grant
MacMillan	Mompou–Lanchberry	Georgiadis	Tempest, Lane, Poole
MacMillan	Searle	Georgiadis	Nerina, Lane, Edwards
Ashton	Glazunov	Levasseur	Fonteyn, Somes
MacMillan	Kenton		Heaton, Hill, Britton
MacMillan	Arnold (*English Dances*)	Heely	Hill
Cranko	Britten	Piper and Heely	Beriosova, Farron, Blair

Date	Title	Place
9 June 1934	SERENADE	White Plains, New York
26 January 1936	JARDIN AUX LILAS	Mercury Theatre, London
19 February 1937	DARK ELEGIES	Duchess Theatre, London
28 February 1940	GRADUATION BALL	Sydney
23 May 1940	LA FÊTE ÉTRANGE	Arts Theatre, London
23 July 1943	NOIR ET BLANC	Théâtre de l'Opéra, Paris
1 June 1945	INTERPLAY	Ziegfeld Theater, New York
27 February 1946	LA SONNAMBULA	City Center, New York
20 November 1946	THE FOUR TEMPERAMENTS	Central High School of Needle Trades, New York
6 February 1948	DESIGNS WITH STRINGS	Edinburgh
21 February 1949	CARMEN	Princes Theatre, London
1 December 1949	BOURRÉE FANTASQUE	New York
11 November 1952	STREET GAMES	Wimbledon Theatre, London
29 May 1954	PAS DES DÉESSES	Kaufmann Auditorium, Y.M.H.A., New York
6 March 1956	THE CONCERT	City Center, New York
24 May 1956	THE WITCH BOY	Amsterdam
April 1957	SONATE À TROIS	Essen
24 June 1957	THE PRISONERS	Dartington Hall, Devonshire
27 November 1957	AGON	City Center, New York
17 January 1958	STARS AND STRIPES	City Center, New York
25 August 1958	THE NIGHT AND SILENCE	Empire Theatre, Edinburgh
September 1958	THE GREAT PEACOCK	Empire Theatre, Edinburgh
27 October 1958	ONDINE	Royal Opera House, London
25 May 1959	HAZAÑA	Sadler's Wells Theatre, London
19 October 1959	ANTIGONE	Royal Opera House, London
28 January 1960	LA FILLE MAL GARDÉE	Royal Opera House, London
10 November 1960	THE INVITATION	New Theatre, Oxford
22 November 1960	LIEBESLIEDER WALZER	City Center, New York
7 December 1960	EBONY CONCERTO	City Center, New York
14 February 1961	THE TWO PIGEONS	Royal Opera House, London
19 April 1962	A WEDDING PRESENT	Empire Theatre, Sunderland
5 May 1962	PIERROT LUNAIRE	New York

Choreographer	Composer	Décor	Dancers
Balanchine	Tchaikovsky	Lurçat	
Tudor	Chausson	Stevenson	
Tudor	Mahler	Benois	
Lichine	J. Strauss	Benois	
Howard	Fauré	Fedorovitch	
Lifar	Lalo		
Robbins	Gould		John Kriza, Janet Reed, J. Robbins
Balanchine	Rieti	Tanning	Danilova, Magallanes, Katcharoff, Tallchief
Balanchine	Hindemith	Seligmann	
Taras	Tchaikovsky	Kirsta	
Petit	Bizet	Clavé	Jeanmaire, Petit
Balanchine	Chabrier	Karinska	
Gore	Ibert	Wilson	
Joffrey	Field		
Robbins	Chopin	Sharaff	
Carter	Salzedo	McDowell	
Béjart	Bartók		
Darrell	Bartók	Kay	Salt, Sunde, Musitz
Balanchine	Stravinsky	Porcher	
Balanchine	Sousa	Hays and Karinska	Kent, Barnett, Adams, Hayden, D'Amboise
Gore	Bach	Wilson	
Wright	Searle	Sonnabend	Algeranova, Poole
Ashton	Henze	de Nobilis	Fonteyn, Somes, Farron, Grant
Morrice	Surinach	Koltai	Chesworth, Martlew, Sandbrook, Morrice
Cranko	Theodorakis	Tamayo	
Ashton	Hérold	Lancaster	Nerina, Blair, Holden, Grant, Edwards
MacMillan	Seiber	Georgiadis	
Balanchine	Brahms	Hays and Karinska	
Taras	Stravinsky	Hays	McBride, Mitchell
Ashton	Messager	Dupont	Seymour, Gable, Anderton, Farley
Darrell	Bartók	Wood	Meyer, Last
Tetley	Schoenberg	Ter-Arutunian	

Date	Title	Place
31 May 1963	DUALITIES	Wiesbaden
13 July 1963	LAS HERMANAS	Stuttgart
15 October 1963	GAMELAN	Kirov Theatre, Leningrad
18 December 1963	MODS AND ROCKERS	Prince Charles Theatre, London
28 January 1964	THE ANATOMY LESSON	Nederlands Dans Theater, The Hague
2 April 1964	THE DREAM	Royal Opera House, London
3 February 1965	HOME	Empire Theatre, Sunderland
25 April 1966	MONOTONES I	Royal Opera House, London
24 March 1965	MONOTONES II	Royal Opera House, London
13 April 1965	ONEGIN	Stuttgart
27 May 1965	DON QUIXOTE	State Theater, New York
7 November 1965	THE SONG OF THE EARTH	Stuttgart
13 April 1966	SUN INTO DARKNESS	Sadler's Wells Theatre, London
November 1966	CONCERTO	Berlin
25 January 1967	SHADOWPLAY	Royal Opera House, London
1967	FREEFALL	Salt Lake City
13 April 1967	JEWELS	State Theater, New York
12 June 1967	HAZARD	Bath
20 June 1967	CAGE OF GOD	Sadler's Wells Theatre, London
20 September 1967	ASTARTE	City Center, New York
20 November 1967	ZIGGURAT	Cochrane Theatre, London
11 January 1968	1, 2, 3	Israel
16 May 1968	PRÉSENCE	Stuttgart
1968	MOMENTS	Holland
25 October 1968	ENIGMA VARIATIONS	Royal Opera House, London
21 November 1968	EMBRACE TIGER	Cochrane Theatre, London
25 November 1968	KNIGHT ERRANT	Manchester
13 December 1968	SOLO FOR VOICE I	Scheveningen, Holland
16 March 1969	THE TAMING OF THE SHREW	Stuttgart
22 May 1969	DANCES AT A GATHERING	New York

FIRST PERFORMANCES—*Continued*

Choreographer	Composer	Décor	Dancers
Keres	Searle	Barth	Gora, Goese
MacMillan	Martin	Georgiadis	Haydée, Barra
Joffrey	Harrison		Kim
Darrell	The Beatles	Downing	
Tetley	Landowsky	Wijnberg	Flier
Ashton	Mendelssohn	Bardon and Walker	
Darrell	Bartók	Cazalet	Nerina
Ashton	Satie		Sibley, Parkinson, Shaw
Ashton	Satie		Lorrayne, Dowell, Mead
Cranko	Tchaikovsky	Rose	Barra, Haydée, Cardus, Madsen
Balanchine	Nabokov	Frances	Balanchine, Farrell, Lamont
MacMillan	Mahler		Haydée
Darrell	Williamson	Waistnage	Jones, Meyer, McDonald, Washington, Sherwood
MacMillan	Shostakovitch	Rose	Seymour, Holtz
Tudor	Schoenberg	Mielziner	
Tetley	Schubel	Tetley	
Balanchine	Fauré, Stravinsky, Tchaikovsky	Harvey and Karinska	
Morrice	Salzedo	Baylis	Bruce, Taylor, Craig
Carter	Rawsthorne	Procktor	
Joffrey	Crome Syrcus	Skelton	Singleton, Zomosa
Tetley	Stockhausen	Baylis	
Morrice	Orgad		
Cranko	Zimmermann	Schmidt-Ochm	Haydée, Clauss, Cragan
Van Dantzig	Webern	Van Schayk	
Ashton	Elgar	Oman	
Tetley	Subotnick	Baylis	
Tudor	R. Strauss	Lazaridis	
van Manen	Cage	van der Wal	
Cranko	Stolze	Dalton	
Robbins	Chopin	Skelton	

BIBLIOGRAPHY

BOOKS on ballet are, of course, extremely numerous, but the following may be of use for those who are particularly interested in the musical side or in the relation between music and choreography:

George Amberg. *Ballet in America*. New York, 1949.
Article 'Ballet Dancing' in *Grove's Dictionary of Music*, 5th Edition, London, 1954.
Cyril W. Beaumont:
  The Complete Book of Ballets. London, 1951.
  Ballets of To-day. London, 1954.
  Ballets Past and Present. London, 1955.
Hector Berlioz. *Memoirs*, trans. David Cairns. London, 1969.
V. Bogdanov-Beresovsky. *Ulanova*. London, 1952.
Caryl Brahms (ed.). *Footnotes to the Ballet*. London, 1936.
M. D. Calvocoressi. *A Survey of Russian Music*. Pelican Books, London, 1944.
Martin Cooper. *Gluck*. London, 1935.
David Drew (ed.). *The Decca Book of Ballet*. London, 1958.
Alfred Einstein. *Gluck*. London, 1936.
Arnold Haskell. *Ballet*. Pelican Books, London, 1951.
Lincoln Kirstein. Article 'Ballet' in *International Cyclopaedia of Music and Musicians*. New York, 1956.
Köchel. *Mozart Verzeichnis*, revised by Alfred Einstein. Leipzig, 1937.
Constant Lambert. *Music Ho!* London, 1966.
Serge Lifar. *The History of the Russian Ballet*, trans. Haskell. Hutchinson, 1954.
Charles Malherbe. *Introduction to Rameau's Collected Works*, Vol. 7. Durand, Paris, 1902.
Wilfrid Mellers. 'Jean Baptiste Lully', in *The Heritage of Music*, Vol. 3. London, 1951.

Serge Moreux. *Béla Bartók*. London, 1953.
Rollo H. Myers. *Music in the Modern World*. London, 1939.
Erik Satie. London, 1948. (Dover reprint)
Israel V. Nestyev. *Serge Prokofiev*. New York, 1946.
Henri Prunières. *Introduction to the Collected Works of Lully*. Durand, Paris.
Roland-Manuel. *Ravel*. London, 1947. (Dover reprint)
Marion M. Scott. *Beethoven*. London, 1934.
Humphrey Searle. 'Boccherini's Ballet Espagnol'. *Monthly Musical Record*. July–August, 1938.
Sacheverell Sitwell and C. W. Beaumont. *The Romantic Ballet*. London, 1938.
Igor Stravinsky. *Chronicles of My Life*. London, 1936.
Ninette de Valois. *Introduction to the Ballet*. London, 1937.
Ernest Walker. *A History of Music in England*. Oxford, 1907.
J. A. Westrup. *Master Musicians—Purcell*, London, 1937.
Eric Walter White. *Stravinsky's Sacrifice to Apollo*. London, 1930.
Stravinsky. London, 1947.

ADDITIONAL BIBLIOGRAPHY

Peter Brinson and Clement Crisp. *Ballet for All*. London, 1970.
Mary Clarke. *Dancers of Mercury: Story of the Ballet Rambert*. London, 1962.
Zoe Dominic and J. S. Gilbert. *Frederick Ashton*. London, 1971.
Ivor Guest. *The Dancer's Heritage*. London, 1968.
Lincoln Kirstein. *Movement and Metaphor*. New York, 1970.
Serge Lifar. *Ma Vie*. London, 1970. (in English)
John Percival. *In the World of Diaghilev*. London, 1971.
Modern Ballet. London, 1970.
F. Reyna. *A Concise History of Ballet*. London, 1965.
Claude Samuel. *Prokofiev*. London, 1971.
Bernard Taper. *Balanchine*. London, 1964.

DISCOGRAPHY

THIS discography attempts to list the most important records of ballet music available in Great Britain in February 1972. Further information may be obtained from the *Stereo Record Guide 5,* by Greenfield, Layton, March, and Stevens, published by LPRL, and the *Second Penguin Guide to Stereo Records,* by Greenfield, March, and Stevens, 1971. The *Gramophone Quarterly Classical Record Catalogue,* compiled by Stanley Day, gives details of the latest releases, and U.S. readers will find the *Schwann Monthly Long Playing Record Catalog* useful in the same way. A number of deleted records are also included in cases where there has been no new recording of the works in question. I have not included all records of ballet music available in Britain, but have attempted to list those which will be of the greatest use to the ballet music lover. The first criterion is completeness, so that recordings of complete ballets are mentioned in preference to ballet suites, where both are available: I have further given preference to conductors and orchestras who have been particularly associated with the ballet, and to composers' own recordings of their music. The list is mainly confined to music written in the first place for ballet, though some works originally written for other purposes which have later become well known as ballets, such as Balakirev's *Thamar,* for instance, are also included.

Adam, Adolphe:
 Giselle. Monte Carlo Opera Orchestra./Bonynge.
 Giselle. Covent Garden Orchestra./Fayer.
Antheil, George:
 Capital of the World (suite). Ballet Theatre Orchestra./Levine.

Arnold, Malcolm:
Homage to the Queen (suite). Philharmonia./Irving.
English Dances (*Solitaire*). London Philharmonic./Boult.
Auber, arr. Lambert:
Les Rendezvous (two pieces). Covent Garden Orchestra./Irving.
Auric, Georges:
Phèdre. Paris Conservatoire Orchestra./Tzipine.
Bach, arr. Walton:
The Wise Virgins. London Philharmonic./Boult.
The Wise Virgins. Vienna Opera Orchestra./Litschauer.
Balakirev:
Thamar. Suisse Romande Orchestra./Ansermet.
Thamar. Royal Philharmonic./Beecham.
Baranovich, Kreshimir:
The Gingerbread Heart. Belgrade Philharmonic./Baranovich.
Barber, Samuel:
Medea (suite). New Symphony Orchestra./Barber.
Souvenirs. Philharmonia./Kurtz.
Bartók, Béla:
Dance Suite. London Philharmonic./Solti.
Dance Suite. R.I.A.S. Orchestra./Fricsay.
The Miraculous Mandarin (suite) and *Music for Strings and Percussion*. London Symphony./Solti.
The Prisoners (Music for Strings, Percussion and Celesta). Concertgebouw./Haitink.
A Wedding Present (Piano Concerto No. 3). Barenboim, New Philharmonia./Boulez.
Home (String Quartet No. 5). Novak Quartet.
Sonata for 2 Pianos and Percussion. B. Bartók, D. Bartók.
Sonata for 2 Pianos and Percussion. Ogdon, Lucas.
Beethoven:
Prometheus. London Philharmonic./van Beinum.
Berlioz:
Symphonie Fantastique. French National Radio Orchestra./Beecham.
The Damnation of Faust (three dances). Suisse Romande Orchestra./Ansermet.

[235]

Romeo and Juliet (soloists and chorus). London Symphony./Davis.
Romeo and Juliet (soloists and chorus). NBC Symphony./Toscanini.
The Trojans (ballet music). Lamoureux Orchestra./Martinon.
The Trojans (complete opera). Covent Garden Orchestra./Davis.
Berners, Lord:
> *The Wedding Bouquet* (two dances). Covent Garden Orchestra./
> Irving.
Bernstein, Leonard:
> *Fancy Free.* New York Philharmonic./Bernstein.
> *Facsimile.* New York Philharmonic./Bernstein.
Bizet:
> *Symphony in C.* Chicago Symphony./Martinon.
> *Jeux d'Enfants.* Paris Conservatoire Orchestra./Martinon.
> *Roma* (suite). New York Ballet Orchestra./Barzin.
> *Carnaval* (from *Rome*). Royal Philharmonic./Beecham.
Bliss, Sir Arthur:
> *Adam Zero* (suite). London Symphony./Bliss.
> *Miracle in the Gorbals* (suite). Philharmonia./Bliss.
> *Checkmate.* London Sinfonia./Bliss.
Boccherini, arr. Françaix:
> *Scuola di Ballo.* London Philharmonic./Dorati.
Borodin:
> *Prince Igor* (Polovtsian Dances). Choir, London Symphony./
> Davis.
Boyce, arr. Lambert:
> *The Prospect Before Us* (Fugue). Covent Garden Orchestra./Irving.
Brahms:
> *Liebeslieder Walzer.* Ensemble.
Britten, Benjamin:
> *Matinées Musicales* and *Soirées Musicales* (Rossini). Vienna State
> Opera./Zeller.
> *Variations on a Theme of Purcell.* London Symphony./Britten.
> *The Prince of the Pagodas.* Covent Garden Orchestra./Britten.
Carter, Elliott:
> *The Minotaur* (suite). Eastman-Rochester Symphony./Hanson.
Casella:
> *La Giara* (two pieces). Hamburg Philharmonic./di Bella.

La Giara (suite). Santa Cecilia Orchestra./Previtali.
Chabrier:
  Bourrée Fantasque (suite). New York Ballet Orchestra./Barzin.
  Suite Pastorale. Suisse Romande Orchestra./Ansermet.
  (N.B. The above two works contain a good deal of the music
  which was used in the Chabrier ballets *Cotillon* and *Ballabile*.)
Chausson:
  Poème (Jardin des Lilas). Zukerman, London Symphony./Macker-
  ras.
Chopin:
  Les Sylphides (arr. Désormière). Paris Conservatoire Orchestra./
  Désormière.
  Les Sylphides (arr. Douglas). Berlin Philharmonic./Karajan.
Copland, Aaron:
  Billy the Kid (suite). Ballet Theatre Orchestra./Levine.
Debussy:
  La Boîte à Joujoux. Suisse Romande Orchestra./Ansermet.
  Jeux. Paris Conservatoire Orchestra./Cluytens.
  Prélude à l'Après-midi d'un Faune. New Philharmonia./Boulez.
Delibes:
  Coppélia. Suisse Romande Orchestra./Bonynge.
  Sylvia. London Symphony./Fistoulari.
  La Source (four numbers). Paris Conservatoire Orchestra./Maag.
Delius:
  Paris (Nocturne). Royal Philharmonic./Beecham.
Dohnányi:
  Suite in F Sharp (The Shadow). London Symphony./Collins.
Dukas:
  La Péri. Monte Carlo Opera Orchestra./Frémaux.
Dutilleux, Henri:
  Le Loup. Champs-Elysées Theatre Orchestra./Bonneau.
Elgar:
  Enigma Variations. Royal Albert Hall Orchestra./Elgar.
  Enigma Variations. NBC Symphony./Toscanini.
  Enigma Variations. London Symphony./Davis.
Falla:
  El Amor Brujo (Love, the Magician). Mistral, New Philharmonia./

Frühbeck de Burgos.
Le Tricorne. Suisse Romande Orchestra./Ansermet.
Fauré:
Pelléas et Mélisande (*Jewels*). Paris Conservatoire Orchestra./ Baudo.
Franck:
Symphonic Variations. Ogdon, Philharmonia./Barbirolli.
Glazounov:
Raymonda (suite). Bolshoi Theatre Orchestra./Svetlanov.
The Seasons (suite). Moscow Radio Symphony./Khaikin.
Glière:
The Red Poppy (suite). Westchester Symphony./Landau.
Glinka:
Russlan and Ludmilla (suite). U.S.S.R. Symphony./Svetlanov.
Gluck:
Don Juan. St. Martin's Academy./Marriner.
Orfeo (excerpts). Paris Conservatoire Orchestra./Froment.
(arr. Mottl:) *Ballet Suite No. 1*. New Symphony Orchestra./Irving.
Gordon, Gavin:
The Rake's Progress (two pieces). Covent Garden Orchestra./ Irving.
Gould, Morton:
Fall River Legend. Ballet Theatre Orchestra./Levine.
Gounod:
Faust (ballet music). New York Philharmonic./Bernstein.
Grétry:
Ballet Suite. English Chamber Orchestra./Leppard.
Céphale et Procris (ballet suite). Belgian Radio Orchestra./ André.
Suite of Dances. Soloistes de Liège./Lemaire.
Jugement de Midas (ballet music). New Philharmonia./Leppard.
Zémire et Azor (ballet). Royal Philharmonic./Beecham.
Handel, arr. Beecham:
The Faithful Shepherd (suite). Royal Philharmonic./Beecham.
Hérold:
La Fille Mal Gardée. Covent Garden Orchestra./Lanchbery.
Hindemith:
Nobilissima Visione (suite). Hamburg Philharmonic./Keilberth.

The Four Temperaments. Berlin Philharmonic./Hindemith.
Holst:
The Golden Goose. English Chamber Orchestra./Holst.
The Perfect Fool (ballet music). London Philharmonic./Boult.
Humperdinck:
Hänsel und Gretel (excerpts). Philharmonia./Karajan.
d'Indy:
Istar. Westminster Symphony./Fistoulari.
Ives:
Central Park in the Dark; The Unanswered Question (*Ivesiana*).
New York Philharmonic./Bernstein.
Khatchaturian:
Gayaneh (suite). Vienna Philharmonic./Khatchaturian.
Gayaneh (suite). London Symphony./Fistoulari.
Spartacus (suite). Vienna Philharmonic./Khatchaturian.
Koechlin:
Les Bandar-Log. BBC. Symphony./Dorati.
Lalo:
Namouna (suite). Suisse Romande Orchestra./Ansermet.
Lambert, Constant:
Horoscope (suite). Philharmonia./Lambert.
The Rio Grande. Greenbaum, Ripley, Philharmonia./Lambert.
Lecocq:
Mamzelle Angot (suite). Covent Garden Orchestra./Fistoulari.
Lhotka, Fran:
The Devil in the Village. Zagreb Opera Orchestra./Lhotka.
Liadov:
Contes Russes. U.S.S.R. Symphony./Svetlanov.
Ligeti:
Nouvelles Aventures. Darmstadt Chamber Orchestra./Maderna.
Liszt, arr. Jacob:
Apparitions (two pieces). Covent Garden Orchestra./Irving.
Apparitions (Cave Scene). Philharmonia./Lambert.
Dante Sonata. Kentner, Sadler's Wells Orchestra./Lambert.
Lully, arr. Mottl:
Ballet Suite. Scarlatti Orchestra./Caracciolo.
Le Temple de la Paix. Oiseau-Lyre Ensemble./Froment.

McPhee, Colin:
Tabuh-Tabuhan. Eastman-Rochester Symphony./Hanson.

Mahler:
Kindertotenlieder (Dark Elegies). Prey, Concertgebouw./Haitink.
Rückert Songs (At Midnight). J. Baker, New Philharmonia./ Barbirolli.
Song of the Earth. New Philharmonia./Klemperer.

Martinů:
Symphony No. 6 *(Symphonic Fantasies)*. New Philharmonia./ Bialoguski.

Massenet:
Le Cid (ballet music). Israel Philharmonic./Martinon.

Mendelssohn, arr. Jacob:
The Lord of Burleigh (two pieces). Covent Garden Orchestra./Irving.
Midsummer Night's Dream. Soloists, New Philharmonia./Frühbeck de Burgos.

Messager:
Les Deux Pigeons (ballet suite). Covent Garden./Mackerras.

Messiaen:
Oiseaux Exotiques. Loriod, Czech Philharmonic./Neumann.
Turangalilâ Symphony. Toronto Symphony./Ozawa.

Meyerbeer, arr. Lambert:
Les Patineurs (suite). Israel Philharmonic./Martinon.

Milhaud, Darius:
La Création du Monde. London Symphony./Carewe.
Le Boeuf sur le Toit. London Symphony./Dorati.
L'Homme et son Désir. Luxembourg Radio Orchestra./Milhaud.

Minkus:
La Bayadère and *Don Quichotte* (excerpts). London Symphony./ Bonynge.

Mussorgsky:
Khovanshchina (Persian Dances). Philharmonia./Karajan.

Offenbach, arr. Rosenthal:
Gaîté Parisienne. Philharmonia./Mackerras.

Orff:
Carmina Burana. Milnes, Boston Symphony./Ozawa.

Petrassi, Goffredo:
Ritratto di Don Chisciotte. Scarlatti Orchestra./Caracciolo.
Ponchielli:
La Gioconda (Dance of the Hours). NBC Symphony./Toscanini.
Poulenc, François:
Les Biches (suite). Paris Conservatoire Orchestra./Désormière.
Prokofiev:
Chout. London Symphony./Susskind.
Cinderella (suite). Covent Garden Orchestra./Rignold.
Le Pas d'Acier. Moscow Radio Symphony./Rozhdestvensky.
Prodigal Son. Suisse Romande Orchestra./Ansermet.
Romeo and Juliet. Boston Symphony./Leinsdorf.
Romeo and Juliet (Suites 1 and 2). Minneapolis Symphony./
Skrowaczewski.
Scythian Suite (*Ala and Lolly*). French National Radio Orchestra./
Markevitch.
Stone Flower. Suisse Romande Orchestra./Varviso.
Summer Day (suite). Champs-Elysées Orchestra./Jouve.
Violin Concerto No. 1 (*Triad*). Oistrakh, Moscow Radio
Symphony./Roshdestvensky.
Purcell:
(arr. Lambert): *Comus* (suite: two pieces). Covent Garden
Orchestra./Irving.
Fairy Queen (dances). Heidelberg Choral./Wehsky.
Rabaud, Henri:
Marouf. Lamoureux Orchestra./Fournet.
Rameau:
Acanthe et Céphise (dances). Caen Chamber Orchestra./Dautel.
Dardanus (two pieces). Lamoureux Orchestra./Froment.
Les Fêtes d'Hébé (suite). Champs-Elysées Orchestra./Allain.
Hippolyte et Aricie (excerpts). English Chamber Orchestra./Lewis.
Les Indes Galantes (suite). Lamoureux Orchestra./Froment.
Les Paladins (suite). Petit Chamber Orchestra./Leppard.
Platée (suite). Lamoureux Orchestra./Froment.
Pygmalion (overture). New Philharmonia./Leppard.
Le Temple de la Gloire (Suites 1 and 2). English Chamber
Orchestra./Leppard.

Zaïs (overture). New Philharmonia./Leppard.
Zaïs (two gavottes). Lamoureux Orchestra./Froment.
Zephyre (sarabande). Lamoureux Orchestra./Froment.
Ravel:
  Boléro. Royal Philharmonic/Monteux.
  Daphnis et Chloë. New England Conservatory Chorus, Boston
    Symphony./Munch.
  Daphnis et Chloë. London Symphony, Choir./Monteux.
  Mother Goose (suite). Suisse Romande Orchestra./Ansermet.
  La Valse. Royal Philharmonic./Monteux.
  Valses Nobles et Sentimentales. Suisse Romande Orchestra./
    Ansermet.
Rawsthorne, Alan:
  Madame Chrysanthème (suite). Pro Arte Orchestra./Rawsthorne.
Rimsky-Korsakov:
  Schéhérazade. U.S.S.R. Symphony./Svetlanov.
  Coq d'Or (suite). Philadelphia Orchestra./Ormandy.
  Snow Maiden (suite). Philharmonia./Fistoulari.
Rossini:
  (arr. Respighi): *La Boutique Fantasque.* Philadelphia Orchestra./
    Ormandy.
  William Tell (ballet music). New Philharmonia./Mackerras.
Roussel:
  Aeneas. French O.R.T.F. and Choir./Martinon.
  Bacchus et Ariane. French O.R.T.F. and Choir./Martinon.
  Le Festin de l'Araignée. Paris O.R.T.F./Martinon.
Saint-Saëns:
  Henry VIII (ballet). Hastings Symphony./Bath.
  Samson and Delilah (excerpts). Royal Philharmonic./Beecham.
Satie:
  Gymnopédies. Royal Philharmonic./Entremont.
  Parade. Monte Carlo Opera Orchestra./Frémaux.
  Relâche. Royal Philharmonic./Entremont.
Scarlatti, arr. Tommasini:
  Good Humoured Ladies. Concert Arts Orchestra./Irving.
Schoenberg:
  Pelléas and Mélisande. New Philharmonia./Barbirolli.

Pierrot Lunaire. Pilarczyk, Domaine Musicale Ensemble./Boulez.
Verklärte Nacht (Pillar of Fire). Domaine Musicale Ensemble./
  Boulez.
Schubert:
  Rosamunde (entractes and ballet music). Suisse Romande
  Orchestra./Ansermet.
Schumann:
  Carnaval. Suisse Romande Orchestra./Ansermet.
Scriabin:
  Poème de l'Extase. U.S.S.R. Symphony./Svetlanov.
Shostakovitch:
  Golden Age (suite). Chicago Symphony./Stokowski.
  Bolt (suite). Bolshoi Theatre Orchestra./Shostakovitch.
  Piano Concerto No. 2. Ogdon, Royal Philharmonic./Foster.
  Symphony No. 1. Czech Philharmonic./Ancerl.
  Symphony No. 7 (Leningrad). U.S.S.R. Symphony./Svetlanov.
Smetana:
  The Bartered Bride (three dances). New York Philharmonic./
  Bernstein.
Stockhausen:
  Gesang der Jünglinge; Kontakte (Ziggurat). [Electronic tape.]
Strauss, Johann, arr. Désormière:
  Le Beau Danube. London Philharmonic./Martinon.
Strauss, Johann, arr. Dorati:
  Graduation Ball. Vienna Philharmonic./Boskovsky.
Strauss, Richard:
  Le Bourgeois Gentilhomme (suite). Vienna Philharmonic./Maazel.
  Don Juan and *Till Eulenspiegel.* Royal Philharmonic./Lewis.
  Schlagobers (Waltz). Berlin Philharmonic./Jochum.
  Salome (Dance of the Seven Veils). Philadelphia Orchestra./
  Ormandy.
Stravinsky:
  Agon. Los Angeles Orchestra./Stravinsky.
  Apollon Musagète. Columbia Symphony./Stravinsky.
  Concerto for Piano and Wind (Jewels). Entremont, Columbia
  Symphony./Stravinsky.
  Ebony Concerto. Goodman, Columbia Symphony./Stravinsky.

[243]

Le Baiser de la Fée. Columbia Symphony./Stravinsky.
Le Chant du Rossignol. Chicago Symphony./Reiner.
The Firebird. Columbia Symphony./Stravinsky.
Jeu de Cartes. Cleveland Symphony./Stravinsky.
Movements. Rosen, Columbia Symphony./Stravinsky.
Les Noces. Columbia Symphony, Ensemble./Stravinsky.
Petrouchka. Columbia Symphony./Stravinsky.
Pulcinella. Columbia Symphony./Stravinsky.
Renard. Soloists, Columbia Symphony./Stravinsky.
Le Sacre du Printemps. Columbia Symphony./Stravinsky.
Scènes de Ballet. Columbia Symphony./Stravinsky.
Subotnick:
   Silver Apples of the Moon (Embrace Tiger and Return to Mountain).
   [Electronic tape.]
Sullivan, arr. Mackerras:
   Pineapple Poll. Royal Philharmonic./Mackerras.
Tchaikovsky:
   Symphony No. 1 (Anastasia). U.S.S.R. Symphony./Svetlanov.
   Symphony No. 3 (Anastasia). U.S.S.R. Symphony./Svetlanov.
   Symphony No. 5 (Les Présages). Israel Philharmonic./Mehta.
   Casse-Noisette. Suisse Romande Orchestra./Ansermet.
   Eugene Onegin (Polonaise). Bournemouth Symphony./Silvestri.
   Eugene Onegin (Waltz). Philadelphia Orchestra./Ormandy.
   The Sleeping Beauty. Covent Garden Orchestra./Irving.
   The Sleeping Beauty. Minneapolis Symphony./Dorati.
   Swan Lake. Moscow Radio Symphony./Rozhdestvensky.
   Piano Concerto No. 2 *(Ballet Imperial).* Zhukov, Moscow Radio
      Symphony./Rozhdestvensky.
Vaughan Williams:
   Job. London Symphony./Boult.
   Old King Cole (suite). London Philharmonic./Boult.
Verdi:
   (arr. Mackerras): *The Lady and the Fool.* Philharmonia./Mackerras.
   Aida (Ballabile). New York Philharmonic./Bernstein.
   Otello (Ballabile). NBC Symphony./Toscanini.
   Sicilian Vespers (Autumn). Covent Garden Orchestra./Braithwaite.
   Il Trovatore (ballet). Philharmonia./Mackerras.

[244]

Macbeth (complete). Soloists, chorus, St. Cecilia Orchestra./
Schippers.

Wagner:
Die Meistersinger von Nürnberg (Dance of the Apprentices). New
York Philharmonic./Bernstein.
Tannhäuser (Venusberg music). Chorus, London Symphony./
Leinsdorf.

Walton, William:
Façade (suite). London Symphony./Irving.
Façade (suite). Philharmonia./Walton.

Warlock, Peter:
Capriol Suite. Royal Philharmonic./Sargent.

Weber, arr. Berlioz:
Invitation to the Dance (*Spectre de la Rose*). NBC Symphony./
Toscanini.
Invitation to the Dance (*Spectre de la Rose*). Czech Philharmonic./
Ancerl.

Webern:
5 Pieces for Orchestra, Op. 10 (*Episodes*). London Symphony./
Dorati.
6 Bagatelles for String Quartet & 5 Movements for String
Quartet (*Moments*). Quartetto Italiano.

Xenakis:
Pithoprakta. Buffalo Philharmonic./Foss.

INDEX

INDEX

SUPPLEMENTARY INDEX
TO CHAPTER VI

[254]

A CATALOGUE OF SELECTED DOVER BOOKS
IN ALL FIELDS OF INTEREST

A CATALOGUE OF SELECTED DOVER BOOKS
IN ALL FIELDS OF INTEREST

AMERICA'S OLD MASTERS, James T. Flexner. Four men emerged unexpectedly from provincial 18th century America to leadership in European art: Benjamin West, J. S. Copley, C. R. Peale, Gilbert Stuart. Brilliant coverage of lives and contributions. Revised, 1967 edition. 69 plates. 365pp. of text.
21806-6 Paperbound $3.00

FIRST FLOWERS OF OUR WILDERNESS: AMERICAN PAINTING, THE COLONIAL PERIOD, James T. Flexner. Painters, and regional painting traditions from earliest Colonial times up to the emergence of Copley, West and Peale Sr., Foster, Gustavus Hesselius, Feke, John Smibert and many anonymous painters in the primitive manner. Engaging presentation, with 162 illustrations. xxii + 368pp.
22180-6 Paperbound $3.50

THE LIGHT OF DISTANT SKIES: AMERICAN PAINTING, 1760-1835, James T. Flexner. The great generation of early American painters goes to Europe to learn and to teach: West, Copley, Gilbert Stuart and others. Allston, Trumbull, Morse; also contemporary American painters—primitives, derivatives, academics—who remained in America. 102 illustrations. xiii + 306pp.
22179-2 Paperbound $3.50

A HISTORY OF THE RISE AND PROGRESS OF THE ARTS OF DESIGN IN THE UNITED STATES, William Dunlap. Much the richest mine of information on early American painters, sculptors, architects, engravers, miniaturists, etc. The only source of information for scores of artists, the major primary source for many others. Unabridged reprint of rare original 1834 edition, with new introduction by James T. Flexner, and 394 new illustrations. Edited by Rita Weiss. 6⅝ x 9⅝.
21695-0, 21696-9, 21697-7 Three volumes, Paperbound $13.50

EPOCHS OF CHINESE AND JAPANESE ART, Ernest F. Fenollosa. From primitive Chinese art to the 20th century, thorough history, explanation of every important art period and form, including Japanese woodcuts; main stress on China and Japan, but Tibet, Korea also included. Still unexcelled for its detailed, rich coverage of cultural background, aesthetic elements, diffusion studies, particularly of the historical period. 2nd, 1913 edition. 242 illustrations. lii + 439pp. of text.
20364-6, 20365-4 Two volumes, Paperbound $6.00

THE GENTLE ART OF MAKING ENEMIES, James A. M. Whistler. Greatest wit of his day deflates Oscar Wilde, Ruskin, Swinburne; strikes back at inane critics, exhibitions, art journalism; aesthetics of impressionist revolution in most striking form. Highly readable classic by great painter. Reproduction of edition designed by Whistler. Introduction by Alfred Werner. xxxvi + 334pp.
21875-9 Paperbound $2.50

VISUAL ILLUSIONS: THEIR CAUSES, CHARACTERISTICS, AND APPLICATIONS, Matthew Luckiesh. Thorough description and discussion of optical illusion, geometric and perspective, particularly; size and shape distortions, illusions of color, of motion; natural illusions; use of illusion in art and magic, industry, etc. Most useful today with op art, also for classical art. Scores of effects illustrated. Introduction by William H. Ittleson. 100 illustrations. xxi + 252pp.

21530-X Paperbound $2.00

A HANDBOOK OF ANATOMY FOR ART STUDENTS, Arthur Thomson. Thorough, virtually exhaustive coverage of skeletal structure, musculature, etc. Full text, supplemented by anatomical diagrams and drawings and by photographs of undraped figures. Unique in its comparison of male and female forms, pointing out differences of contour, texture, form. 211 figures, 40 drawings, 86 photographs. xx + 459pp. 5⅜ x 8⅜.

21163-0 Paperbound $3.50

150 MASTERPIECES OF DRAWING, Selected by Anthony Toney. Full page reproductions of drawings from the early 16th to the end of the 18th century, all beautifully reproduced: Rembrandt, Michelangelo, Dürer, Fragonard, Urs, Graf, Wouwerman, many others. First-rate browsing book, model book for artists. xviii + 150pp. 8⅜ x 11¼.

21032-4 Paperbound $2.50

THE LATER WORK OF AUBREY BEARDSLEY, Aubrey Beardsley. Exotic, erotic, ironic masterpieces in full maturity: Comedy Ballet, Venus and Tannhauser, Pierrot, Lysistrata, Rape of the Lock, Savoy material, Ali Baba, Volpone, etc. This material revolutionized the art world, and is still powerful, fresh, brilliant. With *The Early Work,* all Beardsley's finest work. 174 plates, 2 in color. xiv + 176pp. 8⅛ x 11.

21817-1 Paperbound $3.00

DRAWINGS OF REMBRANDT, Rembrandt van Rijn. Complete reproduction of fabulously rare edition by Lippmann and Hofstede de Groot, completely reedited, updated, improved by Prof. Seymour Slive, Fogg Museum. Portraits, Biblical sketches, landscapes, Oriental types, nudes, episodes from classical mythology—All Rembrandt's fertile genius. Also selection of drawings by his pupils and followers. "Stunning volumes," *Saturday Review.* 550 illustrations. lxxviii + 552pp. 9⅛ x 12¼.

21485-0, 21486-9 Two volumes, Paperbound $10.00

THE DISASTERS OF WAR, Francisco Goya. One of the masterpieces of Western civilization—83 etchings that record Goya's shattering, bitter reaction to the Napoleonic war that swept through Spain after the insurrection of 1808 and to war in general. Reprint of the first edition, with three additional plates from Boston's Museum of Fine Arts. All plates facsimile size. Introduction by Philip Hofer, Fogg Museum. v + 97pp. 9⅜ x 8¼.

21872-4 Paperbound $2.00

GRAPHIC WORKS OF ODILON REDON. Largest collection of Redon's graphic works ever assembled: 172 lithographs, 28 etchings and engravings, 9 drawings. These include some of his most famous works. All the plates from *Odilon Redon: oeuvre graphique complet,* plus additional plates. New introduction and caption translations by Alfred Werner. 209 illustrations. xxvii + 209pp. 9⅛ x 12¼.

21966-8 Paperbound $4.00

DESIGN BY ACCIDENT; A BOOK OF "ACCIDENTAL EFFECTS" FOR ARTISTS AND DESIGNERS, James F. O'Brien. Create your own unique, striking, imaginative effects by "controlled accident" interaction of materials: paints and lacquers, oil and water based paints, splatter, crackling materials, shatter, similar items. Everything you do will be different; first book on this limitless art, so useful to both fine artist and commercial artist. Full instructions. 192 plates showing "accidents," 8 in color. viii + 215pp. 8⅜ x 11¼. 21942-9 Paperbound $3.50

THE BOOK OF SIGNS, Rudolf Koch. Famed German type designer draws 493 beautiful symbols: religious, mystical, alchemical, imperial, property marks, runes, etc. Remarkable fusion of traditional and modern. Good for suggestions of timelessness, smartness, modernity. Text. vi + 104pp. 6⅛ x 9¼. 20162-7 Paperbound $1.25

HISTORY OF INDIAN AND INDONESIAN ART, Ananda K. Coomaraswamy. An unabridged republication of one of the finest books by a great scholar in Eastern art. Rich in descriptive material, history, social backgrounds; Sunga reliefs, Rajput paintings, Gupta temples, Burmese frescoes, textiles, jewelry, sculpture, etc. 400 photos. viii + 423pp. 6⅜ x 9¾. 21436-2 Paperbound $5.00

PRIMITIVE ART, Franz Boas. America's foremost anthropologist surveys textiles, ceramics, woodcarving, basketry, metalwork, etc.; patterns, technology, creation of symbols, style origins. All areas of world, but very full on Northwest Coast Indians. More than 350 illustrations of baskets, boxes, totem poles, weapons, etc. 378 pp. 20025-6 Paperbound $3.00

THE GENTLEMAN AND CABINET MAKER'S DIRECTOR, Thomas Chippendale. Full reprint (third edition, 1762) of most influential furniture book of all time, by master cabinetmaker. 200 plates, illustrating chairs, sofas, mirrors, tables, cabinets, plus 24 photographs of surviving pieces. Biographical introduction by N. Bienenstock. vi + 249pp. 9⅞ x 12¾. 21601-2 Paperbound $4.00

AMERICAN ANTIQUE FURNITURE, Edgar G. Miller, Jr. The basic coverage of all American furniture before 1840. Individual chapters cover type of furniture— clocks, tables, sideboards, etc.—chronologically, with inexhaustible wealth of data. More than 2100 photographs, all identified, commented on. Essential to all early American collectors. Introduction by H. E. Keyes. vi + 1106pp. 7⅞ x 10¾. 21599-7, 21600-4 Two volumes, Paperbound $11.00

PENNSYLVANIA DUTCH AMERICAN FOLK ART, Henry J. Kauffman. 279 photos, 28 drawings of tulipware, Fraktur script, painted tinware, toys, flowered furniture, quilts, samplers, hex signs, house interiors, etc. Full descriptive text. Excellent for tourist, rewarding for designer, collector. Map. 146pp. 7⅞ x 10¾. 21205-X Paperbound $2.50

EARLY NEW ENGLAND GRAVESTONE RUBBINGS, Edmund V. Gillon, Jr. 43 photographs, 226 carefully reproduced rubbings show heavily symbolic, sometimes macabre early gravestones, up to early 19th century. Remarkable early American primitive art, occasionally strikingly beautiful; always powerful. Text. xxvi + 207pp. 8⅜ x 11¼. 21380-3 Paperbound $3.50

ALPHABETS AND ORNAMENTS, Ernst Lehner. Well-known pictorial source for decorative alphabets, script examples, cartouches, frames, decorative title pages, calligraphic initials, borders, similar material. 14th to 19th century, mostly European. Useful in almost any graphic arts designing, varied styles. 750 illustrations. 256pp. 7 x 10.   21905-4 Paperbound $4.00

PAINTING: A CREATIVE APPROACH, Norman Colquhoun. For the beginner simple guide provides an instructive approach to painting: major stumbling blocks for beginner; overcoming them, technical points; paints and pigments; oil painting; watercolor and other media and color. New section on "plastic" paints. Glossary. Formerly *Paint Your Own Pictures*. 221pp.   22000-1 Paperbound $1.75

THE ENJOYMENT AND USE OF COLOR, Walter Sargent. Explanation of the relations between colors themselves and between colors in nature and art, including hundreds of little-known facts about color values, intensities, effects of high and low illumination, complementary colors. Many practical hints for painters, references to great masters. 7 color plates, 29 illustrations. x + 274pp.
20944-X Paperbound $2.75

THE NOTEBOOKS OF LEONARDO DA VINCI, compiled and edited by Jean Paul Richter. 1566 extracts from original manuscripts reveal the full range of Leonardo's versatile genius: all his writings on painting, sculpture, architecture, anatomy, astronomy, geography, topography, physiology, mining, music, etc., in both Italian and English, with 186 plates of manuscript pages and more than 500 additional drawings. Includes studies for the Last Supper, the lost Sforza monument, and other works. Total of xlvii + 866pp. 7⅞ x 10¾.
22572-0, 22573-9 Two volumes, Paperbound $10.00

MONTGOMERY WARD CATALOGUE OF 1895. Tea gowns, yards of flannel and pillow-case lace, stereoscopes, books of gospel hymns, the New Improved Singer Sewing Machine, side saddles, milk skimmers, straight-edged razors, high-button shoes, spittoons, and on and on . . . listing some 25,000 items, practically all illustrated. Essential to the shoppers of the 1890's, it is our truest record of the spirit of the period. Unaltered reprint of Issue No. 57, Spring and Summer 1895. Introduction by Boris Emmet. Innumerable illustrations. xiii + 624pp. 8½ x 11⅝.
22377-9 Paperbound $6.95

THE CRYSTAL PALACE EXHIBITION ILLUSTRATED CATALOGUE (LONDON, 1851). One of the wonders of the modern world—the Crystal Palace Exhibition in which all the nations of the civilized world exhibited their achievements in the arts and sciences—presented in an equally important illustrated catalogue. More than 1700 items pictured with accompanying text—ceramics, textiles, cast-iron work, carpets, pianos, sleds, razors, wall-papers, billiard tables, beehives, silverware and hundreds of other artifacts—represent the focal point of Victorian culture in the Western World. Probably the largest collection of Victorian decorative art ever assembled— indispensable for antiquarians and designers. Unabridged republication of the Art-Journal Catalogue of the Great Exhibition of 1851, with all terminal essays. New introduction by John Gloag, F.S.A. xxxiv + 426pp. 9 x 12.
22503-8 Paperbound $4.50

A HISTORY OF COSTUME, Carl Köhler. Definitive history, based on surviving pieces of clothing primarily, and paintings, statues, etc. secondarily. Highly readable text, supplemented by 594 illustrations of costumes of the ancient Mediterranean peoples, Greece and Rome, the Teutonic prehistoric period; costumes of the Middle Ages, Renaissance, Baroque, 18th and 19th centuries. Clear, measured patterns are provided for many clothing articles. Approach is practical throughout. Enlarged by Emma von Sichart. 464pp.   21030-8 Paperbound $3.50

ORIENTAL RUGS, ANTIQUE AND MODERN, Walter A. Hawley. A complete and authoritative treatise on the Oriental rug—where they are made, by whom and how, designs and symbols, characteristics in detail of the six major groups, how to distinguish them and how to buy them. Detailed technical data is provided on periods, weaves, warps, wefts, textures, sides, ends and knots, although no technical background is required for an understanding. 11 color plates, 80 halftones, 4 maps. vi + 320pp. 6⅛ x 9⅛.   22366-3 Paperbound $5.00

TEN BOOKS ON ARCHITECTURE, Vitruvius. By any standards the most important book on architecture ever written. Early Roman discussion of aesthetics of building, construction methods, orders, sites, and every other aspect of architecture has inspired, instructed architecture for about 2,000 years. Stands behind Palladio, Michelangelo, Bramante, Wren, countless others. Definitive Morris H. Morgan translation. 68 illustrations. xii + 331pp.   20645-9 Paperbound $3.00

THE FOUR BOOKS OF ARCHITECTURE, Andrea Palladio. Translated into every major Western European language in the two centuries following its publication in 1570, this has been one of the most influential books in the history of architecture. Complete reprint of the 1738 Isaac Ware edition. New introduction by Adolf Placzek, Columbia Univ. 216 plates. xxii + 110pp. of text. 9½ x 12¾.
21308-0 Clothbound $10.00

STICKS AND STONES: A STUDY OF AMERICAN ARCHITECTURE AND CIVILIZATION, Lewis Mumford.One of the great classics of American cultural history. American architecture from the medieval-inspired earliest forms to the early 20th century; evolution of structure and style, and reciprocal influences on environment. 21 photographic illustrations. 238pp.   20202-X Paperbound $2.00

THE AMERICAN BUILDER'S COMPANION, Asher Benjamin. The most widely used early 19th century architectural style and source book, for colonial up into Greek Revival periods. Extensive development of geometry of carpentering, construction of sashes, frames, doors, stairs; plans and elevations of domestic and other buildings. Hundreds of thousands of houses were built according to this book, now invaluable to historians, architects, restorers, etc. 1827 edition. 59 plates. 114pp. 7⅞ x 10¾.
22236-5 Paperbound $3.50

DUTCH HOUSES IN THE HUDSON VALLEY BEFORE 1776, Helen Wilkinson Reynolds. The standard survey of the Dutch colonial house and outbuildings, with constructional features, decoration, and local history associated with individual homesteads. Introduction by Franklin D. Roosevelt. Map. 150 illustrations. 469pp. 6⅝ x 9¼.   21469-9 Paperbound $4.00

THE ARCHITECTURE OF COUNTRY HOUSES, Andrew J. Downing. Together with Vaux's *Villas and Cottages* this is the basic book for Hudson River Gothic architecture of the middle Victorian period. Full, sound discussions of general aspects of housing, architecture, style, decoration, furnishing, together with scores of detailed house plans, illustrations of specific buildings, accompanied by full text. Perhaps the most influential single American architectural book. 1850 edition. Introduction by J. Stewart Johnson. 321 figures, 34 architectural designs. xvi + 560pp.

22003-6 Paperbound $4.00

LOST EXAMPLES OF COLONIAL ARCHITECTURE, John Mead Howells. Full-page photographs of buildings that have disappeared or been so altered as to be denatured, including many designed by major early American architects. 245 plates. xvii + 248pp. 7⅞ x 10¾.

21143-6 Paperbound $3.50

DOMESTIC ARCHITECTURE OF THE AMERICAN COLONIES AND OF THE EARLY REPUBLIC, Fiske Kimball. Foremost architect and restorer of Williamsburg and Monticello covers nearly 200 homes between 1620-1825. Architectural details, construction, style features, special fixtures, floor plans, etc. Generally considered finest work in its area. 219 illustrations of houses, doorways, windows, capital mantels. xx + 314pp. 7⅞ x 10¾.

21743-4 Paperbound $4.00

EARLY AMERICAN ROOMS: 1650-1858, edited by Russell Hawes Kettell. Tour of 12 rooms, each representative of a different era in American history and each furnished, decorated, designed and occupied in the style of the era. 72 plans and elevations, 8-page color section, etc., show fabrics, wall papers, arrangements, etc. Full descriptive text. xvii + 200pp. of text. 8⅜ x 11¼.

21633-0 Paperbound $5.00

THE FITZWILLIAM VIRGINAL BOOK, edited by J. Fuller Maitland and W. B. Squire. Full modern printing of famous early 17th-century ms. volume of 300 works by Morley, Byrd, Bull, Gibbons, etc. For piano or other modern keyboard instrument; easy to read format. xxxvi + 938pp. 8⅜ x 11.

21068-5, 21069-3 Two volumes, Paperbound $10.00

KEYBOARD MUSIC, Johann Sebastian Bach. Bach Gesellschaft edition. A rich selection of Bach's masterpieces for the harpsichord: the six English Suites, six French Suites, the six Partitas (Clavierübung part I), the Goldberg Variations (Clavierübung part IV), the fifteen Two-Part Inventions and the fifteen Three-Part Sinfonias. Clearly reproduced on large sheets with ample margins; eminently playable. vi + 312pp. 8⅛ x 11.

22360-4 Paperbound $5.00

THE MUSIC OF BACH: AN INTRODUCTION, Charles Sanford Terry. A fine, nontechnical introduction to Bach's music, both instrumental and vocal. Covers organ music, chamber music, passion music, other types. Analyzes themes, developments, innovations. x + 114pp.

21075-8 Paperbound $1.25

BEETHOVEN AND HIS NINE SYMPHONIES, Sir George Grove. Noted British musicologist provides best history, analysis, commentary on symphonies. Very thorough, rigorously accurate; necessary to both advanced student and amateur music lover. 436 musical passages. vii + 407 pp.

20334-4 Paperbound $2.75

JOHANN SEBASTIAN BACH, Philipp Spitta. One of the great classics of musicology, this definitive analysis of Bach's music (and life) has never been surpassed. Lucid, nontechnical analyses of hundreds of pieces (30 pages devoted to St. Matthew Passion, 26 to B Minor Mass). Also includes major analysis of 18th-century music. 450 musical examples. 40-page musical supplement. Total of xx + 1799pp.
(EUK) 22278-0, 22279-9 Two volumes, Clothbound $17.50

MOZART AND HIS PIANO CONCERTOS, Cuthbert Girdlestone. The only full-length study of an important area of Mozart's creativity. Provides detailed analyses of all 23 concertos, traces inspirational sources. 417 musical examples. Second edition. 509pp. 21271-8 Paperbound $3.50

THE PERFECT WAGNERITE: A COMMENTARY ON THE NIBLUNG'S RING, George Bernard Shaw. Brilliant and still relevant criticism in remarkable essays on Wagner's Ring cycle, Shaw's ideas on political and social ideology behind the plots, role of Leitmotifs, vocal requisites, etc. Prefaces. xxi + 136pp.
(USO) 21707-8 Paperbound $1.50

DON GIOVANNI, W. A. Mozart. Complete libretto, modern English translation; biographies of composer and librettist; accounts of early performances and critical reaction. Lavishly illustrated. All the material you need to understand and appreciate this great work. Dover Opera Guide and Libretto Series; translated and introduced by Ellen Bleiler. 92 illustrations. 209pp.
21134-7 Paperbound $2.00

HIGH FIDELITY SYSTEMS: A LAYMAN'S GUIDE, Roy F. Allison. All the basic information you need for setting up your own audio system: high fidelity and stereo record players, tape records, F.M. Connections, adjusting tone arm, cartridge, checking needle alignment, positioning speakers, phasing speakers, adjusting hums, trouble-shooting, maintenance, and similar topics. Enlarged 1965 edition. More than 50 charts, diagrams, photos. iv + 91pp. 21514-8 Paperbound $1.25

REPRODUCTION OF SOUND, Edgar Villchur. Thorough coverage for laymen of high fidelity systems, reproducing systems in general, needles, amplifiers, preamps, loudspeakers, feedback, explaining physical background. "A rare talent for making technicalities vividly comprehensible," R. Darrell, High Fidelity. 69 figures. iv + 92pp. 21515-6 Paperbound $1.25

HEAR ME TALKIN' TO YA: THE STORY OF JAZZ AS TOLD BY THE MEN WHO MADE IT, Nat Shapiro and Nat Hentoff. Louis Armstrong, Fats Waller, Jo Jones, Clarence Williams, Billy Holiday, Duke Ellington, Jelly Roll Morton and dozens of other jazz greats tell how it was in Chicago's South Side, New Orleans, depression Harlem and the modern West Coast as jazz was born and grew. xvi + 429pp.
21726-4 Paperbound $2.50

FABLES OF AESOP, translated by Sir Roger L'Estrange. A reproduction of the very rare 1931 Paris edition; a selection of the most interesting fables, together with 50 imaginative drawings by Alexander Calder. v + 128pp. 6½x9¼.
21780-9 Paperbound $1.50

AGAINST THE GRAIN (A REBOURS), Joris K. Huysmans. Filled with weird images, evidences of a bizarre imagination, exotic experiments with hallucinatory drugs, rich tastes and smells and the diversions of its sybarite hero Duc Jean des Esseintes, this classic novel pushed 19th-century literary decadence to its limits. Full unabridged edition. Do not confuse this with abridged editions generally sold. Introduction by Havelock Ellis. xlix + 206pp. 22190-3 Paperbound $2.00

VARIORUM SHAKESPEARE: HAMLET. Edited by Horace H. Furness; a landmark of American scholarship. Exhaustive footnotes and appendices treat all doubtful words and phrases, as well as suggested critical emendations throughout the play's history. First volume contains editor's own text, collated with all Quartos and Folios. Second volume contains full first Quarto, translations of Shakespeare's sources (Belleforest, and Saxo Grammaticus), Der Bestrafte Brudermord, and many essays on critical and historical points of interest by major authorities of past and present. Includes details of staging and costuming over the years. By far the best edition available for serious students of Shakespeare. Total of xx + 905pp. 21004-9, 21005-7, 2 volumes, Paperbound $7.00

A LIFE OF WILLIAM SHAKESPEARE, Sir Sidney Lee. This is the standard life of Shakespeare, summarizing everything known about Shakespeare and his plays. Incredibly rich in material, broad in coverage, clear and judicious, it has served thousands as the best introduction to Shakespeare. 1931 edition. 9 plates. xxix + 792pp. (USO) 21967-4 Paperbound $3.75

MASTERS OF THE DRAMA, John Gassner. Most comprehensive history of the drama in print, covering every tradition from Greeks to modern Europe and America, including India, Far East, etc. Covers more than 800 dramatists, 2000 plays, with biographical material, plot summaries, theatre history, criticism, etc. "Best of its kind in English," *New Republic.* 77 illustrations. xxii + 890pp. 20100-7 Clothbound $8.50

THE EVOLUTION OF THE ENGLISH LANGUAGE, George McKnight. The growth of English, from the 14th century to the present. Unusual, non-technical account presents basic information in very interesting form: sound shifts, change in grammar and syntax, vocabulary growth, similar topics. Abundantly illustrated with quotations. Formerly *Modern English in the Making.* xii + 590pp. 21932-1 Paperbound $3.50

AN ETYMOLOGICAL DICTIONARY OF MODERN ENGLISH, Ernest Weekley. Fullest, richest work of its sort, by foremost British lexicographer. Detailed word histories, including many colloquial and archaic words; extensive quotations. Do not confuse this with the Concise Etymological Dictionary, which is much abridged. Total of xxvii + 830pp. 6½ x 9¼. 21873-2, 21874-0 Two volumes, Paperbound $6.00

FLATLAND: A ROMANCE OF MANY DIMENSIONS, E. A. Abbott. Classic of science-fiction explores ramifications of life in a two-dimensional world, and what happens when a three-dimensional being intrudes. Amusing reading, but also useful as introduction to thought about hyperspace. Introduction by Banesh Hoffmann. 16 illustrations. xx + 103pp. 20001-9 Paperbound $1.00

POEMS OF ANNE BRADSTREET, edited with an introduction by Robert Hutchinson. A new selection of poems by America's first poet and perhaps the first significant woman poet in the English language. 48 poems display her development in works of considerable variety—love poems, domestic poems, religious meditations, formal elegies, "quaternions," etc. Notes, bibliography. viii + 222pp.

22160-1 Paperbound $2.50

THREE GOTHIC NOVELS: THE CASTLE OF OTRANTO BY HORACE WALPOLE; VATHEK BY WILLIAM BECKFORD; THE VAMPYRE BY JOHN POLIDORI, WITH FRAGMENT OF A NOVEL BY LORD BYRON, edited by E. F. Bleiler. The first Gothic novel, by Walpole; the finest Oriental tale in English, by Beckford; powerful Romantic supernatural story in versions by Polidori and Byron. All extremely important in history of literature; all still exciting, packed with supernatural thrills, ghosts, haunted castles, magic, etc. xl + 291pp.

21232-7 Paperbound $2.50

THE BEST TALES OF HOFFMANN, E. T. A. Hoffmann. 10 of Hoffmann's most important stories, in modern re-editings of standard translations: Nutcracker and the King of Mice, Signor Formica, Automata, The Sandman, Rath Krespel, The Golden Flowerpot, Master Martin the Cooper, The Mines of Falun, The King's Betrothed, A New Year's Eve Adventure. 7 illustrations by Hoffmann. Edited by E. F. Bleiler. xxxix + 419pp. 21793-0 Paperbound $3.00

GHOST AND HORROR STORIES OF AMBROSE BIERCE, Ambrose Bierce. 23 strikingly modern stories of the horrors latent in the human mind: The Eyes of the Panther, The Damned Thing, An Occurrence at Owl Creek Bridge, An Inhabitant of Carcosa, etc., plus the dream-essay, Visions of the Night. Edited by E. F. Bleiler. xxii + 199pp. 20767-6 Paperbound $1.50

BEST GHOST STORIES OF J. S. LEFANU, J. Sheridan LeFanu. Finest stories by Victorian master often considered greatest supernatural writer of all. Carmilla, Green Tea, The Haunted Baronet, The Familiar, and 12 others. Most never before available in the U. S. A. Edited by E. F. Bleiler. 8 illustrations from Victorian publications. xvii + 467pp. 20415-4 Paperbound $3.00

MATHEMATICAL FOUNDATIONS OF INFORMATION THEORY, A. I. Khinchin. Comprehensive introduction to work of Shannon, McMillan, Feinstein and Khinchin, placing these investigations on a rigorous mathematical basis. Covers entropy concept in probability theory, uniqueness theorem, Shannon's inequality, ergodic sources, the E property, martingale concept, noise, Feinstein's fundamental lemma, Shanon's first and second theorems. Translated by R. A. Silverman and M. D. Friedman. iii + 120pp. 60434-9 Paperbound $1.75

SEVEN SCIENCE FICTION NOVELS, H. G. Wells. The standard collection of the great novels. Complete, unabridged. *First Men in the Moon, Island of Dr. Moreau, War of the Worlds, Food of the Gods, Invisible Man, Time Machine, In the Days of the Comet.* Not only science fiction fans, but every educated person owes it to himself to read these novels. 1015pp. (USO) 20264-X Clothbound $5.00

LAST AND FIRST MEN AND STAR MAKER, TWO SCIENCE FICTION NOVELS, Olaf Stapledon. Greatest future histories in science fiction. In the first, human intelligence is the "hero," through strange paths of evolution, interplanetary invasions, incredible technologies, near extinctions and reemergences. Star Maker describes the quest of a band of star rovers for intelligence itself, through time and space: weird inhuman civilizations, crustacean minds, symbiotic worlds, etc. Complete, unabridged. v + 438pp. (USO) 21962-3 Paperbound $2.50

THREE PROPHETIC NOVELS, H. G. WELLS. Stages of a consistently planned future for mankind. *When the Sleeper Wakes,* and *A Story of the Days to Come,* anticipate *Brave New World* and *1984,* in the 21st Century; *The Time Machine,* only complete version in print, shows farther future and the end of mankind. All show Wells's greatest gifts as storyteller and novelist. Edited by E. F. Bleiler. x + 335pp. (USO) 20605-X Paperbound $2.50

THE DEVIL'S DICTIONARY, Ambrose Bierce. America's own Oscar Wilde—Ambrose Bierce—offers his barbed iconoclastic wisdom in over 1,000 definitions hailed by H. L. Mencken as "some of the most gorgeous witticisms in the English language." 145pp. 20487-1 Paperbound $1.25

MAX AND MORITZ, Wilhelm Busch. Great children's classic, father of comic strip, of two bad boys, Max and Moritz. Also Ker and Plunk (Plisch und Plumm), Cat and Mouse, Deceitful Henry, Ice-Peter, The Boy and the Pipe, and five other pieces. Original German, with English translation. Edited by H. Arthur Klein; translations by various hands and H. Arthur Klein. vi + 216pp.
20181-3 Paperbound $2.00

PIGS IS PIGS AND OTHER FAVORITES, Ellis Parker Butler. The title story is one of the best humor short stories, as Mike Flannery obfuscates biology and English. Also included, That Pup of Murchison's, The Great American Pie Company, and Perkins of Portland. 14 illustrations. v + 109pp. 21532-6 Paperbound $1.25

THE PETERKIN PAPERS, Lucretia P. Hale. It takes genius to be as stupidly mad as the Peterkins, as they decide to become wise, celebrate the "Fourth," keep a cow, and otherwise strain the resources of the Lady from Philadelphia. Basic book of American humor. 153 illustrations. 219pp. 20794-3 Paperbound $1.50

PERRAULT'S FAIRY TALES, translated by A. E. Johnson and S. R. Littlewood, with 34 full-page illustrations by Gustave Doré. All the original Perrault stories—Cinderella, Sleeping Beauty, Bluebeard, Little Red Riding Hood, Puss in Boots, Tom Thumb, etc.—with their witty verse morals and the magnificent illustrations of Doré. One of the five or six great books of European fairy tales. viii + 117pp. 8⅛ x 11. 22311-6 Paperbound $2.00

OLD HUNGARIAN FAIRY TALES, Baroness Orczy. Favorites translated and adapted by author of the *Scarlet Pimpernel.* Eight fairy tales include "The Suitors of Princess Fire-Fly," "The Twin Hunchbacks," "Mr. Cuttlefish's Love Story," and "The Enchanted Cat." This little volume of magic and adventure will captivate children as it has for generations. 90 drawings by Montagu Barstow. 96pp.
22293-4 Paperbound $1.95

THE RED FAIRY BOOK, Andrew Lang. Lang's color fairy books have long been children's favorites. This volume includes Rapunzel, Jack and the Bean-stalk and 35 other stories, familiar and unfamiliar. 4 plates, 93 illustrations x + 367pp.
21673-X Paperbound $2.50

THE BLUE FAIRY BOOK, Andrew Lang. Lang's tales come from all countries and all times. Here are 37 tales from Grimm, the Arabian Nights, Greek Mythology, and other fascinating sources. 8 plates, 130 illustrations. xi + 390pp.
21437-0 Paperbound $2.50

HOUSEHOLD STORIES BY THE BROTHERS GRIMM. Classic English-language edition of the well-known tales — Rumpelstiltskin, Snow White, Hansel and Gretel, The Twelve Brothers, Faithful John, Rapunzel, Tom Thumb (52 stories in all). Translated into simple, straightforward English by Lucy Crane. Ornamented with headpieces, vignettes, elaborate decorative initials and a dozen full-page illustrations by Walter Crane. x + 269pp.
21080-4 Paperbound $2.00

THE MERRY ADVENTURES OF ROBIN HOOD, Howard Pyle. The finest modern versions of the traditional ballads and tales about the great English outlaw. Howard Pyle's complete prose version, with every word, every illustration of the first edition. Do not confuse this facsimile of the original (1883) with modern editions that change text or illustrations. 23 plates plus many page decorations. xxii + 296pp.
22043-5 Paperbound $2.50

THE STORY OF KING ARTHUR AND HIS KNIGHTS, Howard Pyle. The finest children's version of the life of King Arthur; brilliantly retold by Pyle, with 48 of his most imaginative illustrations. xviii + 313pp. 6⅛ x 9¼.
21445-1 Paperbound $2.50

THE WONDERFUL WIZARD OF OZ, L. Frank Baum. America's finest children's book in facsimile of first edition with all Denslow illustrations in full color. The edition a child should have. Introduction by Martin Gardner. 23 color plates, scores of drawings. iv + 267pp.
20691-2 Paperbound $2.50

THE MARVELOUS LAND OF OZ, L. Frank Baum. The second Oz book, every bit as imaginative as the Wizard. The hero is a boy named Tip, but the Scarecrow and the Tin Woodman are back, as is the Oz magic. 16 color plates, 120 drawings by John R. Neill. 287pp.
20692-0 Paperbound $2.50

THE MAGICAL MONARCH OF MO, L. Frank Baum. Remarkable adventures in a land even stranger than Oz. The best of Baum's books not in the Oz series. 15 color plates and dozens of drawings by Frank Verbeck. xviii + 237pp.
21892-9 Paperbound $2.25

THE BAD CHILD'S BOOK OF BEASTS, MORE BEASTS FOR WORSE CHILDREN, A MORAL ALPHABET, Hilaire Belloc. Three complete humor classics in one volume. Be kind to the frog, and do not call him names . . . and 28 other whimsical animals. Familiar favorites and some not so well known. Illustrated by Basil Blackwell. 156pp.
(USO) 20749-8 Paperbound $1.50

EAST O' THE SUN AND WEST O' THE MOON, George W. Dasent. Considered the best of all translations of these Norwegian folk tales, this collection has been enjoyed by generations of children (and folklorists too). Includes True and Untrue, Why the Sea is Salt, East O' the Sun and West O' the Moon, Why the Bear is Stumpy-Tailed, Boots and the Troll, The Cock and the Hen, Rich Peter the Pedlar, and 52 more. The only edition with all 59 tales. 77 illustrations by Erik Werenskiold and Theodor Kittelsen. xv + 418pp. 22521-6 Paperbound $3.50

GOOPS AND HOW TO BE THEM, Gelett Burgess. Classic of tongue-in-cheek humor, masquerading as etiquette book. 87 verses, twice as many cartoons, show mischievous Goops as they demonstrate to children virtues of table manners, neatness, courtesy, etc. Favorite for generations. viii + 88pp. 6½ x 9¼.
22233-0 Paperbound $1.25

ALICE'S ADVENTURES UNDER GROUND, Lewis Carroll. The first version, quite different from the final *Alice in Wonderland,* printed out by Carroll himself with his own illustrations. Complete facsimile of the "million dollar" manuscript Carroll gave to Alice Liddell in 1864. Introduction by Martin Gardner. viii + 96pp. Title and dedication pages in color. 21482-6 Paperbound $1.25

THE BROWNIES, THEIR BOOK, Palmer Cox. Small as mice, cunning as foxes, exuberant and full of mischief, the Brownies go to the zoo, toy shop, seashore, circus, etc., in 24 verse adventures and 266 illustrations. Long a favorite, since their first appearance in St. Nicholas Magazine. xi + 144pp. 6⅝ x 9¼.
21265-3 Paperbound $1.75

SONGS OF CHILDHOOD, Walter De La Mare. Published (under the pseudonym Walter Ramal) when De La Mare was only 29, this charming collection has long been a favorite children's book. A facsimile of the first edition in paper, the 47 poems capture the simplicity of the nursery rhyme and the ballad, including such lyrics as I Met Eve, Tartary, The Silver Penny. vii + 106pp. (USO) 21972-0 Paperbound
$1.25

THE COMPLETE NONSENSE OF EDWARD LEAR, Edward Lear. The finest 19th-century humorist-cartoonist in full: all nonsense limericks, zany alphabets, Owl and Pussycat, songs, nonsense botany, and more than 500 illustrations by Lear himself. Edited by Holbrook Jackson. xxix + 287pp. (USO) 20167-8 Paperbound $2.00

BILLY WHISKERS: THE AUTOBIOGRAPHY OF A GOAT, Frances Trego Montgomery. A favorite of children since the early 20th century, here are the escapades of that rambunctious, irresistible and mischievous goat—Billy Whiskers. Much in the spirit of *Peck's Bad Boy,* this is a book that children never tire of reading or hearing. All the original familiar illustrations by W. H. Fry are included: 6 color plates, 18 black and white drawings. 159pp. 22345-0 Paperbound $2.00

MOTHER GOOSE MELODIES. Faithful republication of the fabulously rare Munroe and Francis "copyright 1833" Boston edition—the most important Mother Goose collection, usually referred to as the "original." Familiar rhymes plus many rare ones, with wonderful old woodcut illustrations. Edited by E. F. Bleiler. 128pp. 4½ x 6⅜. 22577-1 Paperbound $1.00

Two Little Savages; Being the Adventures of Two Boys Who Lived as Indians and What They Learned, Ernest Thompson Seton. Great classic of nature and boyhood provides a vast range of woodlore in most palatable form, a genuinely entertaining story. Two farm boys build a teepee in woods and live in it for a month, working out Indian solutions to living problems, star lore, birds and animals, plants, etc. 293 illustrations. vii + 286pp.

20985-7 Paperbound $2.50

Peter Piper's Practical Principles of Plain & Perfect Pronunciation. Alliterative jingles and tongue-twisters of surprising charm, that made their first appearance in America about 1830. Republished in full with the spirited woodcut illustrations from this earliest American edition. 32pp. 4½ x 6⅜.

22560-7 Paperbound $1.00

Science Experiments and Amusements for Children, Charles Vivian. 73 easy experiments, requiring only materials found at home or easily available, such as candles, coins, steel wool, etc.; illustrate basic phenomena like vacuum, simple chemical reaction, etc. All safe. Modern, well-planned. Formerly *Science Games for Children*. 102 photos, numerous drawings. 96pp. 6⅛ x 9¼.

21856-2 Paperbound $1.25

An Introduction to Chess Moves and Tactics Simply Explained, Leonard Barden. Informal intermediate introduction, quite strong in explaining reasons for moves. Covers basic material, tactics, important openings, traps, positional play in middle game, end game. Attempts to isolate patterns and recurrent configurations. Formerly *Chess*. 58 figures. 102pp. (USO) 21210-6 Paperbound $1.25

Lasker's Manual of Chess, Dr. Emanuel Lasker. Lasker was not only one of the five great World Champions, he was also one of the ablest expositors, theorists, and analysts. In many ways, his Manual, permeated with his philosophy of battle, filled with keen insights, is one of the greatest works ever written on chess. Filled with analyzed games by the great players. A single-volume library that will profit almost any chess player, beginner or master. 308 diagrams. xli x 349pp.

20640-8 Paperbound $2.75

The Master Book of Mathematical Recreations, Fred Schuh. In opinion of many the finest work ever prepared on mathematical puzzles, stunts, recreations; exhaustively thorough explanations of mathematics involved, analysis of effects, citation of puzzles and games. Mathematics involved is elementary. Translated by F. Göbel. 194 figures. xxiv + 430pp. 22134-2 Paperbound $3.00

Mathematics, Magic and Mystery, Martin Gardner. Puzzle editor for Scientific American explains mathematics behind various mystifying tricks: card tricks, stage "mind reading," coin and match tricks, counting out games, geometric dissections, etc. Probability sets, theory of numbers clearly explained. Also provides more than 400 tricks, guaranteed to work, that you can do. 135 illustrations. xii + 176pp.

20335-2 Paperbound $1.50

MATHEMATICAL PUZZLES FOR BEGINNERS AND ENTHUSIASTS, Geoffrey Mott-Smith. 189 puzzles from easy to difficult—involving arithmetic, logic, algebra, properties of digits, probability, etc.—for enjoyment and mental stimulus. Explanation of mathematical principles behind the puzzles. 135 illustrations. viii + 248pp.
20198-8 Paperbound $1.75

PAPER FOLDING FOR BEGINNERS, William D. Murray and Francis J. Rigney. Easiest book on the market, clearest instructions on making interesting, beautiful origami. Sail boats, cups, roosters, frogs that move legs, bonbon boxes, standing birds, etc. 40 projects; more than 275 diagrams and photographs. 94pp.
20713-7 Paperbound $1.00

TRICKS AND GAMES ON THE POOL TABLE, Fred Herrmann. 79 tricks and games— some solitaires, some for two or more players, some competitive games—to entertain you between formal games. Mystifying shots and throws, unusual caroms, tricks involving such props as cork, coins, a hat, etc. Formerly *Fun on the Pool Table*. 77 figures. 95pp.
21814-7 Paperbound $1.00

HAND SHADOWS TO BE THROWN UPON THE WALL: A SERIES OF NOVEL AND AMUSING FIGURES FORMED BY THE HAND, Henry Bursill. Delightful picturebook from great-grandfather's day shows how to make 18 different hand shadows: a bird that flies, duck that quacks, dog that wags his tail, camel, goose, deer, boy, turtle, etc. Only book of its sort. vi + 33pp. 6½ x 9¼. 21779-5 Paperbound $1.00

WHITTLING AND WOODCARVING, E. J. Tangerman. 18th printing of best book on market. "If you can cut a potato you can carve" toys and puzzles, chains, chessmen, caricatures, masks, frames, woodcut blocks, surface patterns, much more. Information on tools, woods, techniques. Also goes into serious wood sculpture from Middle Ages to present, East and West. 464 photos, figures. x + 293pp.
20965-2 Paperbound $2.00

HISTORY OF PHILOSOPHY, Julián Marias. Possibly the clearest, most easily followed, best planned, most useful one-volume history of philosophy on the market; neither skimpy nor overfull. Full details on system of every major philosopher and dozens of less important thinkers from pre-Socratics up to Existentialism and later. Strong on many European figures usually omitted. Has gone through dozens of editions in Europe. 1966 edition, translated by Stanley Appelbaum and Clarence Strowbridge. xviii + 505pp. 21739-6 Paperbound $3.50

YOGA: A SCIENTIFIC EVALUATION, Kovoor T. Behanan. Scientific but non-technical study of physiological results of yoga exercises; done under auspices of Yale U. Relations to Indian thought, to psychoanalysis, etc. 16 photos. xxiii + 270pp.
20505-3 Paperbound $2.50

Prices subject to change without notice.
Available at your book dealer or write for free catalogue to Dept. GI, Dover Publications, Inc., 180 Varick St., N. Y., N. Y. 10014. Dover publishes more than 150 books each year on science, elementary and advanced mathematics, biology, music, art, literary history, social sciences and other areas.